The Craft of Veneering

Date: 3/20/19

A COMPLETE GUIDE from BASIC to ADVANCED

The Craft of Veneering

Craig Thibodeau

The Taunton Press

Text © 2018 by Craig Thibodeau
Photographs © 2018 by The Taunton Press, Inc. (except where noted)
Illustrations © 2018 by The Taunton Press, Inc.

The Taunton Press, Inc.,
63 South Main Street, PO Box 5506, Newtown, CT 06470-5506
Email: tp@taunton.com

Editor: Peter Chapman
Copy Editor: Diane Sinitsky
Indexer: Cathy Goddard
Jacket/Cover design: Alison Wilkes
Interior Design and Layout: Alison Wilkes
Photographer: Craig Thibodeau, except where noted
Illustrator: Christopher Mills

The following names/manufacturers appearing in *The Craft of Veneering* are
trademarks: DeWalt®; Gorilla Glue®; McMaster-Carr®; Pro-Glue®; Q*bert®;
Styrofoam®; Surform®; Titebond®; Vac-U-Clamp®

Library of Congress Cataloging-in-Publication Data

Names: Thibodeau, Craig, author.
Title: The craft of veneering : a complete guide from basic to advanced /
    Craig Thibodeau.
Description: Newtown, CT : The Taunton Press, Inc., 2018. | Includes index.
Identifiers: LCCN 2018011996 | ISBN 9781631869006
Subjects: LCSH: Woodwork--Handbooks, manuals, etc. | Veneers and
    veneering--Handbooks, manuals, etc.
Classification: LCC TT200 .T395 2018 | DDC 684/.08--dc23
LC record available at https://lccn.loc.gov/2018011996
Printed in the United States of America
10 9 8 7 6 5 4 3 2 1

About Your Safety: Working wood is inherently dangerous. Using hand or power
tools improperly or ignoring safety practices can lead to permanent injury or even
death. Don't try to perform operations you learn about here (or elsewhere) unless
you're certain they are safe for you. If something about an operation doesn't feel
right, don't do it. Look for another way. We want you to enjoy the craft, so please
keep safety foremost in your mind whenever you're in the shop.

Dedication

To my loving wife: You provided all the support I needed to get through the long days of writing and photographing for this book. It has been a labor of love and one that I am glad I was able to share with you.
Thank you for always being there.

Acknowledgments

There are so many people who helped make this book a reality that it's hard to thank them all. But the first would have to be Asa Christiana, who has been an avid supporter of my work since our first article for *Fine Woodworking* magazine in 2007. He's been to my shop many times to photograph articles, and we've had some great discussions on life and woodworking over a few beers at the local pub. The real reason to thank him, though, is because he put me in touch with Peter Chapman at The Taunton Press when I mentioned some interest in writing a book. That one connection is what made this book a reality, and without Asa the book might not have happened.

I need to thank my parents for always believing in me and my work and for teaching me from an early age to build and craft things with my hands. We grew up in the country, and playing outside filled my days. I can recall many times when I would be gone exploring the entire day and only return at dark for dinner. I'm lucky to have parents who both know how to make things and took the time to teach me those skills, whether it was helping my mom sew and make crafts or working with my dad building something in his workshop.

The most influential woodworking teacher and friend I've ever had is Paul Schurch. I recall taking my first week-long marquetry class with him in 2005 and realizing immediately that I was watching a true master at work. He and I have worked together on a number of projects over the years since that first class, and I have learned a tremendous amount from Paul—not only about how to run a woodworking business and how to do veneer work or marquetry but also about life in general (and how to take a calmer approach to life). If I hadn't taken that first class from him years ago, I wouldn't be where I am today.

Of course, the folks at The Taunton Press deserve thanks as well, especially Peter Chapman and Rosalind Loeb Wanke, the two minds that made my hundreds of photos and untold pages of text into the final product you see here. Thanks also to everyone else at The Taunton Press who helped make this book a reality.

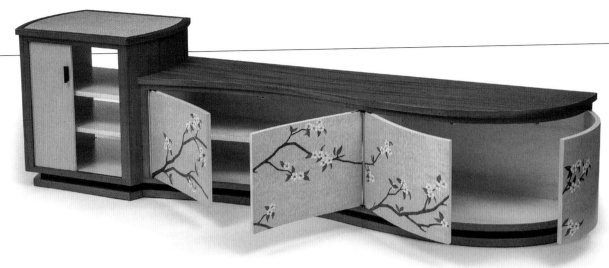

Contents

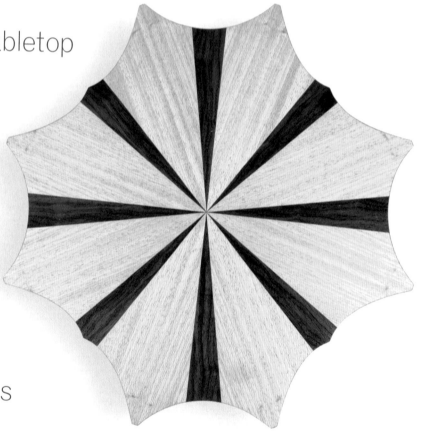

Foreword

I met Craig Thibodeau through his work long before I met him in person. Characterized by elegant veneers, deft marquetry, and impeccable craftsmanship, his cabinets stood alone among aisles of top-notch pieces at the huge annual Design in Wood Exhibition, held at the San Diego County Fair. As editor of *Fine Woodworking* magazine, I was invited each year to hand out the best-in-show award. It was a pleasure and an honor, and whenever Craig had a piece in the show, an easy job. The show is put on by the San Diego Fine Woodworkers Association, one of the largest guilds in the country, and as far as I was concerned, Craig Thibodeau was its rising star.

I was excited to meet him in person, since the magazine was always looking for world-class artisans. But like a lot of the best craftsmen, he's happier to let his work have the spotlight, so I don't think he was there for that first award ceremony. Or maybe he was just busy. Full-time woodworkers don't really have weekends, as they juggle marketing, sales, subcontractors, and when there's a spare minute, woodworking.

But Mr. Thibodeau was on my radar. I soon met him on the phone and was happy to discover that being in *Fine Woodworking* was one of his dreams. Halfway through our first conversation, I knew we'd be doing a pile of articles together.

I found out in that first phone call that Craig had only been a pro for a short time, which made his work even more impressive. I also learned he was a great guy and easy to talk to, an important quality for a collaborative relationship. I also found out that he was still doing product-design work on the side and had a formal design and engineering background—rare but invaluable in a woodworker. And most important, I discovered that his mind was as organized as his work was impeccable.

For a number of years afterward, I shot an article with Craig every time I flew out to San Diego for the big show. We were fast friends from the start. We shared our ups-and-downs as parents and professionals, and I always went to dinner with his beautiful young family at an outdoor Mexican restaurant in Old Town.

The reasons Craig has written so many articles for *Fine Woodworking* are the same reasons this book is extraordinary. Despite being a world-renowned craftsman at this point, with breathtaking work that stands side by side with the 18th-century mechanical marvels of David Roentgen, Thibodeau understands that it's the most fundamental techniques that pave the way for the finest work, and he hasn't forgotten what it felt like to be a beginner.

The whole time Craig was working with us magazine pros, he was going to school on our techniques, too: learning how to clarify a process with photos, how to break it down into crawl-walk-run, and how to craft text that's just as easy to digest.

In one amazing volume, Craig Thibodeau has done something extraordinary: He has created the definitive guide to fine veneer work—one that is likely to remain unchallenged for decades to come. Borrowing equally from old and new techniques and adding his own discoveries, he demonstrates the shortest path to success, guiding you past countless pitfalls and potential frustrations. As a working pro, Craig can't waste time on tricky techniques that don't always deliver, and now you don't have to either.

I'm happy for my friend because I know how good it feels to share what you know and love with others. And I'm happy for all of you, too. You've discovered a gold mine.

—Asa Christiana, former editor of *Fine Woodworking* magazine

Introduction

I can still remember my first official workshop—an old one-car garage on a busy street that I shared with the washer and dryer. It wasn't insulated and had just enough light coming from the two lightbulbs in the ceiling to be able to see what I was doing. There was barely enough power to run my old 1-hp tablesaw, and dust collection was nonexistent. But it was mine, and I loved every minute I got to spend in that shop. It was a place to create and build things with my hands, it was a way to escape the daily distractions that came from life in the 20th century, and it allowed me to build my skills as a woodworker bit by bit until it was time to move on to a larger shop. I've had many shops over the years, but that first one is the only one I think back on with fond memories; all the others were just places to work. That shop was also the place where I was first introduced to veneer in the form of some leftover veneer from a friend's workshop. Veneer was and still is a fascinating material for me, and it continues to amaze me how we can cut such consistently thin slices of wood over and over from huge logs.

I've been working with veneer for more than 20 years now, and during that time I've found it to be a sometimes challenging but always highly satisfying material to work. It can be used in so many different ways to decorate furniture, and the variety of wood species available in veneer is enough to keep any woodworker happy for a long time. One of the best things about veneer is the amazing figure you can find that is rarely seen in solid wood. Because most truly figured logs go directly to the veneer mill, the only way to access this material is through the use of veneer.

During the years I've been using veneer, I've developed a variety of techniques that make working with this relatively delicate material a bit easier. Some of them will seem obvious and others will likely be more obscure. All told, they represent years of trial and error, which I hope many of you can fast-track through because of the information in this book.

I targeted my book at both the beginner and experienced woodworker—and even at the non-woodworker who wants to get started working with veneer. There's very basic information that can help someone who's never touched veneer and more advanced instruction for the experienced woodworker. We'll talk about how and why veneer is made and some of the many ways to incorporate it into furniture and boxes. Then we'll delve into some of the more complex things that can be done with veneer, including marquetry, parquetry, and bent laminations. Each step along the way, we'll go over everything you need to know to get started, and I'll show you a variety of veneering tricks to help ensure that you get the most out of your veneer.

To help demonstrate the many possibilities that are available to the designer or maker when using veneer, there is a variety of veneered furniture and boxes from a wide selection of dedicated makers featured throughout the book. These pieces are from makers who are driven to create new and interesting work, and nearly all of them focus heavily on veneer in their work because of the creative flexibility it allows. I hope you enjoy looking at their work as much as I do.

CHAPTER 1

Introduction to Veneer

There are nearly endless opportunities to learn new woodworking skills, and one of those skills is veneering. Veneer is a beautiful material and gives us the opportunity to explore figure and grain in ways not possible with solid wood. You can create decorative matches with veneer in a wide range of interesting patterns like book-matches and radial matches and make complex geometric parquetry patterns with small pieces of veneer. Even flowers, birds, and animals are available to the veneer artist who learns marquetry cutting, and it takes only a minimal set of tools to begin. Beyond that, you can move into curved veneering and begin to incorporate bent laminations and curved veneering into your work. If you are really motivated, you can try to emulate the work of some of the 17th- and 18th-century masters of decorative furniture—cabinetmakers like Jean-Henri Riesener, David Roentgen, and Pierre Gole.

Where to Use Veneer

There are any number of ways to incorporate beautiful veneered panels into furniture. It can be as simple as a matched set of door panels in figured veneer or as complex as an entire cabinet made from a highly figured veneer log. Even if the

This desk and chair set in mahogany and curly anigre by the author demonstrates how the use of veneer allows for continuity in design as the materials and design details are carried across both pieces in a unified manner.

furniture is not going to have figured grain, the consistency of veneer allows an entire cabinet to be veneered in highly uniform grain-matched material, something that's not easily done with solid wood. Using veneer to enhance your furniture designs makes the work more interesting and decorative and allows for significantly more design freedom for the maker.

When it comes to matching wood grain over large surfaces or multiple pieces of furniture, there really is no substitute for veneer. It allows the builder to stretch grain matching much further than would be possible with solid-wood construction and creates a more uniformly decorative surface with continuity in the wood grain and patterns. The use of veneer also allows us access to a much wider range of wood species than is readily available in solid wood. Many veneers are simply not available in solid form due to their extremely high cost. Because of this, if you want to use highly decorative figured or burl woods in your furniture, you'll really need to learn how to work with veneer.

The straight-grained walnut veneer on this Art Deco chess table by the author is book-matched across the entire table. The lack of figure in the wood allows the form and design of the table to be the focus rather than any dramatic wood grain. The veneer pattern radiates from the centerlines of the table out toward the legs and around the table so that all four sides are identical.

Why Use Veneer?

Using veneer is a very efficient way to get the most from a limited resource. It allows us to use more of a beautiful material than would be possible with solid timber alone. In that way, it also helps with sustainability because a smaller number of trees can create a larger quantity of usable material. Just using veneer alone doesn't really qualify as a sustainable working method because unless we are planting trees in a quantity equal to the ones we are cutting down, there will one day be no more trees to use for veneer or lumber. As the number of trees that produce the most highly sought-after material dwindles, we need to do everything we can to preserve and extend the resource as much as possible. Otherwise, some of those species of trees will simply cease to exist due to overuse and destruction. Once that happens, it will be difficult to get them growing again in any significant quantity.

Species of veneer

The last time I counted, there were more than 100 species of veneer readily available from my veneer suppliers, and of those, many are also available in different figure types and cuts: things like curl, fiddleback, pommele, spalted, bird's eye, quilted, burl, flat cut, quartersawn, rift cut, and rotary cut to name a few (for definitions of these terms—and many others—see the Glossary on pp. 226–227). You'll see in the sample images on pp. 215–224 that there is an almost endless combination of both cut and figure type available in veneer. Seeing the sheer quantity of options available in wood veneer helped me realize that using veneer instead of solid wood for decorative panels in my furniture would enable me to show potential clients many more possible choices of material, figure, and color. It also meant that I could combine those many selections into more interesting figure and color combinations in my marquetry and parquetry work, thereby making my work more interesting and visually attractive to potential clients.

We've all likely seen pictures like this one from the early days of logging and mining in California. This one from 1910 shows a felled giant sequoia; when was the last time any of us saw a tree this large?

CHAIRS AND BOXES

An easy way to begin using veneer is to start incorporating it into your existing work. Whether you make boxes, furniture, or artwork, veneer can be used to enhance your work and bring it to a new level. If you build chairs, you can use it to create decorative back splats and interesting details; I've done this in nearly all my chairs as a way to add visual interest to the designs. If your focus is small boxes, veneer is an ideal material because it allows you to explore a wide array of veneer patterns and techniques with a minimal cost in time or materials. Whatever you build, there is a way to add veneer to it to create more interesting and visually decorative designs.

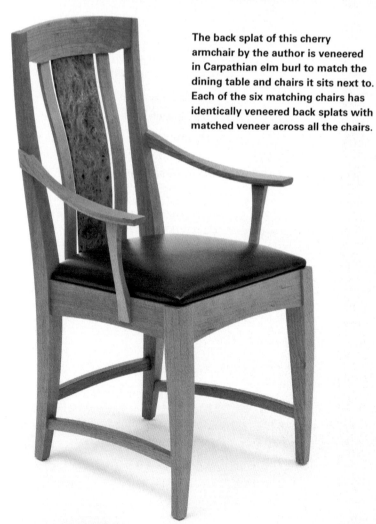

The back splat of this cherry armchair by the author is veneered in Carpathian elm burl to match the dining table and chairs it sits next to. Each of the six matching chairs has identically veneered back splats with matched veneer across all the chairs.

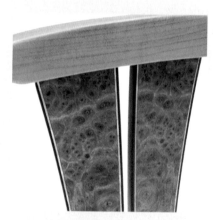

Each of the 10 dining chairs in this set has two-piece back splats veneered in book-matched Carpathian elm burl accented with ebony borders and mother of pearl inlay.

The parquetry box by U.K. maker Kevin Stamper features a beautiful array of dyed veneer squares arranged in a pattern reminding the viewer of a summer field by a lake.

This Amboyna burl and ebony box by Adrian Ferrazzutti demonstrates a striking use of veneer in the matched faces of the box sides and top.

Another lovely box by Adrian Ferrazzutti in pau ferro, holly, sycamore, and ebony shows a decorative parquetry pattern flowing uniformly over the entire surface of the box.

One of a set of two, this Art Deco club chair by the author is veneered in imbuya burl and framed in solid wenge. The veneer work is book-matched around the centerline of the chairs to create a balanced look to the design. The chairs each required approximately 35 sq. ft. of burl veneer to create—you can imagine how much solid imbuya burl would be required to make even a single chair and what that material would likely cost if it was even available. Using veneer for projects like this allows woodworkers to expand their material options into a realm not possible with solid wood.

This log of an unknown burl illustrates how some burls grow as deformations on the outside of trees. Once debarked and rotary cut, the log is likely to yield some unique and beautiful burl veneer.

Where Veneer Comes From

Most highly figured logs end up at the veneer mill to be cut into veneer; that's why you don't see much highly figured lumber at your local lumber store anymore. Occasionally, you'll get lucky and find a nice board of curly maple or something else mildly figured, but almost all really wildly figured wood becomes veneer, as do the majority of truly straight-grained logs. There was a time when you could easily purchase solid burls for low prices to make solid-wood boxes and even furniture, but that time is long gone. From a financial standpoint, it simply makes more sense to cut figured logs into veneer because a single board foot of solid burl would probably be worth only $40 to $50, but the 40 sq. ft. of veneer you could cut from the same board foot of burl would be worth $300 to $400.

Using veneer allows us to extend our wood supply further, which is extremely important with figured or rare woods that are becoming limited in quantity and hard to find. Without veneer, some of those woods would simply not be available to the average user as the cost of the solid boards would be astronomical. This is especially true of burls and highly figured woods: They are cut into veneer so that more usable material comes from each log, which makes the material more affordable for the end user. That also explains why it's possible to buy woods like fiddleback makore and pommele sapele as veneer but not as lumber.

Cutting Veneer

Natural wood veneer is cut from the same logs as solid-wood lumber. The main differences are that veneer tends to be cut from the most uniform and highly figured logs and is cut much thinner at approximately 0.6mm or 0.025 in. thick. As veneer manufacturing technology advances, that thickness will likely decrease and the yield from each log will go up accordingly. Unfortunately, at a certain point, the veneer becomes so thin that it is difficult to use for the kind of veneering you will likely want to do. It might be ideal for plywood manufacturers that can work with ultrathin veneer, but for the average woodworker, anything thinner than 0.025 in. is so delicate and fragile that it is frustrating to work with and very easy to sand through.

To get a clearer understanding of the yield possible with veneer cutting, picture a 1-in.-thick hardwood board. From that board, you can make a single decorative panel, and perhaps if you resaw it, you can make a book-matched panel twice as wide as the board. Now take that same 1-in.-thick board and slice it into veneer of 0.025-in. thickness. You now have 40 leaves of veneer the same length and width as the board. With them you can make an entire cabinet or even multiple pieces of furniture with perfectly

There are woods available to the veneer artist that are rarely, if ever, available in solid-wood form. From left to right, these are a few examples: pommele sapele, maple burl, ash burl, crotch Cuban mahogany, olive ash burl, redwood lace burl, and walnut burl.

Just a quick glance at this rustic oak log cut into veneer and restacked in boulle form clearly demonstrates the massive amount of usable material that comes from a log cut into veneer. This log is nearly 18 in. wide by 10 ft. long, and there are roughly 40 bundles of 32 leaves of veneer in the stack; that roughs out to approximately 34,000 sq. ft. of oak veneer from just this single log. The same log cut into live-edge slabs would yield about nine wood slabs 2 in. thick—enough for only three or four live-edge dining table tops.

matched grain rather than just making a single panel in one piece of furniture.

As with solid-wood lumber, veneer gets cut in a variety of ways to create specific grain patterns. Everything from quartersawn, riftsawn, plainsawn, and rotary cuts are available in veneer. The first three are cut in essentially the same fashion as solid wood. Quartersawn and rift veneers use logs that have been precut to present the appropriate face to the veneer knife so that the wood grain when sliced is quartered or rift in appearance. Plainsawn veneer is created in the same manner as plainsawn lumber, by slicing completely through a log and stacking the slices in the order they are cut; there are just many more slices with veneer.

The one veneer slicing technique that isn't used in solid-wood cutting is rotary cutting. To rotary-cut veneer, a section of log is mounted onto a rotating mandrel as the veneer knife is slowly fed into the surface of the log. This creates veneer in a single con-tinuous, essentially unending slice, producing veneer that can be used to create faces with no seams, which is ideal for stable plywood. The grain pattern produced by rotary-cutting straight-grained veneer is unfortunately a bit odd looking and wouldn't be ideal for a finished piece of furniture. It does, however, make a great substrate for veneer as whole-face Baltic birch plywood. Many burls are also rotary cut, and that method of cutting burls creates grain with unique and interesting patterns.

The cutting process

Logs go through a rigorous selection process before being slated for the veneer mill. The log buyer sees the log only in rough form, so he or she must be able to tell at a glance what the inside of the log will look like when it is cut into veneer. The log buyer initially looks for a clean, straight log with no visible defects or distortions in the surface of the log, then moves to the end grain of the log to determine if any figure could be inside the log. The job of the veneer log buyer is one that requires extensive knowledge of the growth patterns of trees and how they develop figure over time. As there is no way to precut a log

Logs in the veneer storage yard waiting to be cut into veneer are constantly sprayed with water to prevent checking and cracking.

Four Ways of Cutting Veneer

Each method of cutting requires a different system of mounting the log before cutting and a different method of cutting itself.

Rotary cutting

The log is mounted on a large mandrel that is then rotated against a fixed knife.

Plain slicing

Half a log is mounted on a sliding platen that then moves up and down past a fixed blade that slices through the entire half log.

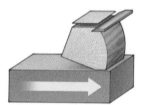

Riftsawn cutting

Riftsawn and quartersawn grain is cut much the same way as plain-sliced veneer, except the portion of the log that gets mounted to the moving mandrel is positioned to present the correct grain orientation for each respective cut.

Quartersawn cutting

Mounting a quartered log as shown creates the trademark ray flecks from the medullary rays in woods such as oak.

to view the wood inside, the final selection of each veneer log depends entirely on the log buyer's knowledge and skill at determining what is hidden inside each log.

Once the logs have been sorted and sent to the mill, the process of turning the logs into veneer is fairly straightforward, although it does require quite substantial and expensive equipment. Many veneer mills have huge yards filled with stacks of logs waiting to be cut into veneer. How long the logs wait in the yard depends on what veneer orders are coming into the slicing company and what type of wood is

being stored. While they wait to be cut, the logs are continuously sprayed with water to help prevent cracking and discoloration in the logs.

As the logs go from the yard to the mill to get cut into veneer, they first go through a debarking process that removes all of the bark and outer skin from the log. Debarking is done by hand with grinders and with large machines that essentially either peel or chip away the bark and outer skin. After the debarking operation, the logs are sent through a large bandsaw mill that cuts them into the necessary shapes and sizes for the particular cut of veneer that has

These log halves are being manually debarked to prepare them for slicing. Debarking removes the bark and outer skin of the logs along with any dirt or grit that might damage the slicing knives.

After being cut into the necessary shapes and sizes for veneer slicing on a large bandsaw, the cut logs are strapped back into log form to prepare them for the soaking process.

been specified. Once cut to size, the logs are strapped back into log form and soaked in extremely hot water for one day to several weeks. This soaking helps soften the wood fibers to make the slicing process more uniform and helps prevent the veneer from checking while being cut. There are any number of variables such as species of wood, thickness of the veneer to be cut, and the hardness of the wood itself that determine the soaking time and the temperature of the water in the soaking vats. This is another area that requires knowledge and experience, and the use of both can greatly influence the quality of the final cut veneer.

Once the log is removed from the hot-water bath, it goes directly to the slicing department. The log section is either mounted to a hydraulic sled that repeatedly raises and lowers the log past a fixed slicing blade or to a rotating mandrel that rotates the log as the blade is fed into it. As the slices of veneer come off the blade, they are stacked in the order they were sliced and kept in that order throughout the entire remaining processes. The individual slices of veneer are sent through a heated dryer and stacked in order as they emerge. Once the veneer leaves are dry, they then get sorted for quality and clipped to final size before being restacked in sequential bundles for shipping. You can see from the photos on the following pages how the entire system is focused on keeping the leaves in the proper order throughout the cutting, drying, and stacking process. This is why you can go to a veneer supplier and purchase one or several bundles of veneer from a specific log—or if you've got the budget, buy an entire log of veneer.

Cut logs are loaded into one of numerous soaking vats filled with hot water so the wood can be softened before cutting. The logs are fed along a conveyor system and loaded into the vats via an overhead crane.

Once the log segment is ready for slicing, it is mounted to a hydraulic sled that will raise and lower the log as it is fed incrementally into the slicing knife. This log half is being prepared to be plain sliced.

The bundles of veneer can then be shipped to one of several secondary businesses for processing into plywood, into veneer faces of matched veneer, or broken down into individual bundles for resale. The majority of sliced veneer gets used by the plywood industry to make a variety of different types and qualities of plywood for any number of end uses from home construction to furniture building. The best-quality veneer goes to veneer face suppliers; these companies create full 4-ft. by 8-ft. veneer faces in paper-backed, adhesive-backed, and two-ply veneer in a wide variety of species and decorative matches.

As the log section is fed into the slicing knife, the veneer leaves move down a motorized conveyor system to be manually stacked in sequential order.

This large maple cluster burl log is being mounted on rotating plates in preparation for rotary slicing, which is very similar to turning a spindle on a small lathe. As the cutting proceeds, the log will become perfectly round and the sliced veneer sheets will be larger and more consistent.

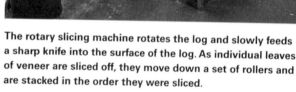

The rotary slicing machine rotates the log and slowly feeds a sharp knife into the surface of the log. As individual leaves of veneer are sliced off, they move down a set of rollers and are stacked in the order they were sliced.

Creating Veneer Faces

The process of creating full sheets of veneer faces requires complex equipment and detailed manufacturing procedures. The end result is high-quality matched sheets of uniformly cut and sanded veneer that can be used for any number of furniture and cabinetry needs.

The first step in creating high-quality veneer faces is to joint the bundles of veneer so they have two parallel edges. This is typically done on large guillotine knife cutters that both measure and clamp the bundles of veneer as they are cut. The bundles of veneer then move to a glue applicator, which applies glue to the edges of the veneer bundles to prepare

After slicing, the veneer leaves are sent to a drying machine. Each individual leaf of veneer is pulled into the dryer by an overhead vacuum system. In just moments, the veneer leaf is dry and ready for trimming.

When the veneer bundles are completely dry, they are restacked in sequential order and sent to the clipping line, where the veneer bundles are cut to specific lengths and widths.

them for the splicing machine. The splicing machine joins the individual leaves of veneer together in whatever match has been selected by heating the glue and pressing the edges of the individual sheets together.

The seamed sheets of veneer are then sent to a grading area to be sorted into different quality levels —the grading changes depending upon the individual species of veneer. Some of these sheets will go on to the veneer face department, where the sheets of veneer will be joined to an appropriate backer material. Anything from paper, adhesive film, or a layer of cross-grain veneer can be used as a backer for high-quality veneer faces. The veneer sheets are glued to the backer material in high-capacity hot presses that

This pearwood log has been cut, dried, stacked, clipped, and bundled in the order it was cut and is ready to be shipped out to any number of veneer wholesalers for conversion into plywood, veneer faces, or bundles for resale.

To prepare the bundles for splicing, they first go to a high-tech jointing machine that digitally measures the width of each bundle and cuts both long edges square and straight with a long guillotine knife.

As soon as the bundles of veneer are jointed, they go through a glue application machine that applies a fine film of heat-sensitive glue to one edge of the entire bundle of veneer. The veneer bundle is then fanned out by the machine to keep the individual leaves from sticking to each other.

The edge-glued leaves are now fed one by one into a splicing machine to join them into larger sheets of veneer. The splicing machine aligns the edges flush and simultaneously applies heat to set the glue on each joint, a process that takes just a few seconds per joint.

When manually grading seamed sheets of veneer for quality, a light table helps highlight defects in the veneer sheet that are then noted and marked.

A backer of paper (or other backer material) is applied to the back face of each sheet of veneer. The sheets are stacked in layers with an adhesive film between the paper and veneer and then go into a high-capacity hot press that permanently adheres the veneer to the paper.

After the backer is applied, the two-ply veneer sheets are sent to the trimming department so they can be cut down to final size, typically 4-ft. by 8-ft. or 4-ft. by 10-ft. sheets.

Finally, the trimmed veneer sheets go through a high-performance sander that lightly sands the face veneer so the end user only needs to finish-sand the veneer once it is applied to the substrate.

permanently adhere the veneer to the backer material. Once the sheet is trimmed to its final size, it goes through a high-performance sander that sands the veneer face to create a high-quality finish-ready surface. You can find many of these ready-to-use veneer faces at your local hardwood supplier, and some suppliers will also take custom orders if you need a specific wood species or grain match.

VENEER RESELLERS

Typically, most veneer resellers photograph the majority of the veneer bundles they sell and post these images on their websites so potential buyers can view the veneer before they buy. That's really the only way to purchase veneer—you should always try to avoid buying veneer sight unseen. At least by looking at a few pictures online, you'll have a decent idea what the grain and figure in the veneer look like before it arrives. If you don't, you may be in for some interesting surprises when you open a package of veneer.

If you ever get the chance to visit a large veneer reseller, you'll see just how large a space is needed to store and properly sort veneer. Most resellers operate from giant warehouses with stacks of veneer going all the way to the ceiling. The majority of veneer sellers don't encourage walk-in sales because just finding and bringing out a stack of a particular species of veneer requires some time and a forklift operator. Typically, you'll want to call ahead and let them know exactly what you'd like to look at so they have time to move the veneer you need to a location where it can be easily viewed. Being able to preview the various veneer choices online ahead of time can really save time and effort for both you and the supplier.

Once the veneer stacks arrive at the supplier's facility, the individual bundles get sorted for quality and are typically photographed so potential buyers can view the veneer online before buying. The staff at Certainly Wood is shown here sorting through hundreds of bundles of walnut burl veneer; it takes skilled workers to sort and photograph veneer correctly so the end user gets just what they order.

Properly storing a large quantity of veneer for retail sales requires a significant amount of warehouse space and the equipment to quickly move, sort, and ship individual orders of veneer. This glimpse into one corner of the Certainly Wood warehouse shows just how much space is needed to store a significant quantity of veneer properly.

Parquetry diamonds in maple and madrone burl veneer adorn the main surfaces of this entertainment center and bring an interesting visual complexity to the overall design.

This decorative two-door cabinet by Timothy Coleman in bird's-eye maple and walnut features decorative parquetry patterns cut into the maple veneer on the doors and complex two-layer fretwork on the top and base.

This unique wall hanging by Kevin Stamper is made entirely from veneer. The base veneer is molded over sculpted foam to create the rippling shapes, then colored parquetry squares are applied, followed by dark English oak veneer, which has been sandblasted to open up the grain.

This mechanical table by Jean-Henri Riesener was commissioned by Marie Antoinette and delivered to her in 1778. It features a mechanical lifting mechanism that can raise the entire top surface to standing height and mechanically activated spring-loaded compartments, as well as a reversible mirror/book stand that rises on a ratcheting mechanism.

Colorful ginkgo leaf marquetry flows across the sides and doors of this small buffet, highlighting the book-matched bird's-eye maple background veneer.

This small nightstand in cherry and maple burl veneer has added detailing in the form of cherry veneer crossbanding and ebony inlay surrounding the maple burl veneered.

Pierre Gole created this table circa 1660 while he was cabinetmaker to Louis XIV. It has exquisite marquetry done in highly exotic materials (some of which are no longer available or legal to use) such as tortoiseshell and ivory. Some of the ivory was even stained a vibrant green color for the leaves of the marquetry flowers.

An extravagant rolltop desk created by David Roentgen around 1785 features a variety of mechanical mechanisms that operate numerous hidden compartments. The desk is composed of an oak, pine, and fir carcase veneered in mahogany on the outside and maple burl and mahogany on the inside.

CHAPTER 2

Working with Veneer

Now that we've seen some of the ways veneer is manufactured and a few of the ways it can be used, let's delve deeper into working with veneer. In this chapter, we'll discuss how to buy veneer and review some of the terminology used to describe veneer in the marketplace (a full listing is provided in the Glossary on pp. 226–227). We'll also talk about how to store your veneer and explain how to flatten buckled veneer. Then we'll demonstrate some of the tools used to cut veneer accurately. To finish, we'll go over a few different ways to tape veneer joints together so you're ready for the next chapter on gluing and pressing your veneer.

Buying Veneer

Buying veneer isn't quite the same as buying lumber from your local lumberyard. Veneer is typically bought online, and you usually won't get to see your veneer in person until it arrives at your door. This can make your first veneer purchase a bit stressful, especially since you likely won't yet know the terminology used in the veneer world. I've been buying veneer from a number of great sources for many years and will explain exactly what you need to know and how to find the veneer you want without frustration.

A bundle of veneer is typically 24 or 32 leaves, all cut sequentially from the log and maintained in sequential order throughout the entire manufacturing process.

Veneer is available from a number of suppliers, primarily online unless you happen to live near one with a retail location (see the list of veneer suppliers on p. 228). As you'll likely be buying your veneer sight unseen except for a few pictures on a website, you'll want to have a clear understanding of what you're buying before making the purchase. Veneer is typically sold in two ways: by the individual leaf from a few select suppliers and by the bundle from most suppliers. There isn't really a typical size for a leaf of veneer. Burl veneers can be very small, down to 4 in. by 6 in. for some species and up to 3 ft. square for others. Some straight-grain veneers can be more than 2 ft. wide and 12 ft. long, but the average size is probably closer to 6 in. to 8 in. wide by 10 ft. long.

No matter the size, a single piece of veneer is called a "leaf," and a "bundle" is a stack of a certain number of leaves, typically 24 or 32. Occasionally, you can find smaller bundles of 12 or 16 leaves; if your projects are large, it's also quite easy to buy multiple sequential bundles or an entire flitch of veneer. Having all the leaves in a bundle of veneer in sequential order is very important for creating uni-

As you can see from this cherry log stacked next to a slicing machine at Atlantic Veneer Corporation, there is virtually zero waste in the process of cutting a log into veneer.

form matches and consistent grain patterns. Every bundle of veneer you buy will have sequentially cut leaves of veneer. In other words, as each leaf of veneer is cut off the log, it is stacked in the order it was cut and kept in that order throughout the drying and sorting process. When you purchase a bundle of veneer, you are purchasing a small section of the tree it came from. Purchasing multiple bundles in sequential order means you are purchasing a larger section of the tree and all the pieces in that section are stacked in order in the bundles.

Veneer, unlike solid wood, is sold by the square foot regardless of the thickness of the veneer. One square foot of veneer is 12 in. by 12 in. by whatever thickness it was cut. Most commercial veneer is approximately 0.025 in. thick, but it is possible to buy thicker veneer up to ⅛ in. thick from some suppliers. Thicker veneers can be used for bent laminations or even for tabletops where you might want some additional thickness to prevent damage and to allow for future resanding and refinishing. There are only a limited number of species available in thicker veneer, however.

Paper-backed, two-ply, and adhesive-backed veneer sheets are tightly rolled and slipped into cardboard boxes for shipping. Make sure to let the sheet lie flat to relax before using it.

One square foot of veneer is a piece 12 in. by 12 in. times the thickness of the veneer leaf.

Paper-backed and two-ply veneers

As mentioned in chapter 1, you can also buy paper-backed and two-ply veneers in a variety of sheet sizes, including full 4-ft. by 8-ft. and 4-ft. by 10-ft. sheets. These typically come in a moderate selection of veneer matches and a large selection of wood types. Paper-backed veneer has a layer of either

COUNTING THE COST

When you purchase a bundle of 32 leaves of veneer, the total cost of the bundle is the combined total square footage of all 32 leaves added together. Because of this, exotic and highly figured veneers can be extremely expensive in large quantities: Rare woods like amboyna burl can cost upward of $25 per sq. ft. It's not necessarily less expensive to use veneer versus solid wood for furniture. Typically, it is quite the opposite when material and labor costs are factored in, more so if you choose to use highly figured veneer. But the design possibilities with veneer are far greater than those of solid wood.

10-mil or 20-mil paper glued to the back side of the face veneer, and the face veneer is extremely thin (roughly 0.015 in.) as it has been presanded by the manufacturer. Great care needs to be taken when gluing and finish-sanding not to damage the show face of the veneer. Two-ply veneer has a second layer of veneer glued cross grain to the back of the primary veneer, which makes it stable and flexible. Both of these can be useful products if you need to veneer a large surface or don't have the equipment to seam and press your own veneers. They are, however, typically much more expensive than raw veneers and again are quite thin, so you need to be careful not to damage the show face while working with them.

Paper-backed and two-ply veneer sheets are rolled into a cylinder and shipped in a cardboard box; make sure to unroll the sheet and let it relax back to a flat state before trying to use it. Most of the information in this book will focus on "raw" wood veneer because it allows us to use both faces of every leaf and create more complex decorative matches, but if you have a project that requires full sheets of matched veneer or simply don't want to cut and seam your own veneer, these premade veneer sheets can be very helpful.

Creating a Cut List

Before placing your veneer order, you'll want to create a project cut list to determine how much veneer you'll need. Measure the overall size of each veneer panel in the piece, remembering that all the panels get veneered on both sides to keep the panel balanced. If you were to veneer only one side of a panel, it would likely warp very quickly and become difficult to use. Depending on your construction, you can either use a less expensive backer veneer for the back of the panel or, if it's a visible interior face, you could use a decorative or contrasting veneer to make your furniture more interesting.

I typically add at least a couple of inches to the width and length of each veneered panel to allow for some trimming and grain alignment. For panels that get a decorative match, like a book-match, you'll want to specify the quantity and size of the leaves needed to create the match. In other words, if you are making a 12-in.-wide door panel in book-matched veneer, you'll need two pieces of veneer at least 6 in. wide to create the book-match. Don't forget to note multiple panels that need to match; for a pair of 12-in.-wide door panels, you'll need four leaves of veneer 6 in. wide to make two door panels that match perfectly. Because of this, the actual number of leaves you order is sometimes more important than the total square footage. Keep in mind that you'll want some extra width for trimming, so in this example I'd look for veneer at least 7 in. wide—and you'll want the same for the backer veneer as well. Lastly, buy extra veneer to allow for mistakes and better

The quartersawn maple interior of this anigre and cherry cabinet brings lightness to the interior space when the doors are opened.

SAMPLE CUT LIST

Overall project part dimensions

- ❖ 2 door panels: 12 in. wide by 30 in. long (interior and exterior visible)
- ❖ 2 side panels: 8 in. wide by 30 in. long (interior and exterior visible)
- ❖ 1 back panel: 24 in. wide by 30 in. long (interior and exterior visible)
- ❖ 2 top and bottom panels: 8 in. wide by 24 in. long (interior and exterior visible)

Oversize veneer panel dimensions

- ❖ Doors: 2 doors x 2 faces per door x 2 leaves per face (book-matched) = 8 pieces, 7 in. wide by 32 in. long
- ❖ Sides: 2 sides x 2 faces per side x 1 leaf per face (single piece) = 4 pieces, 9 in. wide by 32 in. long
- ❖ Back panel: 1 back x 2 faces x 4 leaves per side (double book-match) = 8 pieces, 7 in. wide by 32 in. long
- ❖ Top and bottom: 2 panels x 2 faces per panel x 1 leaf per face (single piece) = 4 pieces, 9 in. wide by 26 in. long

Total veneer square footage

39.4 sq. ft. plus 20% for waste (additional 8 sq. ft.) = roughly 48 sq. ft.

Total number of matched leaves

Match doors and back panels (inside and outside can be different section of bundle) = 8 leaves

Match sides and top and bottom panels (inside and outside can be different section of bundle) = 4 leaves

Summary

Based on the cut list and assuming we're using a nice straight-grained veneer, we'll need 8 leaves of veneer that are 9 in. wide and at least 96 in. long. As most straight-grain veneer is sold in 8-ft. to 10-ft. lengths, you can buy 8 sequential leaves from a single bundle or buy 4 from one and 4 from another if you decide to make the interior a different material than the exterior.

Straight-grained veneer is typically shipped in a roll wrapped in paper; it is less expensive to ship long bundles of veneer if they are rolled.

grain matching. I'll typically add at least 20% to my order for straight-grained veneers and up to 50% extra for figured and burl veneers. The extra cost up front is better than finding out you're one leaf short and that your supplier has already sold the next bundle you need.

Handling Veneer

As we discussed in chapter 1, there are a variety of veneer types available for purchase, but they can essentially be broken down into two types when it comes to shipping and storage: straight-grained veneers and burl veneers. Each requires different handling in the shop. Straight-grained veneer will arrive in a roll wrapped in paper or plastic. The rolls of veneer should be unrolled when they arrive and

You'll often find end checks in the leaves of veneer that need to be taped together. Also, make sure to number the leaves in order so you can keep track of them.

allowed to relax into their natural flat state for a couple hours before use. Ideally, they should also be stored flat, if space is available. Mark defects such as cracks or splits with chalk, and tape any split ends together with blue tape to keep them from spreading. Straight-grained veneers should also be taped across the ends of the leaves to prevent cracks along the grain from starting while they are being handled. It's a helpful practice to number all the leaves of veneer on one face when your order arrives so when you flip them around while cutting or matching, you can easily get them back into sequential order.

Because burl veneers are so fragile, they are shipped flat between pieces of cardboard and are never rolled.

Burl veneers often have defects that will require repair later in the veneering process. Make sure to mark any defects or holes you find with some chalk so you can keep track of them later.

Burl veneers are typically shipped flat between sheets of cardboard because they are fragile and can't be rolled without damage. These veneers can be extremely delicate and should be taped around their perimeter to prevent pieces from breaking off during handling. Carefully tape back together anything that is broken, just in case you need it later. Breaks in burl veneers aren't a big deal because when you tape the pieces back together, the breaks will disappear. Take the time to mark any large defects or holes in the burl with chalk so you can find them easily later.

Storing Veneer

Once you've decided what type and quantity of veneer to purchase, you'll want to set up a good system for storing it. Veneer likes to be stored in somewhat controlled conditions: ideally, 70°F and 50% humidity. Storing veneer in a location that has wild temperature and humidity swings will likely result in veneer that becomes buckled or cracked over time and is difficult to work with. If ideal conditions aren't available or possible, it can help to store your veneer wrapped lightly in plastic tarps and weighed down between sheets of plywood or medium-density fiberboard (MDF). This will minimize the swings of temperature and humidity on the veneer and help to keep it flatter over time.

Flattening buckled veneer

You'll likely remember the first time you receive a shipment of buckled veneer. It tends to stick in the memory because it looks as though it couldn't possibly be used for anything, and you'll feel as though you just wasted a bunch of money. Luckily, all is not lost, and flattening buckled veneer is actually pretty easy. Once you've got it flattened, your veneer will be surprisingly easy to work with. It might seem intimidating at first, but using a commercial flattening solution and a simple system for pressing the veneer flat make the process very user-friendly.

The ideal way to store veneer is to lay it flat on shelves in a somewhat climate-controlled environment.

One of the many varieties of commercial veneer softener on the market, Pro-Glue Veneer Softener, made by Vac-U-Clamp, works well with all buckled veneers and requires no mixing to use.

Most burl veneers will arrive somewhat buckled. You can glue down mildly wavy veneer, but buckled or heavily distorted veneer needs flattening first. Flattening burl veneers makes them much easier to work with and removes most of the brittleness from the veneer. There are a variety of homemade recipes for flattening solution containing numerous ingredients, but commercial flattening solution is reliable, easy to use, and readily available. The commercial solutions are typically a combination of alcohol, glycerin, water, and a glue product; the homemade versions have similar ingredients. I tend to use Pro-Glue Veneer Softener from Vac-U-Clamp® because it works quickly and I can buy it locally.

If you have a vacuum bag system, which we'll discuss in detail in chapter 3, it will make flattening much easier; if not, clamps will also work but require more effort and you'll need quite a few if your veneer leaves are large. For flattening in the vacuum bag, make a set of cauls from ¼-in. MDF that are slightly larger than your veneer sheets. You'll also need large sheets of paper to absorb the flattening solution. Unprinted newsprint works well as does brown paper, but don't use anything with print on it

It's easy to see the difference between flattened veneer and severely buckled veneer. Shown here are flattened madrone burl and maple burl stacked on top of two bundles of buckled Carpathian elm burl.

or the ink will likely transfer onto the veneer. Begin by spraying the veneer with flattening solution; the idea is to wet the veneer uniformly but not soak it. Let the veneer sit for 15 to 20 minutes so the flattening solution can absorb into the grain fully.

Next, stack the veneer leaves in order based on the chalk numbering you did when they arrived, but flip every other one end for end so the buckled grain is reversed and will be pressed out more completely. Start with an MDF caul, then lay down a sheet of

Soak the veneer leaves one by one with flattening solution. The goal is to wet the leaves thoroughly but not soak them until they are dripping wet.

Stack the wet veneer with sheets of paper between the layers and MDF cauls on both sides in preparation for pressing flat.

You'll find that after about 30 minutes, the paper is completely soaked with flattening solution and needs to be switched out for dry paper so the drying process can continue.

The freshly flattened veneer is flexible and easy to cut, but it still has a bit of moisture in it, so it needs a bit more drying time outside of the press. Store it between sheets of MDF for a few days to finish the drying and to keep it flat.

paper and place the first leaf of veneer on top of the paper. Then add another piece of paper and another leaf of veneer. You can flatten an entire bundle of veneer at one time using this method. Continue stacking until all the leaves are stacked evenly with a layer of paper between each of them and between the veneer and the top and bottom cauls. Place the entire stack in the vacuum bag and press the stack flat for about 30 minutes. Now remove it from the bag and change out the wet paper for new dry paper. If you used the right amount of flattening solution, you'll find the paper is quite wet.

To continue the drying process, you need to replace the paper with fresh dry paper that will be

able to pull more moisture from the veneer. Return the stack to the vacuum bag and continue pressing. Remove the stack again in a couple hours and repeat, switching the wet paper for dry paper. After three or four paper replacements, the veneer will be close to dry and it can be removed from the vacuum bag and the leaves restacked in order without the paper layers. Keep the dried veneer stored between sheets of MDF for a couple more days to continue the drying process, and then the leaves will be ready for use. It's a good idea to leave them between the MDF sheets if you're not going to use them for a while—otherwise, the leaves will tend to buckle again.

This large Italian Art Deco desk by the author is made entirely of matched myrtle burl veneer. The veneer leaves were roughly 3 ft. square and needed extensive flattening before use. Once flattened, the veneer cut like soft leather and was quite easy to work with; even bending the burl veneer around the curved edges of the desktop, feet, and door edges was not overly difficult.

The process of flattening veneer with clamps is essentially the same as with a vacuum bag. The primary difference is the need to increase the thickness of the outer MDF cauls from ¼ in. to ¾ in. so they distribute pressure from the clamps more evenly throughout the veneer. All other details of the process are the same, from soaking the veneer in flattening solution through changing the wet paper for dry paper after set time periods.

Cutting Veneer

Learning how to cut veneer is a lot like learning how to cut dovetails: Everyone's got an opinion on how to do it correctly, and all the methods seem to be different. It can be challenging to sort the good methods from the bad and figure out which will work for you. I struggled with this when I was starting to cut veneer as well. There are a variety of tools used to cut veneer, from a handheld veneer saw to a modern powered track saw. Each has advantages and disadvantages.

Whichever tool or method you use to cut your veneer, the process is essentially the same. Mark the location of the cut on a taped-together stack of veneer, align the straightedge with the marked cut line, and methodically cut through the veneer either one piece at a time or as an entire stack. Over the years, I've cut veneer using just about every tool that can be used to

cut wood, and I've developed a simple system that works well and is easy to learn. We'll discuss a few different tools below, but in reality, you can do virtually everything with just a handheld veneer saw and a straightedge—how much simpler could it be?

Handheld veneer saws

The traditional tool for cutting veneer is a handheld veneer saw. There are essentially two versions of the veneer saw available today, and both work very well. One has a double-sided blade with an elongated handle, and the other has a single-sided blade with a large wooden handle. They are both designed to be used with the back of the blade running against a straightedge, and the teeth have no bevel on the back

There are only two handheld veneer saws currently on the market. Either makes a great saw for cutting veneer and should last for many years.

SHARPENING A VENEER SAW

Begin by sharpening the teeth with a small triangular file, following the angles already on the teeth and keeping the file perpendicular to the surface of the blade. Follow that up by beveling the edge of the blade with the flat face of the file to taper the teeth to a fine point. Most blades do not come tapered, so you'll be adding a new taper with the file. Finally, remove the burr from the back of the blade on a fine waterstone or some 320-grit sandpaper glued to a flat block of wood.

Use a small triangular file to sharpen the teeth of the saw, making sure to follow the existing angle of the teeth with the file.

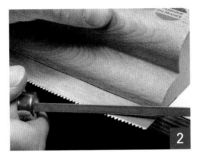

Once the teeth are sharpened, lay the back of the saw flat on your bench and use the flat side of the file to create a bevel on the blade. Continue filing until the teeth reach a sharp point.

Use a fine-grit waterstone or a flat block with a piece of 320-grit sandpaper glued to it to remove the burr from the back of the blade. It should take only a few light passes to get a smooth back.

edge so the cut will always be vertical. Both saws will quickly cut a clean, straight edge on a stack of veneer. Both are also relatively inexpensive, but they do need a quick sharpening to work their best (see the sidebar above).

To cut an accurate straight line through a leaf of veneer requires the use of a straightedge to run the sawblade against. Typically, a piece of straightened hardwood about 1 in. thick by 2 in. wide and at least a few inches longer than the veneer leaf makes an ideal straightedge. It can be improved by applying coarse sandpaper (P100) to the underside to prevent movement while cutting. One edge of the straight-edge must obviously be straight and square to the bottom face of the board or the cuts will not end up straight and square. You can straighten and square the edge quickly with a properly set-up jointer or with a handplane and machinist's square.

Before you cut into your just-purchased bundle of veneer, you'll want to align the leaves so the grain

from leaf to leaf lines up perfectly. Look for telltale grain markings that appear on each leaf, and line them up leaf by leaf in the stack. Tape the stack together in that spot and then move on to another

Every bundle of veneer you buy will have some obvious grain markings that you can use to line up the individual leaves before cutting. Lining up obvious markings that travel from leaf to leaf helps to ensure that when you cut through the stack of veneer, each leaf is cut in the same location and they can all be used to make uniform veneer matches with consistent grain patterns from leaf to leaf.

Once the stack of veneer is taped together, make a couple of pencil marks to get your first cut line laid out.

Line up your straightedge with the pencil marks made previously and gradually cut through the stack of veneer, making sure to keep the back of the sawblade tight against the straightedge.

location and repeat the alignment and taping process; do this several times around the perimeter of the bundle. Now when you cut through the bundle, you'll be able to create veneer matches that have perfect grain alignment from leaf to leaf. I find I can efficiently cut through stacks of 8 to 12 leaves of veneer with a handheld veneer saw without any problem; more than that and I'll either break the stack down into a couple of thinner stacks or switch to a powered track saw.

Place the veneer to be cut on a self-healing cutting mat like those available from sewing-supply stores; these mats will keep your blade sharper much longer than if you were to cut into a sheet of MDF or plywood. Mark the line to be cut with two marks, one on each end of the stack (there's no need to mark the entire line). Simply line up the edge of your straightedge with the two marks. You'll be cutting off the waste side of the line, so keep the straightedge on the side you plan to keep. Hold the straightedge firmly in place and start gradually cutting along the full length of the veneer. Don't try to cut through each piece in a single cut; rather, make multiple lighter passes and let the saw do the work. Continue cutting until all the leaves are cut through. Make sure to keep the back of the sawblade pressed firmly against

JOINTING THE EDGE

Occasionally, your cut edge might require a light sanding to remove small chips or torn grain. With the cut stack of veneer still taped together, slide the stack to the edge of your bench and let it overhang about ⅛ in. Place your straightedge on top of the stack, set back from the edge by about the same ⅛ in. Make a long, straight sanding block in a similar fashion to how the cutting straightedge was made, with one flat face that has P100-grit sandpaper glued to it. Hold the sanding block perpendicular to the cut edge of the veneer and gently sand back and forth a few times along the entire length of the cut. Check your progress by examining the cut edge to see if the flaws have disappeared. If they haven't, continue sanding evenly until they are gone.

Sometimes the veneer you cut with a handsaw or even a track saw might have a bit of tearout or some small chips along the edge (this is especially noticeable in burl veneers). A couple of quick passes with a sanding block will remove any flaws.

the straightedge the entire time. This is a skill that can take some practice to get right, but there really isn't much more to handsaw cutting than that.

Other cutting tools

Another tool that can be used to cut veneer is a scalpel or utility knife. I don't recommend using these to regularly cut long veneer joints because they tend to follow the grain of the wood rather than the straight-

Scalpels aren't so great at cutting long-grain veneer joints, but they make fantastic tools for cutting small pieces of decorative banding and occasional marquetry pieces.

A modern track saw can make fast work of cutting a clean, accurate line through a stack of veneer, and the cut will always be straight and true.

❖ TIP ❖ Making parallel cuts in a stack of veneer simply requires marking one cut line, cutting it, and then marking the second line off the first cut with a tape measure. The same method works for cutting the tapered veneer pieces necessary for the radial match and parquetry projects coming later in the book.

edge. They both also have a cutting edge that is beveled on both sides, so while cutting the blade must be held at a slight angle to make truly vertical cuts. The scalpel is quite useful for cutting small pieces of veneer for borders and inlay, however.

For cutting larger stacks of veneer or multiple bundles at the same time, a powered track saw makes an excellent cutting tool. The edge of the track functions as the straightedge, and with the saw riding in the grooved track, the cuts are always perfectly straight. There are a number of brands of track saws, with several track lengths available for each, so it's possible to create a track of essentially unlimited length.

The process for cutting a stack of veneer with a track saw is similar to cutting with a handsaw. Mark the line to be cut, place the edge of the track on the line, and make the cut with the saw. Be sure to start and stop the saw past the edge of the veneer and cut just through the thickness of the stack of veneer. Press down firmly on the track to hold the bundle of veneer flat while cutting. Also, since we're using a powered saw, don't cut on the cutting mat—cut into a sheet of inexpensive plywood instead. It works best if the location of the cut is changed slightly with each cut so the cuts don't overlap. By moving the cut to a new location each time, you are essentially making a zero-clearance bottom surface for the sawblade so the veneer can't tear out on the bottom. It would be quite difficult to align the sawblade exactly with the kerf of a previous cut, so it's easier to just move a bit and make a new cut.

Taping Veneer Joints

I started taping my veneer joints with blue tape from a home center, and I still use it for the majority of the veneer taping I do in the shop. It's easy to find and reasonably affordable. There are a few other tapes that work well for taping veneer joints beyond

TAPES FOR VENEER

Regular blue tape from a home center is very strong and does a great job pulling veneer joints together tightly. It's a bit thick to put in the press, though, because it might leave an impression in the veneer, and that's where thin blue tape and gum tape come in. Sold as 60-day painter's tape, **thin blue tape** is thinner than regular blue tape and has a weaker adhesive, which is handy when you need to peel it off after your panel comes out of the press. **Gum tape,** a thin paper tape with dry hide glue adhesive on one side, is used by lightly moistening the back of the tape on a wet sponge just before it's applied. Gum tape shrinks slightly when it dries, so it can help pull together seams in veneer sheets. It is also easy to remove by simply moistening the top side of the tape with water. The moist tape can then be quickly peeled or scraped off your glued-up panel. Gum tape is available in a variety of types, some solid and some perforated, in widths from 1 in. to 2 in.

Blue tape is the workhorse of the tape world. We'll use regular blue tape for a variety of things while making decorative veneer panels. It's great for temporarily tacking together joints while doing large layouts so the wood grain can be seen and the parts stay together. It also works well pulling joints together on the back side of matched joints so the face veneer can then be taped with either gum tape or thin blue tape. It's available in a variety of widths from ¾ in. up to 3 in.

Thin blue tape, blue tape, and gum tape (from top to bottom) are the most useful tapes in veneering, and each has its own purpose. Try to keep some of all three in the shop.

just regular blue tape—gum tape and thin blue tape being the most prevalent. Each has a use in veneer work, and you'll find it handy to have all of them around while you're working; each takes a slightly different approach as discussed in the sidebar above.

Taping book-matched veneer

Continuing on with the process we started in the previous section, you've now got a stack of veneer leaves, each with a clean sanded or cut edge that can be joined to another edge to create a larger panel. Let's take two of those leaves and tape up a quick book-match just to see how the different tapes work; we'll cover book-matching in greater detail later, so this is just a quick exercise in taping.

Take two leaves in order and fold them open like a book along the cut edge. You should see a mirrored effect in the grain pattern flowing from one leaf across to the other. Lay a couple of short strips of

1-in. blue tape across the joint at about 4-in. intervals. It works best if you press the tape firmly down on one piece of veneer and then, while holding the two pieces of veneer down, pull the tape across the joint and press it firmly down on the second piece of veneer. Blue tape has a slight bit of stretch to it and applying it in this fashion helps the tape pull the joint tighter. Follow this up with a single piece of blue tape along the length of the joint. I've found that a good method for ensuring the tape won't loosen while I'm working is to rub along all the tape strips with a long brass brush (mine is a long-handled one from McMaster-Carr®). Burnishing the tape this way helps press the tape adhesive firmly into the veneer, which holds the veneer together better while you work on the opposite face. Once you've got one side fully taped, flip the veneer sheet over and you're ready to use a different tape to finish taping before pressing.

There are essentially two sides to a sheet of veneer: the glue face and the show face. As the names suggest, the glue face gets glued to the substrate and the show face goes up and is the visible face once the veneer is glued to the substrate. On the sample bookmatch we just taped together, we were working on the glue face. Now we'll apply a different tape to the show face to get it ready for glue-up. There are two tapes that I find useful in this situation: thin blue tape and gum tape. Each behaves slightly differently and has a place in veneering; where to use each is a topic we'll cover throughout the book.

Let's start by taping the show face of our joint with thin blue tape. Apply roughly 3-in.-long pieces across

Blue tape is inherently stretchy, and you can use this to your advantage when taping joints. Lay the tape down on one side of the joint, and pull it tightly across to the other side. You should be able to feel the tape pull the joint tighter.

To ensure that the tape is firmly seated on the veneer and won't peel off accidentally, give it a good burnishing with a stiff brass brush.

both ends of the joint and at about 4-in. intervals along the length of the joint. Repeat the same procedure of pressing the tape down on one side of the joint and pulling it across to the other side to pull the joint tightly together. Make sure to rub the tape down firmly because the adhesive in thin blue tape is fairly weak. Now run a single piece of tape along the length of the joint, overlapping it equally on both sides. Follow this up with a good burnishing with the brass brush to press the tape down.

One key note about thin blue tape is that because the adhesive is weaker, it only seems to hold for a short time (usually less than an hour before it begins releasing), so you'll want to use it only on panels that will be glued up fairly quickly. If you need to leave the veneer unglued for a period of time or if you have other work to do on the panel before gluing it down, the best tape option is probably gum tape.

Now let's practice the same procedure with gum tape. Take another two leaves of your cut veneer and book-match them together. Blue-tape the joint on the glue face and flip the sheet over to be ready for gum taping. Gum tape is a thin paper tape with a dry adhesive on the back side that's ideal for veneer joints that need to be worked with and left out of the press for longer periods of time, as the glue on the tape adheres to the veneer until moist-

Thin blue tape doesn't have the adhesive power of regular blue tape, so try to use it only on joints that will be getting pressed fairly quickly. They should be in the press within an hour after taping.

ened again. The key with gum tape is to get just the right amount of water on the adhesive: too little and it doesn't stick well, too much and you end up with water and glue smeared on your veneer. Excess water tends to make the veneer expand and move, which we don't want.

With gum tape, you really don't need a bunch of tape strips going across the joint; the one main piece running the length of the joint is plenty to hold veneer leaves together. Tear off a piece of gum tape the length of your joint and run it over the wet sponge. You should have a wet piece of tape that isn't dripping water on your veneer; if it's dripping wet, you've used way too much water, and if it feels dry to the touch, you haven't used enough. Lay the tape down the length of the joint, and wipe over the tape with a paper towel to both press the tape more firmly into the veneer and to remove any excess moisture. Don't pull hard on the tape to stretch it when you lay it down or the tape will tear. The shrinkage that occurs with gum tape while it dries will pull the joint tight.

Once you're finished taping the show face with either thin blue tape or gum tape, it's time to remove the regular blue tape from the glue face of the joint. Flip the sheet over and gently peel off the tape you applied across the joint. Once all the tape is removed, you're ready to glue the veneer to your substrate, as explained in the next chapter.

❖ **TIP** ❖ To help keep the veneer flat, I cover freshly gum-taped joints with a sheet of ¾-in. MDF until the tape is dry (roughly 20 minutes). Otherwise, the joints can tend to buckle and move.

GUM TAPE DISPENSERS

There are a few models of gum tape dispensers on the market that have a small sponge built in for moistening gum tape. You can also make your own with some scrap materials and a dish sponge as I did; mine is made of a couple of pieces of plywood glued to a narrow base with a dowel pushed through a hole in the sides to hold rolls of tape (below). Add a dish sponge in a small plastic cup in front and you're done. Or, if you are just starting out with gum tape, a wet sponge in a shallow bowl will work great and cost you almost nothing in time or money. I know of one veneer expert who has used this method for many years.

Gum tape shrinks slightly as it dries, so it helps pull together veneer joints. Just make sure to let it dry fully before removing the blue tape from the glue face of the joint.

Once the gum tape has dried, flip over the veneer and remove the blue tape from the glue face. Now you're ready to glue it down.

CHAPTER 3

Substrates, Glues, and Presses

When it comes time to glue down your first sheet of veneer, you'll find there is a variety of glues, substrates, and presses available to do the job, and each behaves a little differently than the others. In this chapter, we'll discuss the different substrates used for veneering and why to choose one over another for a particular veneering situation. Then we'll explore some of the many glues that can be used for veneer work and how to use them correctly. Lastly, we'll take a look at the two primary ways you can press veneer onto your substrate—either with hand clamps or with a vacuum bag system. Don't let the wide variety of choices seem overwhelming, though: You can achieve great results with a minimal set of tools and equipment that won't cost you a bundle of money, and we'll discuss that along the way, too.

Choosing a Substrate

Because veneer is so thin, it needs to be glued onto another more rigid material to make it stable and more durable. This material is called the substrate, which can be made of any number of things. For our work, we'll be concentrating on three main substrate materials: medium-density fiberboard (MDF), plywood, and solid wood.

The three main substrates used for veneering are (from the bottom up) MDF, plywood, and solid wood. Each has a place in your veneering toolkit and there are advantages to using each in certain situations.

Each of these substrates has benefits and drawbacks when used as a base for veneer, as you'll see below.

Medium-density fiberboard (MDF)

MDF is the most frequently used substrate in veneering today. It is made by mixing wood fibers and a resin binder together and then pressing that mixture into flat sheets under high pressure and high heat. It differs from particleboard in that particleboard is typically made from larger particles of wood dust and tends to break down and crumble more easily. By contrast, MDF is extremely uniform in thickness and very stable and dense; there is essentially no wood movement in an MDF panel. These two properties make MDF a preferred substrate for veneering.

MDF is the most commonly used substrate for veneering. It is extremely flat and uniform in thickness but heavy and not structural. The dust from cutting and sanding MDF is very fine and unsafe to breathe, so it's important to wear a good dust mask and vacuum as you sand.

Unfortunately, MDF also has a few drawbacks, the most significant of which is weight. A sheet of MDF is very heavy due to the density of the wood fibers and resin—upward of 80 lb. for a ¾-in. sheet. MDF also doesn't take fasteners or joinery well because it's composed primarily of shredded wood fiber, so some additional structure is usually necessary to give strength to an MDF-veneered piece. Working safely with MDF can also be a challenge if your workshop doesn't have adequate dust collection. MDF dust, like most dust, is hazardous to your health. Recent developments in MDF have introduced lower formaldehyde resins that reduce the health risk from chemical exposure to MDF, but the dust is still very unhealthy to breathe.

Plywood

When it comes to using plywood as a substrate for veneer, there is really only one good option: Baltic birch plywood. It has the flatness and stability necessary for veneering and is available in a variety of thicknesses. One thing to note when using Baltic birch plywood is always to orient your veneer grain direction at right angles to the grain on the face of the plywood. This way, you are essentially adding another layer to the plywood core and it will be more likely to remain stable once veneered. Baltic Birch plywood is

Baltic birch plywood can be purchased with single-piece faces and is very strong structurally. Be sure to veneer in the opposite direction to the grain of the plywood faces to maintain stability.

Baltic Birch Plywood Substrate

For thinner parts, you can veneer directly onto thin Baltic birch plywood. Make sure the veneer grain runs perpendicular to the plywood face grain.

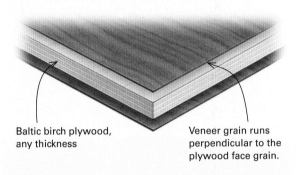

Baltic birch plywood, any thickness

Veneer grain runs perpendicular to the plywood face grain.

quite heavy, nearly the same weight as MDF, but it does have great fastener-holding capabilities and is structurally very strong compared with MDF.

Solid wood

Solid wood makes a great substrate for veneer if you are veneering narrow or long pieces where wood movement isn't going to be a problem or if you veneer wider boards with the grain. Wide solid-wood panels have all the wood movement issues typically seen in solid-wood construction and therefore should be veneered with the grain. I'll typically use resawn veneer over a solid-wood base for tabletops to give some extra durability, but you can veneer over solid wood with commercial veneer as well. Just make sure your panel is flat and smooth before veneering because any milling marks might transfer through to the show face of the veneer, and veneer both sides of the panel just as you would any substrate to help keep it flat.

Narrow parts like legs and trim molding can easily be veneered without any wood movement issues

CUSTOM PLYWOOD

One way to use MDF to advantage is to combine it with other substrates. I've developed a system I use for nearly all my case furniture that incorporates a ¾-in.-thick lumber-core plywood faced on both sides with either ⅛-in. or ¼-in. MDF. By using this custom-thickness core, I get the flatness and stability of MDF without the extra weight, and the lumber-core plywood center holds fasteners and joinery better than pure MDF would. It also allows me to vary the thickness of my panels to create setbacks and reveals between different parts by changing the thickness of the MDF skin or the lumber-core center without adding significantly to the weight of my panels.

Start making the custom core by cutting all the parts 1 in. oversize in all directions so alignment isn't critical. Then apply polyvinyl acetate (PVA) glue to one face of each layer and put the sandwich in the vacuum bag for about an hour. Once it's dry, you can move right on to veneering; however, if you accidentally got some glue on the face of the core, make sure to sand it off completely or your veneer glue might not adhere properly to the MDF. Making the custom substrate doesn't take much extra effort. It's just one more glue-up before the veneering stage—and it saves me the effort of moving around heavy sheets of MDF.

Leave everything oversize at this point, but leave one edge of the plywood core slightly proud to act as a reference edge when trimming the panel to size later. Apply glue to just one face of each layer using PVA glue and a ¼-in. nap adhesive roller.

Cover the stack of glued parts with breather mesh, and place it in a vacuum bag for an hour or two to let the glue set. Leave the lamination to finish drying for 24 hours, and stand it where there is airflow to both sides of the panel so it cures flat.

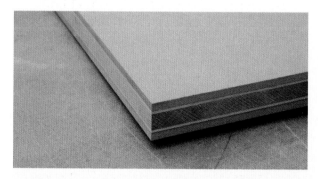

I've developed my own custom substrate for veneering that combines two readily available core materials into one that has the advantages of both but none of the drawbacks. By gluing thin sheets of uniform MDF to a lightweight core of lumber-core plywood, I created a flat, lightweight substrate that can take veneer and fasteners and has some structural stability.

Custom Case Panel

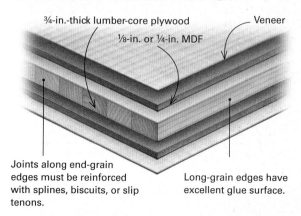

¾-in.-thick lumber-core plywood

⅛-in. or ¼-in. MDF

Veneer

Joints along end-grain edges must be reinforced with splines, biscuits, or slip tenons.

Long-grain edges have excellent glue surface.

Solid wood can be used as a substrate for veneer on narrow parts and on decorative trim pieces. On this Art Deco cabinet by the author, the entire exterior of the cabinet is veneered in etimoe veneer, and the majority of the trim and frame pieces (including the legs) are veneered over a solid-wood substrate. Typically, you'll want to keep the wood parts no more than a couple of inches wide so wood movement doesn't become an issue.

The half-round moldings on this Art Deco bench in myrtle burl veneer are made of veneered solid wood, as are the feet. Wood movement isn't an issue on such narrow parts, and there is no need to veneer the back side of any of these pieces.

because the solid-wood component is typically only a few inches wide. I use solid wood as a substrate for veneer when making furniture designs that are entirely veneered, like many Art Deco pieces where legs, trim pieces, and moldings are all veneered in matching material. I also use it when making furniture where the wood selection is not available in solid wood and therefore parts must be made with veneer. It's also possible to veneer long strips of solid wood with cross-grain veneer because solid wood doesn't really move in the length dimension. Making structural parts out of solid wood adds strength to your furniture, and covering them with decorative veneer that matches the rest of the piece creates a more unified design esthetic.

Glues for Veneer

When I first started using veneer, it didn't seem as though there were as many glues available as there are today. I used primarily polyvinyl acetate (PVA), urea formaldehyde (UF), and hide glue for nearly all my veneering. It turns out there are a number of other glues that can be used to glue veneer, and many of them have benefits over my old favorites in certain situations. Let's start with the basic glues and work our way to more specialized glues later in the discussion. In the project section of this book, each project will demonstrate the use of a different glue, so you'll get a chance to see how the different glues behave and learn their working properties. I've found that having a variety of glues in the shop allows me to be prepared for just about any glue-up that needs to be done. However, the majority of my veneering is done with only three glues: PVA for simple flat panels, UF for marquetry and parquetry veneering, and polyurethane for complex panels and curved work. As a beginning veneer artist, however, you can get by with just a single glue for a long time before needing to invest in more varieties. Whether you choose something like hot hide glue or PVA will depend on your workshop setup and the type of work you like to do.

Polyvinyl acetate (PVA)

The easiest and most readily available glue to use in your veneer work is PVA glue. My personal preference for PVA glue is Titebond® 1, which is easy to apply, dries fast, and forms a fairly rigid glueline. I tend not to use the more water-resistant type 2 and 3 varieties of PVA glues because not much of my work needs to be waterproof—and if it does, I'll switch to epoxy or polyurethane glue because they are both truly waterproof. I've also found that type 2 and 3 PVA glues tend to have softer gluelines and therefore more cold creep, neither of which is beneficial in

❖ TIP ❖ Make sure to stand glued panels in a location that gives them airflow on both sides, and let them sit for 24 hours so the glue can fully cure before you sand the veneer or untape any joints. If you remove the tape from the joints before the glue has fully cured, the joints tend to open up a bit as the glue dries.

veneering. I use Titebond 1 for a variety of veneer jobs but primarily for flat panels with simple veneer work like book-matches; more complex veneer jobs get a different glue.

When using PVA to glue veneer, roll a thin, even coat of glue onto the substrate (never on the veneer or you'll end up with a buckled sheet of veneer that's impossible to press flat). I find that adhesive rollers from the local home center work well as glue rollers for most of the glues I use. Double-check that the glue is evenly spread over the entire surface, especially around the edges, where it can sometimes be thinner. When you place the veneer into the glue, try to get the alignment correct as you put it down; PVA glues have good initial tack, and you'll risk tearing the veneer if you try to pull it up and move it around. PVA glue dries quickly enough that panels

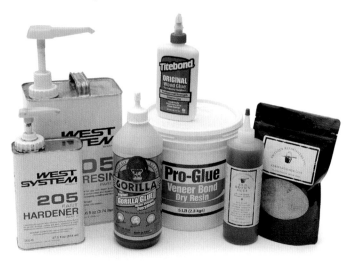

There are many glues that can be used to glue veneer: PVA, polyurethane, epoxy, hot hide glue, liquid hide glue, and urea formaldehyde glue all work well with veneer. Each has its own working characteristics and applications.

Titebond 1 is a great all-around glue for veneering and woodworking in general. It dries fast, has a hard glueline, is easy to clean up, and doesn't require any particular safety precautions during use.

Applying the correct amount of PVA glue doesn't take much practice. You'll want the substrate surface to be completely wet with glue but not so wet that you can pour it off. Make sure there are no puddles or dry spots.

can be taken out of the press in one to two hours. This makes it an ideal glue for pressing multiple panels in a short time.

Urea formaldehyde (UF)

UF-based glue is another glue that frequently gets used for veneering, especially in marquetry and parquetry work and often in bent laminations as well. There are a few brands on the market today, but the one I use most is made by Pro-Glue®, called Pro-Glue Veneer Bond Dry Resin. It comes in white and brown colors that can be mixed together in different quantities to create custom glue colors if you need to match a particular wood tone on something like a bent lamination where the glue color should blend in with the wood grain. Unlike other UF glues, Pro-Glue is a dry powder that you mix with water when you're ready to use it. The formaldehyde content is low, but it's still a good idea to wear gloves and a chemical respirator when mixing and sanding this glue.

UF glue is applied similarly to PVA glue. Roll on a thin, even coat, and make sure you've coated the entire substrate, especially the edges. When you lay the veneer onto the glue, you'll notice that it doesn't have the initial tack of PVA glue. Instead, it is slightly slippery and the veneer can be moved around a bit in the glue, which makes it easier to

position the veneer on the substrate but also easier for the veneer to move around while in the press (all the more reason to have a few pieces of tape around the perimeter to hold the veneer in place).

Pro-Glue, like most UF glues, takes between 6 and 8 hours in the press to cure, depending on the temperature of your shop. Higher temperatures speed curing and lower temps slow it. Either way, you'll want to wait 24 hours before removing any tape or sanding your panel to allow the glue to finish curing completely. When you're ready to clean up the panel after the glue has cured, be aware that UF glues dry very hard and the squeeze-out around the edges of panels can be very sharp. Wear safety glasses while trimming the panel edges because those sharp bits of glue seem to fly everywhere, and they aren't fun to get in your eyes.

Urea formaldehyde glues come in multiple colors that can be mixed together to create new colors in case you need to match a particular wood tone. This brand, Pro-Glue Veneer Bond Dry Resin, is a powder that gets mixed with water to create the active glue. It's formaldehyde based, so you'll want to wear gloves and a chemical respirator while using it.

Hot hide glue

Traditional hot hide glue is a time-honored adhesive for veneering. Typically applied with a veneer hammer, it can be used to veneer small or large surfaces as well as curved parts. If you're not familiar with using hot hide glue, you'll definitely want to practice a few glue-ups with some scrap material before working on an important project. Hot hide glue comes in pearl or granulated form and gets heated

Liquid hide glue (see p. 48) fresh from the bottle is a thick gel, but warm up the bottle in a container of warm water and the glue becomes nice and runny, ideal for veneering. There are several manufacturers of liquid hide glue on the market today, but I've found Old Brown Glue to be the best. It's made in small controlled batches and is always fresh.

Hot hide glue comes in pearls and granules that get dissolved in cold water then heated in a double-boiler system over a hot plate. Water goes in the bottom pot, and the glue gets heated in the upper pot. Temperature control is a must with hide glue to prevent burning the glue; the ideal temperature range is between 140°F and 160°F. If you don't have a glue pot with temperature control, you can use a meat thermometer to monitor the temperature of the glue.

and kept hot in a two-layer glue pot much like a double boiler. Just place some granules in a plastic container and cover them with cold water; in about an hour the granules will have absorbed the water and will be ready to go into the glue pot for heating. Temperature control is very important with hide glue. If the glue is too cold, it will not liquefy properly; too hot and the glue can be ruined. The ideal temperature range is between 140°F and 160°F. Try to keep the glue below 160°F; if you go much higher than that, you'll risk ruining the glue.

Most hide glue made in the U.S. comes from just one company, Milligan & Higgins, and luckily, they are extremely helpful if you have technical questions regarding hide glue (see the Resources list on p. 228 for their contact information). Hide glue is available in a variety of gram strengths. The strength part of that description can be misleading because it doesn't actually refer to the strength of the glue but rather to the set time and stiffness of the glue. Higher num-

bers set faster and dry stiffer. For veneering, 192-gram strength hide glue is the best option, providing an ideal combination of set time and stiffness.

It takes an hour or so for a glue pot to warm up and get the hide glue fully liquefied, so you'll want to plan your glue-ups well in advance. As with all the other glues, hide-glued panels need to rest for at least 24 hours to continue curing before any cleanup is done. As you'll see in chapter 4, when you use hot hide glue, the veneer gets covered in hide glue on both the show and glue faces. Cleaning the show face before the glue has cured is pretty easy: Simply wipe the surface with a cloth dampened with water and scrub off the excess glue. Try not to soak the veneer with water because too much could release the glue that holds the veneer to the substrate. Just wipe the surface and then use a scraper or stiff brush to remove the excess. If you leave any glue on the surface to fully cure, you'll need to sand or scrape it off later.

Since the entire surface of the veneer gets covered with hide glue in hammer veneering, it's not possible to tape joints together ahead of time for more complex veneer matches. Instead, each piece of veneer is glued down individually and the joints between them are cut and forced tight while they are hammered flat. I find this to be a time-consuming method of veneering complex panels, so I use hot hide glue only for veneering small projects with single sheets of veneer and use other glues for more intricate veneering where I am able to tape joints together ahead of time and glue the veneer down in a single operation.

Gorilla Glue® is the most readily available brand of polyurethane glue on the market and the one I use the most. You'll be able to find it in most home centers and a variety of other stores. It does take some practice to get the hang of using it properly though, and you'll want to wear gloves to keep it off your hands. Keep a spray bottle of water handy when using polyurethane glues because they need moisture to cure.

Liquid hide glue

Liquid hide glue has become a staple glue in many woodshops for a variety of processes over the past few years. I like to use it for veneer glue-ups where my standard glues won't work quite the way I need them to. For example, when veneering columns, the veneer needs to completely wrap around the surface of the column, leaving the final seam in the veneer to be cut after the glue is partially cured. To do this necessitates using a glue that can be reversed temporarily by applying heat and then reactivated after the final joint is cut and the veneer is re-pressed. (See the article by Patrick Edwards in *Fine Woodworking* magazine issue 173 on veneering columns for a complete set of instructions.)

Liquid hide glue is relatively easy to use. Just place the bottle of glue in a hot-water bath for about 20 minutes and start gluing much as you would with any other woodworking glue. You can use liquid hide glue in a vacuum press or with clamps, but either way it does take quite a while to dry fully as the drying is primarily accomplished through evaporation of the water in the glue. Cleanup of veneer work glued with liquid hide glue is done in the same manner as with hot hide glue. Wipe the surface with water and scrape or scrub any excess glue off the surface.

There are two main brands of liquid hide glue on the market right now, one made by Titebond and another made by Patrick Edwards called Old Brown Glue (my personal favorite for liquid hide glue). Knowing the process Patrick uses to manufacture Old Brown Glue, I'm always confident that the glue I buy from him is fresh, and I can buy it in a variety of sizes so it doesn't expire before I get through a bottle.

Polyurethane glue

Polyurethane glue is the most misunderstood glue for veneering. Because of the glue's lack of moisture, your veneer sheets won't start to curl as soon as they touch the glue, which is a big benefit when gluing large pieces of veneer. It is also inherently slippery, so it's possible to move the veneer sheet around a bit to fine-tune alignment of the veneer on the substrate. And any glue that penetrates the veneer and appears on the show face is easy to sand off and doesn't affect how the wood takes stain or finishes. Poly glues are also great for bent laminations because they have a rigid glueline that keeps bent-laminated panels the

When using polyurethane glue, it's easy to tell whether you've used enough or too much glue. These three panels show a veneered panel with, from left to right, way too much glue, just the right amount, and not enough glue. It's all in the amount of glue that bleeds through to the show face of the veneer.

Two-part epoxy

Two-part epoxy may not seem like an ideal glue for veneering, but it can be used where no other glue can get the job done successfully. I learned a variety of techniques for using two-part epoxy with veneer while working on a large yacht renovation. On this project, we were faced with the prospect of re-veneering curved panels already installed on the boat. It would have been extremely challenging to create a vacuum bag system that would properly press the veneer onto the cabinetry, so instead we used paper-backed veneer in large sheets that were cut to exactly fit each panel on the boat. We then used thickened epoxy spread with a notched trowel as the adhesive and pressed the veneer into the epoxy, pressing it flat with hard rubber blocks.

exact shape of the form they were made on. Sounds pretty good so far, doesn't it?

The only real drawback to working with polyurethane glue is the cleanup. As the glue cures, it creates foam, and any excess glue you've got on your parts will turn into messy, sticky foam until it's cured hard. I found out the hard way that it's best to leave the foam alone until it cures and chisel it off once it's fully dried. The foam is soft and doesn't have any structural strength, so don't use it where you might need gap-filling strength. That's a job for epoxy.

Because polyurethane glues are isocyanate based, you'll want to keep them off your hands by wearing gloves while working. If you get some on your bench or tools, you can clean it off with acetone or denatured alcohol while it's still wet. It takes a bit of moisture to start the curing process in polyurethane glue, so keep a spray bottle handy while veneering. After you have the glue spread on your substrate, lightly mist the glue face of the veneer panel with water. It barely needs any water to start curing, so don't overdo it or the veneer will start to buckle.

Two-part epoxy is a useful glue to have around. You won't often need it for veneer work, but when you do, it's probably the only glue that will do the job. Just keep in mind that you'll need to wear safety gear to protect your health while using it: ideally, nitrile gloves and a chemical respirator.

VENEERING WITH THICKENED EPOXY

Start with a mixture of two-part epoxy and add enough thickening filler to create a paste similar in consistency to mayonnaise. (Don't worry about the reddish color of the epoxy shown in the photos; old hardener can change color to a deep red but still works fine. I wouldn't use it on a veneering job where the glue might bleed through to the surface of the veneer, though.)

Spread the mixture over the substrate with a notched trowel to create uniform lines of glue over the entire surface. Then align the veneer and press it into the epoxy surface, fair it flat with either a scrap of MDF or stiff rubber trowels that distribute pressure over a large area of veneer, and even out the epoxy gluelines into a single flat uniform glue layer. The process is similar to hammer veneering except that the hammer in this case is a piece of MDF to prevent damaging the delicate veneer with the hammer face. Keep in mind that epoxy contains chemicals you don't want to breathe or get on your hands, so wear gloves and a respirator with chemical cartridges for protection.

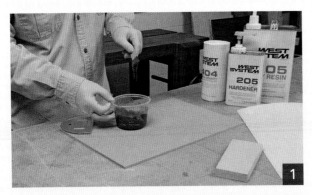

Make a small batch of two-part epoxy and mix in enough adhesive filler to make the epoxy the consistency of mayonnaise. Be sure to thoroughly mix the epoxy before and after adding the filler.

Spread the epoxy mixture over your panel with a notched trowel. Grout and drywall trowels work well and are inexpensive. Make sure the epoxy is completely spread over the panel in uniform ridges so you have a visible, even set of epoxy lines on the substrate.

Lay your paper-backed or two-ply veneer into the epoxy, making sure the alignment is correct. If you partially pull off the sheet of veneer, you should see a uniform set of epoxy lines on the veneer, which means you've got the correct amount of glue.

Use a scrap of MDF or a hard rubber trowel to spread the epoxy over the entire panel. Start in the center and work outward using quite a bit of force. Check your progress occasionally by running your hand over the veneer surface; you should feel a uniformly flat surface. If there are any ridges or bumps, use the trowel to continue smoothing them down until the entire surface is flat and smooth.

This technique is definitely a specialized one with limited use in everyday veneering, but thickened two-part epoxy does work extremely well at adhering paper-backed and two-ply veneer to flat and curved surfaces where a vacuum press or clamps wouldn't be possible. I wouldn't consider this a technique for beginners because it is technically complex to complete all the steps properly, but it can be a handy tool to have in your toolbox for some future project.

Pressing Veneer

It doesn't take much equipment to press small pieces of veneer. You can do it with a few clamps and some simple cauls made from scrap material, or skip the clamps entirely and hammer-veneer your panel with hot hide glue. If you are planning to make larger veneered panels or make veneering a more significant part of your furniture making, you might want to invest in a vacuum bag system. These systems can seem expensive at first, but there are ways to create a system that will work for years without having to spend a lot of money.

To press veneer with either clamps or a vacuum bag system requires essentially the same set of tools: cauls, plastic sheet, glue, and an adhesive roller. The real difference between the two is that

You'll need a wide variety of clamps to press a panel of any significant size. The bigger the panel, the more clamps you'll need and the more likely you'll need a few bowed cauls as well to get pressure into the center of the panel.

using clamps necessitates thicker cauls to help distribute pressure better, while in a vacuum bag, thinner cauls work fine.

Pressing with clamps

Let's start by going over what you'll need to do a simple veneer glue-up with clamps. First, you'll need lots of clamps, and if your panel is wide, you'll need some deep-throat clamps or a few sets of bowed cauls to help apply pressure in the center of the panel.

You'll need to make a set of flat clamping cauls from ¾-in. MDF or particleboard; the cauls should be about ⅛ in. larger than your substrate in each direction. Also, cut two pieces of plastic sheet (available from your home center in large rolls) about ½ in. or so larger than the cauls. Then make two spacers to lift the assembly off your bench so you can apply the clamps easily. I use scrap pieces of 4-in.- to 5-in.-wide 8/4 lumber or pieces of plywood nailed together in a T shape as spacers, and make them as long as the panel is wide. With these items prepared, you're ready to do a veneer glue-up with clamps.

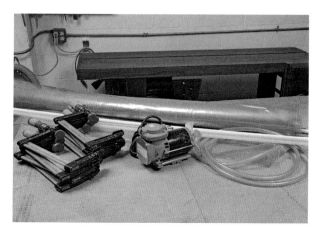

There are essentially two ways to press veneer onto your substrate: using clamps or a vacuum bag. Both work well, but each has advantages in certain situations.

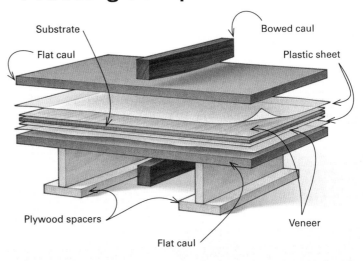

Pressing Setup

Substrate

Flat caul

Bowed caul

Plastic sheet

Plywood spacers

Veneer

Flat caul

Make your clamping cauls out of ¾-in. MDF or particleboard, and cut them just a bit larger than the dimensions of your substrate to ensure you get clamping pressure right to the edge of the panel. Raising the whole assembly up on some T-shaped plywood spacers will make clamping the panel much easier.

Start by placing the first caul on top of the spacers, then cover the caul with plastic sheet and set your substrate on top of the plastic. Apply an even layer of glue to the substrate and then carefully place the veneer on the glue. Flip the panel over and place it veneer side down on the plastic-covered caul. Repeat

Using shopmade bowed cauls to apply pressure to the center of wide panels can save you the cost of purchasing deep-reach clamps, and they don't take very long to make. The wider your panel, the longer your cauls will need to be.

spreading glue on the second side of the substrate and then place the top veneer sheet on the glue. Quickly tape the veneer in place around the perimeter with several pieces of blue tape. Cover the top veneer with the second sheet of plastic and the second caul and then begin applying clamps. Space the clamps evenly around the perimeter of the stack, reaching as far into the center of the panel as possible. Add the upper and lower bowed cauls with a clamp on each end to increase pressure in the center of the panel and leave the panel to dry.

Pressing with a vacuum bag setup

The alternative to using clamps for pressing veneer is to use a vacuum bag system. These systems can be quite simple (see top photo on p. 54) or extremely complex depending upon your needs and budget. My first vacuum bag was an inexpensive 4-ft. by 8-ft. vinyl bag that cost around $100, and my first vacuum pump came from a surplus equipment store and only cost $15—not much in terms of the cost of shop equipment for the value it gives. I used that

MAKING BOWED CAULS FOR CLAMPING WIDE PANELS

Bowed cauls are a great tool used to apply clamping pressure to the center of wide panels when you don't have access to deep-reach clamps (which also happen to be expensive). The bowed cauls can be made with any scrap wood you have handy, but hardwood does work better than softwood like 2x4s. Ideally, the cauls should be roughly 1¼ in. wide by 2 in. high and as long as necessary to reach both edges of the panel. Start by drawing a gentle, smooth curve on one edge of the board that starts about ¼ in. up from the bottom on each end and gradually curves down to the bottom of the board. The resulting curved line should be uniformly smooth with no bumps or hard corners.

Cut along the marked line with a bandsaw or jigsaw, and smooth the cut surface with coarse sandpaper. When you're done, the caul should rock back and forth smoothly and have about ¼ in. of space at each end of the curve; this will close down when you apply clamping pressure. Make enough cauls to have sets of two wherever necessary: one top and one bottom caul at each location. Typically, you'll want to have a set of cauls every 3 in. to 4 in. across the panel where you aren't able to place deep-reach clamps.

Draw a smooth, flowing curved line along the bottom edge of the caul with a marker. You can draw the line freehand and smooth the curve out with sandpaper later, or you can use a flexible batten to lay out a more uniform curve right from the start. Make the curve rise about ¼ in. at the ends so the caul will create good pressure along its entire length.

Use a bandsaw or jigsaw to cut the curved line along the bottom edge of all the cauls, then sand off any bumps or hard edges.

pump for 10 years before it finally burnt out, and I still use the bag. Not many other tools in your shop will last as long and get so much use without requiring any significant maintenance.

Vacuum bag materials

The least expensive material available for vacuum bags is vinyl, which tends to be less resilient than polyurethane bag materials (and less expensive) but is still durable. Polyurethane bags are much less likely to stretch permanently when used with large forms or cauls with sharp corners because the material is much more elastic than vinyl and can handle heat better. There are two primary thicknesses available for both materials: 20mm and 30mm. Either will work for a vacuum bag, but the thicker material will be more durable and less likely to develop pinholes over time. You should be able to purchase a new 4-ft. by 8-ft. vinyl or polyurethane bag for around $200. Keep in mind that there are several vacuum bag sizes available, so if you are planning to make only small items with your vacuum press, there's no need to buy a large bag.

The cheapest way to get into vacuum bag veneering is with a vinyl vacuum bag and a used vacuum pump from a surplus store. There are also a few online sources for used vacuum pumps that will work quite well. I've found Veneer Supplies (www.veneersupplies.com) to be a great source of refurbished vacuum pumps.

Vacuum pumps

There are a variety of pump options you can choose for a vacuum bag system, from a surplus shop—refurbished piston-style pump to a high-end rotary vane–enclosed pump system and a few options in between. Personally, I've always been a fan of the piston-style pumps because they are continuous duty (meaning they run the entire duration of the pressing process) and are essentially maintenance-free. If having the pump running constantly is a deal breaker for you, then you've really only got two options. Either invest in a more expensive pump with a built-in vacuum switch to turn the pump on and off as needed to maintain the correct vacuum level, or make your own vacuum switch from a variety of parts for use with a less expensive pump.

A starter-level continuous-duty piston pump will cost between $150 and $350; less if you find a refurbished one and more if you buy a newer, more powerful pump. A new full-featured pump system with built-in controls and fast evacuation can run upward of $2,000. For beginning veneer work, you really don't need an expensive pump system. Start out with an inexpensive piston or diaphragm pump and make sure you really like doing veneer work before dropping thousands of dollars on a full-featured pump system. The only real negative to using a lower-cost pump is that evacuation speed is slower, so it takes a bit longer to get the bag to full vacuum. There are work-arounds for this, though; several plans on the Internet detail how to incorporate a vacuum tank into your pump system, which allows you to precharge the vacuum and rapidly evacuate the bag on startup.

REPAIRING HOLES IN VACUUM BAGS

The most significant maintenance you'll ever need to do to a vacuum bag is to repair small holes likely caused by cauls with sharp corners. A quick method to repair these is to place a piece of clear packing tape on both the inside and outside face of the bag directly over the hole. Press the tape firmly onto the bag, and you'll effectively seal the hole from both sides. To prevent these types of holes from occurring in the first place, I recommend using a breather mesh on top of your glue-ups.

Apply a piece of clear packing tape to the inside of the vacuum bag directly over the hole. Press it on firmly.

Apply a second piece of packing tape to the outside of the bag, again directly over the hole, and press it down hard onto the bag. This should effectively seal the hole.

The lowest-cost vacuum pump you can buy is a used diaphragm pump from a surplus store. Typically, they have been removed from old equipment but still have many years of life left in them. Expect to pay between $15 and $50 for one of these pumps. They are suited for continuous duty and can achieve a high vacuum of 24 in. Hg but are fairly slow at 1.1 cfm—which is ideal for a small bag system but pretty slow for a large one.

One of many double piston–style vacuum pumps that can be used for vacuum bag systems, this one is a continuous duty–style pump with moderately fast evacuation of 3 cfm and high vacuum of 24 in. Hg. Expect to pay between $150 and $250 for a refurbished model or between $400 and $850 for a new one, depending on the strength and speed of the pump.

For those without budgetary constraints, this full-featured rotary-vane vacuum pump from Vac-U-Clamp, model VHP, will provide very fast evacuation of 10 cfm and extremely high vacuum of 29 in. Hg. It is rated for continuous duty and has enough power to run multiple bags simultaneously. These features come with some added cost (nearly $2,000 for the complete pump system), but if you need a high-power, ready-to-go pump, this is a good option.

Breather mesh

To effectively use a vacuum bag system for veneering requires essentially the same tool set as you would use to press veneer with clamps; the only real differences are the thinner cauls and the addition of breather mesh. Breather mesh is a plastic mesh made of thin crisscrossing plastic ribs. It does two important things in a vacuum-bagged veneer glue-up. First, it allows the vacuum pressure to spread evenly over the surface of the panel, and, second, it protects the vacuum bag from the sharp corners of the cauls. Breather mesh is relatively inexpensive and well worth the cost. I use a piece of mesh that is large enough to completely cover the top caul of my glue-up and reach the inlet hose for the vacuum pump.

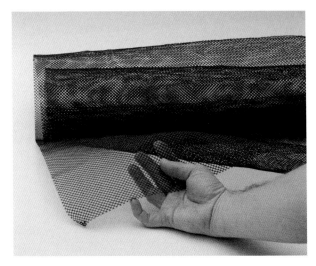

Breather mesh is a woven plastic mesh designed to allow free airflow across large surfaces. It's not overly expensive but is highly useful for vacuum bag veneering.

FLIP-TOP PRESSES

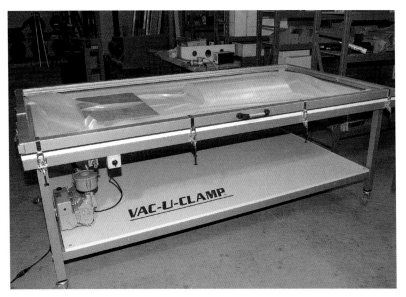

For a home shop or even a small professional, one of the best vacuum systems you can buy is a flip-top press. This entry-level press from Vac-U-Clamp is the SP series 4-ft. by 8-ft. flip top with an integral continuous-duty pump. It combines the best attributes of a vacuum bag with easy access, fast evacuation, and high-quality construction for around $8,500.

If you've got extra money to spend on a vacuum system, you can quickly move up to a flip-top vacuum press. This press is essentially a flat table with a hinged top frame that has vacuum bag material inside it. You place the material to be pressed on the table and close down the top, effectively sealing it to the tabletop. Start the vacuum pump and in just a few seconds the vacuum will be pressing your veneer. Flip tops are much easier to use than a bag system because they don't require you to slide heavy panels in and out of the vacuum bag. The tabletop also functions as the bottom caul, so you'll only need a top caul for all your pressing. Unfortunately, they do cost significantly more than a vacuum bag system.

CHAPTER 4

Creating Your First Veneered Panels

There are a variety of ways to decoratively match pieces of veneer to create interesting patterns: book-matching, four-way matching, and radial matching to name just a few. In this chapter, we'll go over two ways to use veneer: a one-piece glue-up done with just a single piece of veneer for a nice decorative box top and a book-matched panel made of two sequential leaves of veneer for an inset door panel.

A single piece of figured sycamore veneer glued to ¼-in. Baltic birch plywood adds visual complexity to what might otherwise have been a simple mahogany box.

The basic tools for cutting and taping a book-matched panel are a veneer saw, a straightedge, a cutting mat, blue painter's tape, a brass brush, and gum tape.

A single piece of mirror can be used to see what a book-match will look like by placing the mirror on the proposed center of the book-match. A two-piece hinged mirror will be necessary to see four-way and radial matches.

The Tools You'll Need

The basic tool set you'll need for cutting and taping together your first veneer panel is composed of all the tools we discussed earlier: a veneer saw, a cutting mat, and a straightedge, along with some tape and a brass brush. To make visualizing the different veneer matches easier, we're going to add one new tool to your arsenal—a set of rectangular mirrors with a simple tape hinge joining them together. These hinged mirrors will become a surprisingly useful tool for the different veneer matches we're going to be working on later in the book.

With a single piece of mirror, you can easily see what a book-match of veneer will look like by placing the mirror on what will be the joint between the two leaves of veneer. Looking into the mirror then shows you both sides of the book-match, and you can move the mirror around until you find the most pleasing grain match. Once you've found the perfect match, just make a couple of pencil marks along the bottom edge of the mirror so you'll know where to cut the veneer.

Backer Veneer

An important design decision for any veneered project is what to use for backer veneer—the veneer that goes on the back side of all veneered panels to balance them and help keep them flat. Backer veneer can be one of two things: either an inexpensive, unattractive species of wood used only to balance the panel without any decorative properties or a chance to add more decoration to your work.

The golden anigre–veneered interior of this small cabinet was intended to bring lightness to the interior but also blend well with the exterior panels of matching anigre veneer that are inlaid into the walnut doors and side panels.

USING A TWO-PIECE MIRROR

The cheapest way to create your own hinged mirror is to buy two rectangular mirrors from a glass-supply store. There is likely one near you that can cut the mirror to size for you. I've found that a set of mirrors ¼ in. thick by roughly 6 in. wide and 20 in. long works great.

Lay the two mirrors end to end (mirror side up) with about ¼ in. of space between them, and apply a strip of blue tape across the joint. Flip the mirrors over, and tape the other side of the joint as well. This effectively creates a flexible hinge between the two mirrors. Be careful when handling the mirror glass because the cut edges can be quite sharp. If you find they are too sharp to touch, use a hard block covered with some coarse sandpaper to break all the edges before taping the mirrors together.

Using a set of mirrors with the tape hinge connecting them allows you to see a variety of veneer matches, everything from a four-piece match with the mirrors held at 90° to each other to an eight-piece radial match with the mirror faces held 45° apart and a whole variety of matches in between.

Freshly cut glass edges are very sharp. Break them with a piece of coarse sandpaper on a hard wood block so you don't get cut while taping them together.

Taping two mirror panels together to create a hinged pair of mirrors allows you to see a variety of veneer matches beyond just a simple book-match. Butt the mirrors together end to end and leave about ¼ in. of space between them, then tape the joint on both sides of the mirror with blue tape.

Holding a set of taped-together mirrors at 90° to each other will allow you to see a complete four-way match from a single piece of veneer.

Using the same set of hinged mirrors held at different angles allows you to see different radial matches. Here, they are held 45° apart to show an eight-piece radial match of veneer.

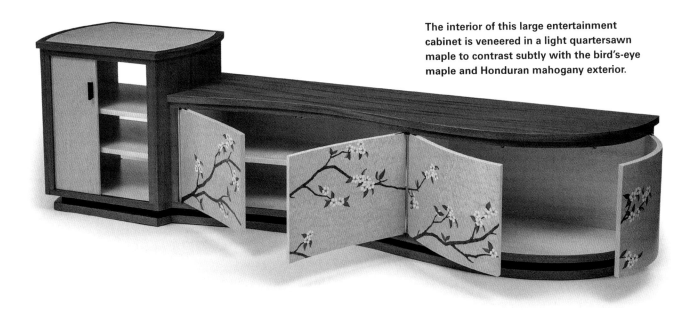

The interior of this large entertainment cabinet is veneered in a light quartersawn maple to contrast subtly with the bird's-eye maple and Honduran mahogany exterior.

For me, backer veneer is an opportunity to do something creative with the interior of my furniture. I'll nearly always veneer the inside of a cabinet with something that contrasts with the exterior veneer, typically a veneer light in color and figured like a curly maple or anigre. The lighter veneer adds an element of intrigue and interest for the client when they open a door and find something unexpected on the inside rather than a bland, plain wood. The lighter veneer also helps brighten the interior of what might otherwise be a confined inside space.

A great way to start veneering is to make a simple veneered box top like this one where the decorative veneer adds a nice detail to an otherwise plain box.

A One-Piece Veneered Panel

A good project to use as an introduction to the world of veneering is a decoratively veneered top panel for a small box. This simple project is a great place to learn some basic veneering skills, including how to work with hot hide glue and hammer veneering. Vacuum bagging and more complex glues will be saved for later chapters. For now, we'll focus on the basics: proper preparation for gluing the veneer and the correct techniques to spread the glue and hammer it down.

Cutting the veneer to size is easy with the right tools: A sharp veneer saw, a straightedge, and a cutting mat are all you need to get clean, accurate cuts.

INTERIOR VENEERS FOR CONTRAST

When I veneer door panels, I also take into account what the interior of the cabinet will look like. If the design calls for an interior that essentially matches the exterior, then I'll veneer the inside of the door panel with veneer that matches what's used on the outside of the panel. This gives the appearance of a solid-wood panel but the variety of a veneered one. If the interior needs to be veneered in something different, I'll veneer the inside faces of the doors with material that matches the rest of the interior.

The same can be done with boxes or nearly any project that you plan to veneer. Box interiors are a great place to experiment with different materials and add interest to small pieces. This attention to detail becomes something that helps potential clients remember your work long after they've put the box down.

This marquetry cabinet by the author features an exterior veneered in ash burl and an interior veneered in light white quartersawn maple.

This box by Adrian Ferrazutti showcases some exquisite parquetry on the exterior, but the real delight comes when you open it to find a vibrant figured sycamore interior.

An Art Deco cabinet like this amboyna burl and etimoe–veneered piece by the author becomes even more interesting when the doors open because the interior is veneered in strikingly bright curly sycamore.

The first step is to determine the overall size of your panel. For this example, we'll make the top of the small box approximately 6 in. wide by 9 in. long. Cut a piece of Baltic birch plywood 1 in. over the size of your panel with the grain running opposite to the direction of the veneer. In other words, if your finished box top needs to be 6 in. wide by 9 in. long, the plywood should be 10 in. wide by 7 in. long and the grain on the plywood should look as though it is 10 in. wide and 7 in. long.

Then cut the veneer 7 in. wide by 10 in. long so it is oversize and matches the plywood piece rather than the exact size of your finished panel. Use the techniques discussed in chapter 2 to cut the veneer with a veneer saw and a straightedge on the cutting mat. Remember to cut a second piece for the back of the panel as well, possibly in the same veneer as the front.

Working with hot hide glue

Now let's get some hide glue cooking. (Ideally, you'd do this part a few hours before you want to glue your veneer as it takes a while for the glue to get hot.) Start by scooping about ½ cup of hide glue granules into a plastic container, then cover the glue with cold water to just above the level of the granules. Set this aside for about an hour to gel.

After an hour, the granules of hide glue should have completely absorbed the water. Pour the mixture into the glue pot of your double-boiler setup. The outer pot should be filled about two-thirds full with hot water and be warming on a hot plate. I find that heating up the water pot first and using a meat thermometer to check the temperature is a good way to ensure the temperature of the water is not too high. You'll want to keep the temperature of the hide glue between 140°F and 160°F.

While your glue is cooking (it will take 45 to 60 minutes to get up to the correct temperature),

Pour some granules of hide glue in a plastic container, and fill to just above the level of the glue with cold water. In about an hour, you'll have hide glue gel ready to be heated in the glue pot.

Gather all the tools you'll need for hammer veneering while the glue is cooking: a veneer hammer, plastic sheeting to cover your work area, the plywood substrate, your veneer sheets, and the glue pot.

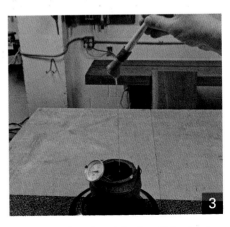

Check the viscosity of the hot hide glue by lifting the brush out of the glue pot. The continuous stream of glue coming off the brush should be about 10 in. long before it breaks into drops.

you can be cutting your veneer and substrate to size. Cover your work area with a sheet of plastic to make cleanup faster. Get all your tools ready: glue brush, veneer hammer, water, and some paper towels. Hot hide glue sets quickly as it cools, so you'll want to have everything ready when you start spreading glue.

Check the hide glue for proper viscosity. It should run in a single continuous line down from a brush lifted about 10 in. out of the glue pot. If it's too thick, add a bit of hot water to the mix; if it's too thin, let it cook a while longer before use. When it's just the right consistency, it's time to start gluing the veneer.

Start by spreading a moderate amount of hide glue onto the substrate with the glue brush, working the glue into the wood. Then quickly lay the veneer show face down onto the glued substrate and spread more hide glue onto the glue face of the veneer with the glue brush. The glue that is getting onto the show face will act as a lubricant for the hammer when you hammer the veneer down.

Once the glue is spread uniformly on the veneer, lift it up and flip it over so the glue face is down on the substrate. Grab your veneer hammer and start working it back and forth down the center of the panel. Slowly move outward toward the edges of the panel, applying a significant amount of pressure to the front of the hammer. Use one hand on the handle to steer the hammer and press firmly on the head of the hammer with the other. Continue working the hammer back and forth across the entire surface of the panel until all of the veneer is pressed evenly to the substrate.

Begin spreading hide glue on the substrate, making sure to work the glue into the wood grain and moving quickly as the glue begins to set very fast.

Place the veneer show face down onto the substrate, and spread glue on the glue face of the veneer. The glue that gets on the show face will act as lubrication for the veneer hammer.

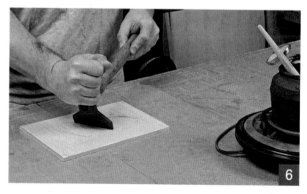

Flip the veneer over and place the glue face down on the substrate. Begin pressing down on the veneer with the hammer, starting in the center and working outward. It takes quite a bit of pressure, so work two handed if you need to but concentrate your pressure on the head of the hammer. Continue working from the center out until all the veneer is pressed flat.

FITTING THE BOX TOP

The veneered top can be made a number of different ways, but I've found that the easiest method is to start with a thin piece of plywood, maybe ¼ in. thick, for the top panel. Veneer both faces, then cut a rabbet around the perimeter of the top that then gets recessed into a narrow dado cut into the sides of the box before assembly. Locate the dado so the veneered top ends up flush with the sides of the box. Sand the top and sides flush after assembly.

The veneering in this project is pretty simple because you're only veneering a small panel; the complexity comes in accurately cutting the rabbet on the panel so that it fits exactly inside the dado in the box with no gap around the perimeter of the panel. Even that can be fixed with a bit of decorative inlay though, so it isn't really a problem.

The quickest way to fit this kind of top to the box is to make a single saw kerf in each of the box sides located exactly the thickness of the veneered top panel down from the top of the sides. Then gradually sneak up on a snug fit in that kerf with the rabbet cut on the top panel.

Start with a tight fit between the rabbet and dado, and keep fine-tuning the fit either on the tablesaw or with a rabbet plane until the top slips into the kerf in the sides.

You should notice hide glue squeezing out all along the edges of the panel as you work; the idea is to get all the extra glue out from underneath the veneer before it hardens. Once you start to hear a cracking sound, you're done hammering. Wipe off any excess glue with a paper towel dampened with warm water (don't use too much—just enough to make the towel damp). Once one side of the panel is completed, flip it over and repeat the same steps to veneer on the back face.

A Book-Matched Veneer Panel

Creating a book-matched veneer panel is a great way to practice the precision needed to work with veneer when creating decorative matches. One way to do this in your regular woodworking is to make a set of veneered panels to be placed in frame-and-panel doors in a cabinet instead of solid-wood panels. The veneered panels won't take much more effort to create, and you'll have lots of interesting options for decorative grain and figure that you wouldn't have with solid wood.

A book-matched veneered panel can add interest to what might have been a simple frame-and-panel design, as in this walnut desk built by Loy Davis Martin with beautiful book-matched curly walnut panels in solid walnut frames. The curly walnut veneer is even book-matched across the outer panels of the desk, adding unity to the whole design.

This sideboard by Loy Davis Martin features book-matched door panels in curly spalted maple veneer and parquetry-decorated drawer fronts.

Timothy Coleman used book-matched Japanese ash panels in the doors of this small cabinet to frame a figured ash central panel. The wildly flowing grain in the ash panels clearly shows the pattern book-matched across the two doors.

This curly maple and mahogany cabinet by the author features curly maple veneer book-matched across the two doors. The side panels are also book-matched from left to right to maintain design continuity.

To make a book-matched panel, you need two leaves of veneer for the front of the panel and two more to create the book-match on the back of the panel. Lining up the grain lines in the four leaves of veneer before cutting them allows you to cut through all the leaves in the same location, which will make it easier to line up the grain in your book-match.

Because my veneered panels for frame-and-panel doors are inserted as part of the door-assembly process, I tend to make them on a substrate of ¼-in. MDF. This makes the panels very stable and allows me to glue them into the door frame, strengthening the door structure. You could make the substrate out of ½-in. MDF or Baltic birch, but I find it generally doesn't leave enough material in a ¾-in.-thick frame once the ½-in. panel has been veneered. This can be a judgment call you make based on the overall design of your cabinet and door parts. For now, let's assume you've decided to go with ¼-in. MDF as the substrate for your panel and we'll proceed accordingly.

To start, you'll need two leaves of your selected veneer for the front of the panel and two more leaves for the back of the panel. For this sample panel, we're going to be using a walnut veneer for both the front and back of the panel, so we'll need four leaves of sequential walnut veneer at least 8½ in. wide and 25 in. long to create our roughly 16-in. by 24-in. door panel. Begin by aligning the grain pattern in the veneer from leaf to leaf as we did in chapter 2, then tape the stack of four leaves together in a few spots. That way, when you cut through the stack to create

your book-matched veneer pattern, the grain orientation of all four leaves will be nearly identical. Once you've found the book-match you like (as explained in the sidebar on the facing page), mark the veneer with a pencil in a few places at the bottom edge of the mirror. Since you've already aligned and taped the veneer leaves together, you can move right to cutting the veneer.

Cutting the veneer

Lay your straightedge on the marked line with the blade side facing the waste part of the veneer and begin cutting through the stack with the veneer saw. Remember to cut gradually through the stack and take your time; making multiple light passes is better than trying to force the veneer to cut in a single pass of the saw. Also, be sure to keep the back of the saw-

DIFFERENT VIEWS FROM THE MIRROR

Using the hinged mirror panel we created earlier, fold one mirror out of the way and set the edge of the other mirror along the line you'd like to use to create the center seam of your book-match. Take some time and move the mirror around to find the perfect pattern in the grain. By looking into the mirror, you should be able to see what your book-match will look like when you cut the veneer. A slight change in the angle of the mirror can bring out a more interesting book-match and create grain that has either more or less uniformity. It all depends on how you want the grain at the center of the panel to look: Would you like it to be an obvious joint where the grain has more dramatic cathedral patterns, or would you prefer something more subdued where the grain at the center is more uniformly vertical from one side to the other? The choice is yours and is all part of the process of learning the craft of veneering.

To view a book-match with the hinged mirrors, fold the extra mirror out of the way and place a single mirror on your chosen veneer seam.

Moving the mirror over the surface of the veneer allows you to change the look of the book-matched grain. It's easy to see what the different grain orientation will do to the appearance of the panels; here, we've created a look that has more dramatic cathedral grain in the center.

Moving the mirror in the opposite direction creates an entirely different grain pattern. It can be very useful to play with these different patterns when designing your veneered panel.

Once you've selected the perfect grain pattern from the mirror image, mark along the bottom edge of the mirror with a pencil. This will become the cut line for your veneer saw.

Cut through the stack of veneer using the instructions detailed in chapter 2 (see pp. 34–36). The only tools you need are a veneer saw, a straightedge, and a mat to cut on.

Sometimes you'll need to touch up the fresh cut edge on your veneer. Slide the stack just off the edge of your bench, and place the straightedge on top of it to hold the veneer flat. Sand the edge of the stack with a hard sanding block, making sure to sand evenly down the entire edge.

blade pressed firmly against the straightedge to keep the cut edge vertical.

Check the quality of the cut edge before untaping the stack, and if it has any tears or rough grain, give it a quick sanding with the hard sanding block we made in chapter 2. Follow the procedure outlined previously to get a nice clean vertical edge on the stack of veneer.

Taping the veneer

Once you've cut the veneer, untape the stack and lay out the two sets of leaves with the book-match joints in the center. You'll be looking at the show face of the veneer so this is what you'll see when the veneer is glued down. Line up the grain markings from one side of the joint to the other by gently sliding one piece of veneer along the joint until the grain matches perfectly from side to side. As you align the joint, look for any telltale grain lines that need to carry across the joint to create a better book-match. Apply a few pieces of blue tape across the joint to hold it together once you've got the grain perfectly aligned.

Next, flip the veneer over so you can tape the glue face of the joint tightly together. We'll use regular blue tape for this taping. Begin by applying strips of

tape across the joint about 4 in. to 6 in. apart, and pull the tape tight as you press it down so it pulls the joint together. Now run one long strip of tape down the length of the joint and burnish the tape down with a brass brush to seat the tape firmly into the veneer.

Flip the taped veneer over, and remove the few pieces of blue tape from the show face. Double-check the alignment of the grain in your book-match. If it needs adjustment, repeat the above taping steps until it looks the way you want. For this panel, we'll use gum tape to hold the show-face joint together. We've already gone over how to use gum tape in detail in

Initially, tape the book-match together in just a few spots so you can check the grain alignment. If it's not quite right, adjust the pieces of veneer until the grain lines up perfectly.

Tape the glue side of the joint together with regular blue tape. Applying a number of pieces across the joint helps pull the seam tight before you apply a long piece along the length of the joint. After that, rub the tape down by burnishing it with a brass brush.

chapter 2, but here's a quick refresher. Moisten the adhesive side of a strip of tape lightly with a damp sponge and gently press it down along the length of the joint, keeping it roughly centered on the joint. Then take a piece of paper towel and pat down the tape to help seat it onto the veneer and remove any excess moisture from the tape. Place the taped veneer sheet under a piece of MDF for 20 to 30 minutes to allow the tape to dry. Once the gum tape is dry, flip the veneer over and remove all the blue tape from the glue face. This book-matched sheet of veneer is now ready to be glued down to the substrate. Repeat the same procedure for the second book-matched veneer leaves.

Gluing up the veneer

Now that you've got the veneer sheets gum-taped and ready to glue up, assemble the rest of the equipment you'll need to press this veneer with liquid hide glue and clamps. First, you'll need to make up a few sets of bowed cauls so you can get clamping pressure to the center of your door panel. Make them as we discussed in chapter 3 with some scrap wood and a bandsaw or jigsaw. You'll probably want at least three pairs for this glue-up. In addition to the bowed cauls, you'll need a set of ¾-in. MDF flat cauls for clamping that are just a bit larger than your substrate. For this panel, they should be just over 17 in. wide by 25 in. long.

Because we're using liquid hide glue for this project, you'll need a small bottle of that along with a glue roller and a container of hot water. Go ahead and get your bottle of liquid hide glue ready by setting it in the container of hot water for about 20 minutes to make it more fluid. When it comes to rolling out glues, I find that adhesive rollers from the home center work very well for most glues. I buy the 9-in.-long rollers and cut them into thirds so I can use them on my 3-in.-wide roller handle.

You'll also need two spacers to lift up the assembly and allow you to get the clamps applied more easily. I made mine from a few scraps of plywood nailed together into a T shape. They're about 4 in. high and

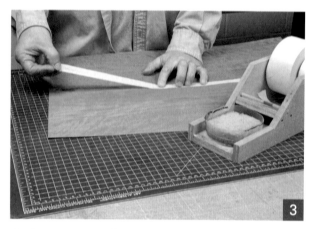

Apply gum tape as discussed in chapter 2, first by moistening the glue face of the tape, then by centering the tape on the veneer joint as you lay it down.

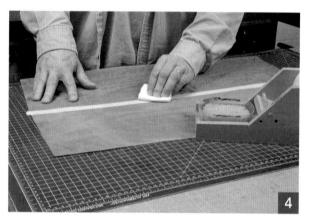

Remove any extra moisture from the tape by patting it down hard with a paper towel before placing the veneer under a piece of MDF to dry for 20 to 30 minutes.

When both joints are gum-taped and dry, you can remove the blue tape from the glue face of the veneer and it will be ready for pressing.

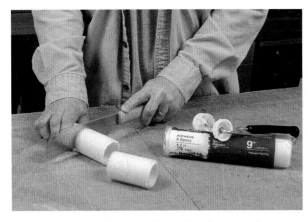

Adhesive rollers make great glue rollers for veneering. Buy 9-in. rollers and cut them into 3-in. lengths for use on a 3-in. roller.

You can make spacers with pieces of 8/4 lumber 4 in. to 5 in. wide or with scraps of plywood nailed together to form a T shape. These work great for a variety of tasks in the shop, so they are handy to have around in a variety of lengths.

When you are ready to spread glue on the substrate, make sure you have everything ready to clamp it as well. You'll want to have one caul covered with a plastic sheet on top of the spacers you made earlier.

Roll an even layer of liquid hide glue onto the substrate, making sure to get uniform coverage everywhere and avoiding any puddles of glue.

Once the glue is spread, you've got only a couple minutes to get the veneer in place and the clamps on, so work quickly.

17 in. long, so they span completely across the width of the panel. Get things set up for gluing by setting one of the cauls on top of the two spacers, placing the spacers a few inches in from each end of the caul. Lay a single sheet of plastic over the caul, and set your ¼-in. MDF substrate on top of the plastic.

Begin spreading the glue and roll it evenly over the surface of the substrate. Work quickly because the glue starts to cure as soon as it comes out of the bottle. With liquid hide glue, you've probably got only a couple of minutes to get the glue spread and the veneer down, so I'll typically glue only one side of each panel at a time. Make sure to get extra coverage around the edges. There should be a uniform layer of glue over the whole surface; you're aiming for an even spread of glue but not so much that it's puddling up on the panel. Lay the first sheet of veneer carefully onto the glue surface and press it down lightly all around. Try to work quickly because the glue will not take long to start curing, and the longer you leave the veneer in the glue without clamps, the more it's going to want to buckle and move.

Place a layer of plastic over the veneer, then lay on the top caul. Begin clamping the panel, starting with the bowed cauls that reach into the center of the panel and then working your way outward to the clamps around the edges. Tighten all the clamps uniformly and make sure you have a clamp every couple of inches over the entire surface of the panel. Leave

the assembly to dry overnight, then remove all the clamps, cauls, and plastic and evaluate how your book-matched veneer panel looks. If all went well, the veneer should be pressed uniformly flat and there should be light spots of glue bleed-through spread evenly over the face of the veneer. If the first side turned out as well as it should, flip the panel over and glue your second piece of veneer to the other side using the same procedure. Once the second side is dry and out of the clamps, set the panel aside in a location that gets airflow to both sides of the panel and leave it to continue drying overnight.

With the veneer placed and the plastic sheet and caul on top, apply the clamps and bowed cauls. Start with the bowed cauls that apply pressure into the center of the panel and work outward, making sure you have clamps every couple inches around the perimeter of your panel.

It can take quite a few clamps to press even a moderately sized door panel. Anything larger than this and you'll want to move up to a vacuum bag system to press your veneer because it simply takes too long to get all the clamps tightened while the glue is setting.

The final step is to place the finished book-matched veneer panel in a frame-and-panel door.

Sanding through a veneered panel is a disappointing experience and will require the veneer to be either repaired or replaced. Depending on the severity of the damage, it might be easier just to start over with a new panel. Small sand-throughs can often be touched up with touch-up markers. It's helpful to have a wide selection of markers in your shop—just in case.

Sanding Veneer after Gluing

There are few things in woodworking more disappointing and soul destroying than sanding through a completed veneer panel. Typically, it happens on the last stage of sanding when you think you're nearly done with the project and decide to give it just a touch more finish sanding. First, you'll start to see a change in the color of the veneer, and then the grain will begin to disappear; by the time you realize what's happened, you've sanded even more of the veneer away. Some sand-throughs can be repaired and some can't without leaving obvious traces that a repair was done.

Small sand-throughs like the edge that I oversanded (above) can be touched up with touch-up markers and made to essentially disappear to everyone but the maker; this takes practice and a steady hand. Keep in mind that natural wood is made up of several layers of color and to accurately replicate it, you need to apply a few different layers of color with various tools. Re-creating grain lines can be done with fine-line pens, and replacing sections of background color can be done with wider markers, but

figure and iridescence (from curl or fiddleback grain) are nearly impossible to re-create. To do more extensive veneer repair requires many more tools than touch-up markers. There are powdered pigments that can be mixed with finish to paint on missing grain, wax crayons for filling dents, shellac fill sticks, paint pens, finish pens, and so on. The best advice I ever received about fixing sand-throughs (though I didn't think it was so great at the time) was to learn not to sand through my veneer in the first place. It takes practice but is well worth the effort.

Current slicing methods produce veneer that is thinner than ever before, which makes using proper sanding technique even more important. If you're working with resawn veneer in $1/16$-in. to $1/8$-in. thicknesses, you can just about sand all day and not worry about sanding through your veneer. With commercial veneer, if you sand a bit too long or use an overly heavy grit to start sanding, you'll burn through the veneer in no time at all.

I've learned the hard way to be somewhat minimal when sanding commercial veneer. I typically start sanding with 150-grit on a random-orbit sander to quickly level the surface and remove any glue squeeze-out, then switch to hand sanding with a hard rubber or foam block and 180-grit sandpaper for my

I frequently start my veneer sanding with a random-orbit sander and 150-grit sandpaper. I rarely sand with anything coarser than 150-grit because the sanding marks can be difficult to remove without risking sanding through the veneer.

Once the sander has leveled the surface, I go over the entire panel with a hard foam block and some 180-grit sandpaper, which helps to further level the surface and remove any orbital sanding marks.

primary sanding. After that, I'll finish up with 180- and 220-grit on the random-orbit sander and I'm done. I'll very rarely sand with anything coarser than 150-grit, and you don't typically need to go beyond 220-grit if you are finishing with sprayed lacquer or conversion varnish because they both build decent film thicknesses. If you're going to French polish or oil your veneered pieces, you might consider sanding up to 320- or 400-grit by hand. Burl veneers can also benefit from sanding to 320-grit.

As with any finishing system, make some samples and test your sanding and finishing methods to see the final outcome before using them on a completed project. You'll be able to see very quickly what works and what doesn't. Without the samples, you'd be experimenting on a project that may have hundreds of hours of labor and expensive materials tied up in it.

What's Next?

Another way to incorporate veneer into your woodworking would be to make a set of doors that don't have the solid-wood frame but are instead full ¾-in.-thickness veneered panels with either thin solid wood

or veneer edging. These doors take a bit more effort to make but can give a nice clean appearance to a cabinet front. A good method for making these doors is to prefit the veneer substrate to the assembled cabinet and then edge them in either thin wood or veneer edging before veneering the faces with matched veneer. Done this way, the view you'll see from the outside of the cabinet is of the full veneer surface and not the edging around the perimeter. We'll go into more detail about edging veneered panels later in the book.

Beyond these more introductory projects, the sky's the limit as to where you can use veneer in furniture and boxes. In a lot of Art Deco furniture from the 1920s, veneer was used to cover the entire outside surface of the furniture, and it was accurately matched and aligned using many of the techniques we'll be exploring in detail in later chapters. Even earlier than the Art Deco period, there was extravagant furniture decorated in marquetry veneer work being made for hundreds of years. Some of the most expensive and opulent furniture ever created was made with veneer in the 17th and 18th centuries. Now that you've experienced book-matching veneer, let's move on to more complex topics so you too can create your own veneered masterpiece.

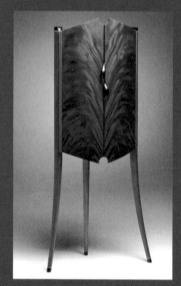

This tall jewelry cabinet by Michael Singer features a pair of book-matched doors in crotch mahogany veneer. The edging on doors like this is applied before the veneer, so the viewer only sees the fantastic mahogany veneer faces.

The doors on this calla lily marquetry buffet by the author are made with book-matched leaves of quarter-sawn koa veneer, which is also book-matched across the drawer fronts and buffet sides.

For a completely different look, you can run the wood grain horizontally across the doors and cabinet sides as the author did on this small side cabinet in cherry and maple.

Created in the late 18th century, this is one of many masterpieces of veneering made by the David Roentgen workshops. It incorporates nearly every form of veneering.

Emile Jacques Ruhlmann designed extremely precise and ornate Art Deco furniture in the early 1920s. This buffet in macassar ebony with ivory detailing has book-matched veneer decorating most of the surface.

This small end table by Emile Jacques Ruhlmann features book-matched Carpathian elm veneer wrapping completely around its oval shape to create undulating waves in the wood grain.

CHAPTER 5

A Four-Way Matched Panel

Now that you've made it through your first veneering projects and learned some of the techniques required, it's time to move on to more interesting veneer work. Our next project will involve working with burl veneer and making a four-way matched panel to use as an attractive box top. Burl veneers can display some of the most unique and interesting grain patterns available in wood veneer and therefore are an ideal material for showcasing beautiful wood on boxes and panels. Lining up the swirling grain of burl veneers in decorative matches is a bit more difficult than doing the same with straight-grained veneer. The somewhat random-looking grain of burls can change quickly from leaf to leaf, so it's imperative that your stack of burl veneer be sequentially cut and organized; otherwise, your four-way match will have grain that doesn't actually match.

A four-way book-matched olive ash burl panel makes a
great decorative addition to a small custom box. It doesn't
take many tools or a large shop to lay up panels this size.

Selecting Your Burl Veneer

There are quite a few wood species to choose from
when it comes to burl veneers, and the size of the
burl veneer leaves can vary widely. Some burls are
available only in relatively small sizes; camphor burl,
for one, is difficult to find in large sheets. Olive ash
burl and ash burl, on the other hand, can often be
bought in bundles several feet wide and long.
Obviously, the type of wood you'd like to use for
your burl project and how its wood grain and color
relate to the other materials in the project will affect
your choice of burl veneer. Along with that, you
should factor in the size of the burl panel you are

planning to create and how many leaves of burl it
will take to create that panel. Although you could
make a four-way matched box top in ash burl veneer
cut from the corner of a large bundle, it might make
more sense (and be more cost-effective) to limit
yourself to a smaller bundle to make the box top.
Since many burls are available in smaller bundles,
you should have no problem finding a burl veneer
that is perfect for your project.

Once you've selected the specific burl veneer to use
for this project, you'll need to determine whether it
should be flattened before working. For my box, I'm
using a nice bundle of olive ash burl veneer for the
top, and it definitely needs to be flattened before use.
Many burls arrive quite brittle and wavy; those
should be flattened before working them in any way.
Follow the flattening instructions in chapter 2, and

Burl veneer is available in a variety of colors and patterns, everything from subtle to complex in a wide range of sizes and wood species. In this stack are walnut burl on the bottom, and then, from left to right, redwood lace burl, madrone burl, Carpathian elm burl, walnut sap burl, and olive ash burl in the front right corner.

you should end up with pliable, easy-to-cut veneer. Keep in mind that it takes a few days to properly flatten and dry veneer soaked in flattening solution, so plan for the necessary time in advance.

Now select four leaves from the bundle of burl veneer to use for your box top. Ideally, you'd select the top four leaves and leave the remainder of the bundle for another project. Sometimes you'll find the outermost leaves have been damaged and pieces of the burl may be broken or missing. If this is the case, set those leaves aside and select the first four undamaged consecutive leaves you find. Restack the rest of the bundle, making sure the remaining leaves are numbered correctly so you know in the future that four leaves were removed from the bundle.

For this project, we'll be making the top for a medium-size jewelry box. The final top will be 12 in. long by 9 in. wide, so to make a four-way matched top we'll need to start with four pieces of burl veneer

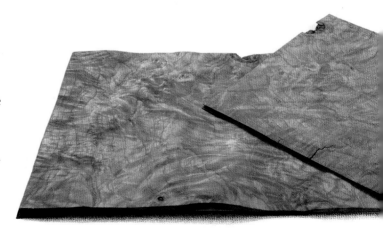

Olive ash burl makes quite a dramatic background veneer with its varying light and dark swirls. It is frequently quite buckled when it arrives, so plan to flatten it before cutting to size. The end result will be flexible, flat veneer like the stack on top.

USING THE MIRROR TECHNIQUE

The easiest way to preview burl veneer matches is to use the mirror technique we discussed earlier. To create a four-way match, you'll need the hinged mirrors we made in chapter 4. Start by selecting the most heavily figured area of your burl veneer bundle. Make this point the center of the four-way match and arrange the two mirrors so they are 90° to each other. This will give you a clear picture of how the match will look with the selected grain at the center. Now move the mirrors around to preview some other grain-matching options in your burl.

Frequently, burl matches look most interesting when the busiest part of the burl is located in the center of the match. It really depends on the specific burl you've chosen though, so be sure to try the mirrors in a few different locations until you find one that looks appealing. Hold the mirrors in place and mark the veneer at the bottom edge of both mirrors with a pencil so you can keep track of your perfect match.

Now mark the outer edges of the perimeter so you can cut the veneer bundle down to a more manageable size. I do this by just measuring out from the base of the mirrors with a tape measure and putting a few pencil marks at the correct location. Then connect the marks to get your perimeter cut lines.

Using the hinged mirrors we made in chapter 4, you can quite easily preview a variety of four-way book-matches. If you keep the mirrors 90° apart and move them around on the burl veneer, you'll get a good idea of the best book-match possible before you cut any veneer. Once you've found the most attractive book-match for your veneer, mark along the bottom edges of both mirrors with a pencil.

Measure with a tape measure from each mirror out to the oversize dimension of your burl veneer, and mark both edges with the pencil as before. Connect these marks with full-length lines and you'll have marked the overall perimeter of your veneer.

Splits in the burl veneer like these are a challenge to repair without them being visible in the finished piece, so try to avoid using sections of the burl that have them. You can always save those leaves for any repair work you might need to do later.

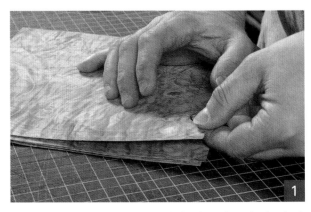

Find a prominent grain detail and line it up from leaf to leaf through the stack of veneer. Then repeat this process with a few other marks around the perimeter of the stack. Tape the stack of veneer tightly together once you've got all the leaves aligned.

at least 6½ in. long by 5 in. wide that can be cut, seamed together, and trimmed down to create our 12-in. by 9-in. box top. Starting ½ in. oversize on all sides allows room to trim and fine-tune the seams in case the grain pattern varies a lot from leaf to leaf.

Stacking and Cutting

Once you've got your burl veneer flattened and you've marked out your perfect match with the hinged mirrors (see the sidebar on p. 79), it's time to cut the veneer leaves to size. Start by lining up the grain pattern from leaf to leaf so that all four leaves have perfectly aligned grain when you cut through them. With burl veneers, aligning the grain can be slightly more challenging than with straight-grained veneer because the grain patterns in burl veneer can change quite rapidly from leaf to leaf.

The process is essentially the same either way though, so start by selecting a prominent grain detail in each leaf and line it up from leaf to leaf until the marks are perfectly aligned through all four leaves. Then tape the stack together in that spot, move to another location, and repeat the aligning and taping

Line up your straightedge with the center seam marks, and carefully cut through all four leaves of veneer with the veneer saw. Take your time and don't try to cut through each leaf in just one pass.

process. Repeat this on all four sides of the burl. When finished, you should have a well-aligned stack of veneer.

Line up your straightedge with what will be the long center seam of the book-match, and carefully cut through the stack of veneer. Slide the stack to the edge of your bench, and sand the cut edge with your sanding block to clean up any tearout or chips in the veneer (top left photo, p. 82). We're going to cut only the first joint for now, so go ahead and untape the stack of burl after making this cut (top right photo, p. 82). Take a pencil or some chalk and mark the four leaves in one corner, numbering them 1, 2, 3, and 4 to keep track of them while you flip them around.

REPAIRING HOLES AND DAMAGE TO BURL VENEER

Burl veneer will often arrive slightly damaged or with holes that need to be repaired. It's always a good idea to keep any of the bits and pieces of the burl veneer you find when you unpack it so you can use them later for repairs like these. Most of the time, simple repairs can be done quite easily with a scalpel and some regular blue tape. Try to work from the glue face of your veneer so the show face will be less damaged if something goes wrong during the repair.

Start by checking to see if all four leaves of veneer need the same amount of repair work; it's possible that holes and splits will fade and get smaller as they go deeper into the bundle. When filling small holes, a quick way to make essentially hidden repairs is to first place a piece of blue tape over the hole, then use small bits of burl scraps to fill the holes.

Frequently, there will be sections of the burl you won't be using anyway, so you can simply cut off a small area of similar color and grain to the area with the hole and use that for filler. Try to roughly replicate the shape of the hole with the new piece by trimming around the perimeter with a scalpel or sharp chisel. Now place the new piece in the hole and press it firmly onto the blue tape. You'll likely be able to see small areas of blue tape around the perimeter of the hole. Fill these with smaller pieces of the scrap burl by cutting them with a chisel while pushing the scrap into the hole. This should make the smaller holes all but disappear. To finish the repair, spread PVA glue over the repair and smear it into the cracks with your finger. Then lightly sand over the repaired area with 120-grit sandpaper to fill the remaining defects with a combination of dust and glue.

To repair splits and cracks, try to pull them back together with blue tape. If you pull the tape tight, it should make them virtually disappear. If they don't, you'll need to fill the splits with slivers of scrap burl veneer as well. Trim and fit these as you did when filling the hole by carefully cutting them to shape with a scalpel and test-fitting the slivers until they are the right shape to fill the splits.

Apply blue tape to the back of the hole you plan to repair. This makes it easier to see, and the tape will hold the small pieces of burl together during the repair process.

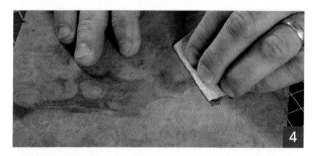

Find a scrap piece of burl that closely matches the grain around the hole you're planning to fill. Gradually cut the filler piece down in size until it fits into the hole. Trim off excess material and insert the filler piece of burl into the hole.

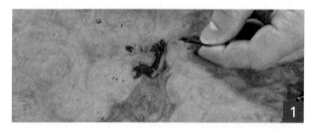

Press extra pieces of burl into the remaining holes and trim them flush with the surrounding veneer. Then spread PVA glue over the repair and smear it around with your finger.

Gently sand the wet glue and repaired area with 120-grit sandpaper until it is flush with the surrounding veneer. Your repair should be nearly invisible at this point.

Burl veneers typically benefit from a light touchup of the cut edge with a long sanding block. Keep the sanding block square to the cut edge, and sand only enough to clean up any torn or chipped grain.

Untape the stack, but before flipping the veneer leaves around, make sure to number them in one corner so you can keep track of the proper order while you move them around.

Assembling Joints

Take the first two leaves (1 and 2) and open them like a traditional book-match along the joint you just cut and sanded. Carefully line up the grain across the joint. Don't worry whether the ends of the leaves line up at this point because you're going to cut that seam later. Apply a few pieces of blue tape tightly across the joint to hold the veneer in place. Now take leaves 3 and 4 and repeat the same aligning and taping procedure. At this point, you should have two sheets of book-matched burl veneer. Ideally, the grain between the book-matches will be well aligned and the two sheets will look almost identical.

Now you need to align and cut the center seam of the four-way book-match. A good way to do this is to lay out the two sheets as though they are about to be taped together in the center (book-matched just like the first two joints), then flip one of them over the seam and down on top of the other sheet (see the top photos on p. 84). Align the grain between the two sheets at the joint as you did on the initial stack of veneer before you cut it. There should be a few nice grain lines you can use to line them up correctly. Tape the two sheets together, and mark a line perpendicular to the first joint you cut. Getting the

Take the first two leaves of veneer and open them like a book along the joint you just cut. Line up the grain markings across the joint. Once you're happy with the alignment, tape the joint together with a few pieces of blue tape pulled tightly across the joint. Repeat the alignment and taping operation on the second pair of leaves.

seam perpendicular is fairly easy to do with a plastic drafting triangle: Line up one edge of the triangle with the taped joint, then slide the perpendicular edge of the triangle back and forth until you have it where you want the center joint. Mark this line with a pencil.

Next, remove the plastic triangle and lay your straightedge on the line you marked. Cut through the veneer so you are cutting off the waste side of the joint. Once the seam is cut, slide it off the edge of

The maple burl veneer on this dresser is book-matched across the front, and each drawer face is made from consecutively matched leaves of veneer to create a unified appearance to the overall design. Each of the panels is edged in cherry crossbanding to match the cherry framework.

A four-way book-match of olive ash veneer is the center-piece of this Art Deco–inspired oval table by David Marr. The olive is bordered by macassar ebony crossbanding that radiates from the center of the table and flows down over the edges to the matching ebony base.

This Torah cabinet by Paul Schurch features a four-way book-matched walnut burl veneer front panel framing a central lighted panel of stone pomegranates.

Jefferson Shallenberger used a six-piece redwood burl match to create the intriguing pattern on the top of this curvaceous cabinet. He also carried the burl down the door faces and matched them around the perimeter of the cabinet.

A four-way book-match of Carpathian elm burl veneer surrounded with a border of macassar ebony creates a stunning desktop for this matched desk and chair set by the author. Leaving a bit of the lighter sapwood on the burl created a more visually inter-esting top than if it were simply a single uniform color.

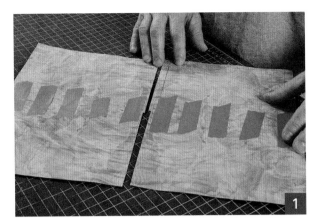

Lay out the two sheets of veneer as if you were book-matching them in the center.

Flip one sheet on top of the other along the seam so you can cut the center joint. Carefully line up the grain between the two sheets at the seam, and tape them together when the alignment is perfect.

Mark a line perpendicular to your first book-matched joints using a drafting triangle or square. This is the center joint of the four-way book-match, so getting the joint exactly perpendicular to the first joints is important. If it's off a bit, you'll see it in the final assembly.

Cut through both sheets of veneer at the marked line with your veneer saw and straightedge. Then lightly sand the cut veneer with a hard block to remove any tearout or damage, making sure to sand the entire edge evenly.

your bench and sand the joint lightly to clean up any tearout or damage.

Untape the sheets and flip the top one over so you can see the final joint. Carefully line up the center point where all four pieces of veneer meet, and apply a few pieces of tape across the joint. Double-check the alignment of all the joints and the grain matches between each pair of leaves. You should have nearly perfect grain alignment throughout all four seams. If you do, flip the sheet over so the glue face is up, and tightly tape across and along all the joints with blue tape to hold them together while you retape the show-face joints. If any of the joints need adjustment, untape them and slide the veneer leaves until

the grain lines up properly. You'll also need to recut the surrounding joints, which is why we kept extra veneer right from the start.

Flip the sheet again so the show face is up and remove the pieces of blue tape you applied earlier. We're going to use gum tape to finish-tape the show face of these seams. Apply long pieces of gum tape along the entire length of both seams. Burnish the tape down with a folded paper towel, then quickly place the sheet under a piece of MDF to hold it flat until the gum tape dries (typically an hour or two). Once the gum tape is dry, flip the sheet over and remove all the blue tape from the glue face.

Untape the two sheets and unfold them along the seam. Line up the grain along the joint, taking care to get the center point exact between all four leaves, and then tape across the final joint in a few spots to hold it tightly together.

Flip the sheet over and apply blue tape across and along all the joints, making sure to stretch the tape across the joints so it pulls them together tightly.

Flip the sheet again so the show face is up and remove all the blue tape from joints. Tape the show-face joints with gum tape as described previously. Dry and burnish down the joints with a folded paper towel, and then place the sheet under a piece of MDF to dry. When it's dry, remove all the blue tape from the glue face.

Final Sizing

You can cut the sheet of veneer to final size now in preparation for gluing to the substrate. Since the final panel size is 12 in. by 9 in., make sure to leave some extra material around the edges for gluing—about ¼ in. or so on each edge should be enough since this is such a small panel. Be careful when trimming the perimeter not to chip or break the delicate burl veneer.

Once you've got the sheet cut down to about 12½ in. by 9½ in., it's essentially ready to be glued to the substrate. All you need to do is to cut a piece of veneer for the backer and you're done. Try to select a backer veneer that complements the box design you've created; in my case, I'm using a nice straight-grained anigre veneer to contrast with the olive ash burl veneer used for the box top. Cut your backer veneer to 12½ in. long by 9½ in. wide.

Measure and mark lines about ¼ in. over the size of your final panel. We're leaving it oversize about ¼ in. all around so there will be material to trim off after glue-up. I find it easiest to mark the panel edges on the glue face so I can measure out from the joints and keep them centered on my final panel.

Trim all four edges of the veneer sheet on the marked lines.

❖ TIP ❖ Polyurethane glues stick to just about everything but plastic sheet, so always make sure you have a sheet of plastic between the veneer and the caul and the veneer and your press.

Prepare all the supplies you'll need for the glue-up: plastic sheet, caul, substrate, polyurethane glue, breather mesh, glue roller, and a spray bottle of water.

Gluing in a Frame Press

We'll be using polyurethane glue and my shopmade flip-top frame vacuum press to adhere the burl veneer to the substrate—in this case, a piece of ¼-in.-thick MDF. One of the benefits of using a frame press is that all you need to do to start applying vacuum is to close the press—there's no sliding things in and out of bags and wondering if the veneer moved while going into the bag. There's also no need for a second caul because the bottom face of the frame press becomes the bottom caul.

We discussed polyurethane glues earlier (see pp. 48–49), but here's a quick refresher. Poly glues are moisture activated, so they need a bit of moisture to cure, which we'll add with a mist of water on the veneer from a spray bottle right before it goes onto the glue. Prepare the supplies you'll need for this glue-up: two pieces of plastic sheet about 13 in. by 10 in., a ¼-in. MDF caul roughly 12½ in. by 9½ in., a glue roller, a bottle of polyurethane glue, a small

spray bottle of water set to spray a fine mist, and your vacuum system, including the breather mesh. Also cut your ¼-in. MDF substrate to final size, 12½ in. wide by 9½ in. long.

You need to have everything assembled in the proper order so you can work efficiently because poly glues start to cure after only 5 to 10 minutes in open air. Lay out your two sheets of veneer so you can keep track of their orientation and have the plastic sheet and caul nearby as well. Roll an even coat of polyurethane glue on the back side of the substrate, making sure there are no puddles or dry spots. Spray a very light mist of water on the glue face of the backer veneer and lay it down onto the glue. Press the veneer in place quickly, then flip over the substrate and spread glue on the top surface. Again, make sure the glue is evenly spread. Now spray a fine mist of water on the glue face of the burl veneer and lay it down onto the glue. Make

Spread an even layer of glue on the substrate. There should be no puddles or drips running off the edges. It takes a bit less polyurethane glue than PVA glue to do the same glue-up, so note how much you're using.

Mist the glue face of the backer veneer lightly immediately before placing it on the glue. Then quickly flip the panel over and spread the glue on the substrate and mist the burl veneer glue face.

Apply a few pieces of blue tape around the perimeter of the panel to hold the veneer in place. You'll likely notice that the burl veneer starts to buckle and curl quite quickly once you mist it with water.

Cover the caul with the breather mesh and close the vacuum press; leave it under pressure for about two hours. One great benefit of a frame press is not having to slide veneered panels into and out of the press.

sure it is lined up with the substrate, and apply a few pieces of blue tape around the perimeter to hold the veneer in place.

Place a piece of plastic on the face of your vacuum table, lay the veneered substrate on top of the plastic, cover the veneer with another piece of plastic, the top caul, and then the breather mesh (make sure the mesh reaches all the way to the vacuum hose inlet), and close the press. With poly glues, you should be able to remove the panel from the vacuum bag in about 2 hours, but leave the tape on the panel for 24 hours so the glue can fully cure. Make sure to set the panel in a location where it can get airflow to both sides or it may warp.

Sanding Burl Veneer

After removing the panel from the press, set it aside to finish curing for 24 hours. After that, your panel will be ready to be cleaned up and sanded. Start by removing all the gum tape from the panel. Just moisten the tape with a wet paper towel and you'll see it start to become translucent. A few passes with the wet towel and the tape adhesive will be loose enough to allow the tape to be peeled off in long strips. After removing all the tape, set the panel aside so the veneer can dry completely before doing any sanding—typically an hour or two is plenty of time.

Sanding burl veneer is a bit different from sanding straight-grained wood because the sanding marks from a hand-sanding block would essentially be going across the grain of the burl and be highly visible even if you sanded with a high grit. For this reason, I hand-sand burls only at the beginning of the sanding process and do all my finish sanding with a random-orbit sander. Start with a hard block and some 150-grit paper. Use this to level the burl and bring the panel to an initial flat surface. Don't overdo it. At this stage, you're really only trying to get the panel flat and remove any glue squeeze-out. You're not trying to finish-sand with this one grit.

Moisten the gum tape with a wet paper towel until it becomes translucent. Using a putty knife to get under the edge of the wet tape will allow you to peel it off in long strips. Once all the tape is removed, set the panel aside to dry for a couple hours.

Hand-sand the panel with a hard block and 150-grit paper. This is just to cut through the polyurethane bleed-through and flatten the veneer. Don't overdo this sanding or you might sand through the burl veneer.

Next, move to your random-orbit sander with 150-grit paper. Sand the panel as you would any other veneered panel, carefully and not overdoing the sanding in any one location. Work your way through the grits from 150 through 180, 220, up to 320, mak-

WHEN TO SAND

Keep in mind that when you sand a veneered panel is very important. For example, on panels that get solid-wood edging that will be flush with the veneer, I don't do any sanding until the solid edging is applied; otherwise, you might end up over-sanding areas and have burn-throughs in the veneerwork. On the other hand, if your panel will be recessed inside a frame or between cabinet legs, you'll want to finish-sand it before it gets glued into the surrounding parts. If you don't finish-sand it first, you'll have a hard time sanding into the tight corners of the assembled parts.

This folding screen by Paul Schurch features multiple four-piece book-matches of laurel burl veneer surrounded by walnut veneer crossbanding. Whether you do the crossbanding along with the veneering or as an inlay after veneering, you'll be less likely to sand through the burl veneer if you wait to sand everything flush until after all the crossbanding work is done. But keep in mind that you'll need to finish sanding the veneer before you glue the panel into the frame; otherwise, you'll struggle with sanding the recessed veneer properly.

The wide solid cherry edge that surrounds book-matched Carpathian elm burl veneer with an ebony and macassar ebony crossbanding between makes this dining table top a challenge to sand without potentially sanding through the delicate veneer. Waiting to sand the top until everything is done could work, but along the way you'll still need to bring the inlays flush with the veneer before you can add the crossbanding. I've found that sanding them until they are just flush with the veneer but no further helps me not sand through the veneer at later stages.

Known as the "Hawksmoor Desk," this monumental project by Andrew Varah features multiple types of burl veneer, including olive ash, madrone, and maple, along with a variety of other decorative woods. Determining when and how to sand each portion of a project this complex would take some advance planning. In essence, though, it's the same as any other project: Sand as much of each layer as possible before adding another layer to it.

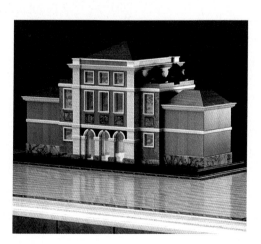

This curvy box by Andrew Crawford features a four-way book-match of myrtle burl veneer that is joined at the seam of the front and top panels. It is also decorated with Andrew's trademark harlequin diamond parquetry and a variety of inlaid edging. On a box like this, it's best to hold off on sanding until all the inlay work is done.

ing sure to vacuum off all the dust between grits. After sanding with 320-grit paper, you shouldn't be able to see any sanding scratches and the panel is ready for finish.

Complete your sanding schedule with a random-orbit sander, starting with 150-grit and moving up through 180-, 220-, and 320-grit paper. This will leave you with a blemish-free surface ready for finish. Make sure you vacuum off the panel after each sanding grit and be careful not to sand too much in any one location.

The finish-sanded burl panel is ready to become the top of your decorative box.

CHAPTER 6

A Radial-Matched Tabletop

Radial matches (or sunbursts or starbursts as they are also known) are an interesting way to incorporate decorative veneer patterns into furniture. Most frequently they are seen in the form of round tabletops, though they can also be used in a variety of places like doors and side panels in case furniture to add complexity to a design (see the Gallery on pp. 94–95). Often, they showcase wildly figured grain patterns like crotch veneer and burls, but you can use essentially any veneer to make a radial match and add some decorative veneering to your work. In essence, a radial match is a circular pattern of pie slice–shaped pieces of veneer either book- or slip-matched to create a repeating pattern of wood grain.

Creating a Radial Match

There are a variety of ways to create radial matches. The most common involves book-matching the leaves of veneer around a central point, but you can also slip-match the leaves to create an interesting spiral pattern. Slip-matching works well with some veneers and not as well with others—you wouldn't typically see it used

Damion Fauser has made a series of small tables like this one in jarrah and silver ash by combining a radial-matched center panel with decorative contrasting crossbanding.

Making the template

To make a radial match, you'll need an accurate method for cutting identical triangular pieces of veneer. I've found that the easiest method is to make a full-size drawing of a section of the tabletop I'm making and then use that to lay out how many pieces will be needed for the top veneer pattern. With that information, I can make a simple drawing of one of the radial-match pieces to use as a template for cutting all the veneer.

To illustrate the techniques used to make radial matches, I'll be making a 16-piece radial-matched round tabletop in flatsawn walnut veneer. The table-top needs to be 32 in. across, so my veneer leaves need to be at least 16 in. long plus some extra for trimming later (about ½ in. or so). To make it around the 32-in.-dia. circle, I need the leaves to be just over 6.25 in. wide. I determine this with some basic geometry. To calculate the circumference of a circle (the distance around the outside perimeter), multiply the diameter times pi (3.14). Divide that number by the number of leaves in your radial match, in my case 16, and you get the width of the widest part of the pie-shaped piece required for each part of the radial match. For my tabletop, the circumference is 100.5 in.; dividing that by my 16 leaves gives me a width of roughly 6.25 in. for each leaf. I always go over this by a little to account for the curve of the circle and because I want my veneer pieces a bit long (½ in. on each piece), so let's say a minimum of 6.5-in.-wide leaves will be necessary to make my 32-in.-dia. radial match from 16 matched pieces of veneer.

You can also do the same thing without the math by using a digital angle gauge to determine the shape of your pie slices. Let's use the same tabletop as an example. A full circle is 360°; divide that by 16 and you get 22.5° for each piece of the pie. Set your angle gauge to 22.5°, and trace both sides of it on a piece of paper. Because the table needs to be 32 in. in diameter, each pie slice needs to be at least 16 in. long plus a bit to account for trimming later. Just extend the lines from the angle gauge until they are about 16½ in. long and you'll have a drawing ready to use

with burl veneer, for instance, because the pattern shift would not be very obvious.

The most basic method for making a radial match is to cut multiple pie slice–shaped pieces of veneer from the same location in a bundle of veneer and book-match those pie slices into a circle to form something like a round tabletop that will end up with a repeating decorative pattern in the wood grain. The typical number of veneer leaves used to make a radial match can vary from 4, 8, 12, 16, all the way up to 32 or more depending on the complexity desired. The most common are 16 and 32 leaf matches. The number of leaves needs to grow by 2 every time so that the pattern is balanced around the circle; odd numbers of leaves would create a pattern where the final 2 leaves would not line up correctly. Increasing by 2 gives a pattern balanced in pairs, which is most apparent in book-matches where the 2-leaf pattern repeats as many times as necessary to create the final design.

16-Piece Radial Match

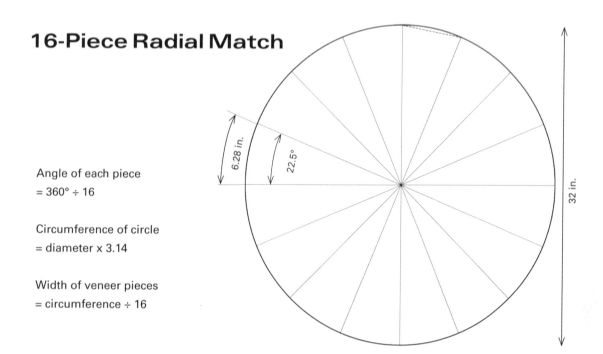

Angle of each piece
= 360° ÷ 16

Circumference of circle
= diameter x 3.14

Width of veneer pieces
= circumference ÷ 16

6.28 in.

22.5°

32 in.

Use a digital angle gauge to lay out your pie slice–shaped drawing, if you don't have access to a system for printing large images. Just draw one straight line down the page, set the angle gauge to 22.5°, and mark the angle directly from the gauge.

Spray-glue the drawing to a piece of ¼-in. MDF, and cut just outside the lines with a bandsaw or jigsaw. Then sand or handplane it right to the line.

for making the template. As with anything like this, the more accurate you are when making the initial layout measurements, the more accurate the final piece will be.

Once you've created your full-size paper template, spray-glue it to a piece of ¼-in. MDF and cut the

MDF exactly along the lines of your drawing. Rough-cutting close to the line on the bandsaw, and then gradually working right up to the line with a hand-plane or hard sanding block makes the process fairly painless; keep the lines straight by using a long sanding block, if necessary. This final template is the exact

Patrick Edwards combined radial-matched background veneer with stunning, highly complex marquetry in his pair of mirror-imaged Louis-Phillipe tilt-top tables.

Paul Schurch used a 16-piece radial match in madrone burl decorated with satinwood marquetry ribbons and inlaid stone butterflies to create this low coffee table. It has a matching lower level created with an 8-piece radial match and more marquetry ribbons.

The author created a 24-piece radial match in satinwood veneer as the background for his campion flower marquetry, which is bordered by pau ferro crossbanding and ebony inlay.

This cherry cabinet by Damion Fauser features two doors with 12-piece radial-matched panels. Damion added another decorative detail by leaving a slice of sapwood on the edge of each piece to create a beautiful star pattern on both doors.

Peter Young combined parquetry patterns with radial-matched veneer work to create a unique pattern in his coffee table design, alternating the colors of the parquetry with each piece of the radial match.

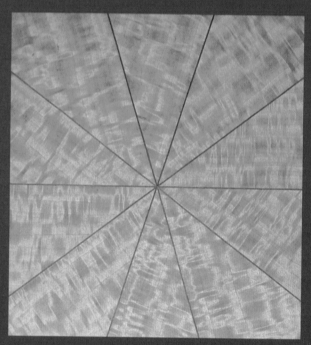

This table has a 10-piece slip-matched top in block-figured anigre with thin lines of walnut inlaid between the leaves of veneer. You can see the way the pattern repeats in a more noticeable manner with a slip-matched versus a book-matched top.

The doors of this walnut buffet are 12-piece book-matches of flatsawn walnut veneer. For a piece like this, the template should be of the longest piece in the radial match so you can trim the veneer sheet down to the size of the doors after taping the veneer together.

A more complex radial match like this one by David Marr made of 16 pieces of veneer in two different woods and with two sizes of veneer requires more planning and layout than a traditional radial match of identical parts.

This Art Deco bed with built-in nightstands by Gray Hawk features a variety of radial-matched and bent-laminated veneer work that would require a number of different bending forms and highly detailed, accurate drawings to complete properly.

size of one of your radial-match veneer pieces, and with it you can use the hinged mirrors we made in chapter 4 to visualize exactly what the final radial match will look like without cutting any veneer.

Take the time to number your leaves of veneer in order before doing any cutting or sorting; you'll regret it later if you don't.

One important note to add is that since we're making a 16-piece radial match, we obviously need 16 sequential pieces of the same veneer from a single bundle. Ideally, you'd have an extra piece or two in case one gets damaged or cut overly narrow by accident. I've got a bundle with 18 leaves of sequentially matched walnut veneer. The first thing I want to do is number all the leaves in one corner from 1 to 18 so that when I'm moving them around I can keep track of which leaf needs to go where.

Mocking up the radial match

Once all the leaves are numbered, set the hinged mirrors on top of one veneer leaf and slide the MDF template between the two mirrors to set them at the exact angle needed for the tabletop veneer. Then remove the template to see the radial pattern displayed in the mirrors. This system allows you to preview the radial

Using the MDF template and a set of hinged mirrors, you can mock up your radial match using a variety of different veneers to see what looks best. I use the template to get an exact spacing between the mirrors so I'll know precisely what the radial match will look like before cutting any veneer.

Aligning all the veneer leaves precisely is important with a radial match because the book-matched veneer leaves will be difficult if not impossible to align later and your book-matched pattern will show wide variation at the seams if you don't line them up correctly from the start.

I use the MDF template as a guide throughout the entire process of making a radial match. Here, it's being used to double-check that the hinged mirrors were accurately spaced when the radial match was traced onto the veneer.

match in full and move the mirrors around on the veneer to preview other options for your radial-match design. Keep moving the mirrors until you find the most pleasing look for your radial match. Quite often the busiest area gets placed in the center of the table so the eye is drawn in when looking at the table. Once I find the best look, I'll mark along the bottom edges of the mirrors with a pencil. We've done this a few times already in earlier chapters—it gives you the exact shape of the parts you need to cut, assuming the mirrors are at the right angle.

Now place the MDF template on the top piece of veneer and double-check that it lines up with your pencil marks from earlier. If it does, all is well and you're ready for the next step. If not, something was wrong with the alignment of the hinged mirrors when you were placing them and you'll need to recheck the look of your radial match with the mirrors and template as before. Once you've confirmed the location of the template, trace around it again with a pencil.

You need to line up the 16 leaves of veneer in the stack so the grain flows as closely as possible from one leaf to the other. Any misalignment will be obvious in the final tabletop and hard to correct later, so take the time to get them lined up correctly now. This is another skill that we have practiced a few times in earlier chapters, and like so many things, practice does make perfect. Tape the stack of veneer together in a few places around the perimeter to hold the alignment while cutting.

Cutting the veneer

Use your straightedge and veneer saw to cut along the first of the two lines marking your radial-match leaves. You can cut in either direction, but I tend to cut in the direction that goes with the wood grain rather than against it, which seems to leave a slightly better cut. Once one side is cut, slide it off the side of your bench and sand it smooth with a hard block and some 120-grit sandpaper. Make sure the edge is straight and vertical. Now tape the stack together along the sanded edge. Place the template on top of the stack, line up one edge with the freshly cut and sanded edge, and then mask the other edge.

When you place the straightedge on the second cut line, move the straightedge a hair over the marked line at the widest end of the stack so you end up cutting slightly wider leaves than planned. For a tabletop this size, I would move the straightedge out by just the smallest amount, possibly 1/64 in. or so. The key is not to undercut the angle or you'll have a hard time making things line up in the end. The system we're using depends on taping together two halves of the full circle, then cutting them to fit each other while always maintaining the fine points at the center of the circle. Cut through the stack as before. Once the second line is cut, repeat the sanding process from before, keeping the sanding block straight and square the entire time. Now untape the stack of veneer. Your numbers should still be visible on all the leaves; if not, renumber them all from 1 to 16 before moving on.

Cutting through 16 layers of veneer takes time and patience. It also takes some skill to hold the saw at exactly 90° to the fence the entire time.

I nearly always sand the cut edges to make sure they are straight and square; this also helps to eliminate any tearout or chips in the veneer edge.

Another small table by Damion Fauser illustrates again what creative grain layout can do for your radial matches. By leaving a little sapwood on each piece of veneer, he's created a lovely star pattern in the center of the tabletop.

Use your MDF template to mark the second cut line off the first cut line. Move the outer edge of the template a little past where it should be located so you are cutting pieces just slightly larger than desired. A bare 1/64 in. or so is plenty when you multiply it over 16 pieces.

Radial-Match Numbering System

Using a system taught by Paul Schurch, it's possible to create a radial-matched pattern with only a minimal grain pattern shift from leaf to leaf.

Black numbers are face up. Red numbers are flipped upside down.

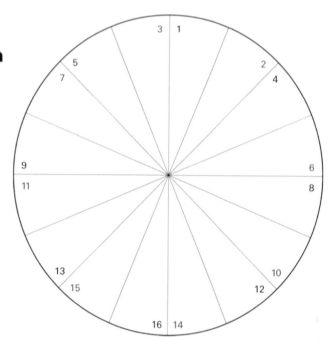

Layout

I learned the system I use for making radial matches with minimal pattern shift from Paul Schurch. His method involves merely altering the placement of the numbered leaves so that adjacent leaves are never more than two numbers apart. Begin with leaf 1, then flip leaf 2 over and place it to one side of leaf 1. Now take leaf 3 and flip it over, then place it on the opposite side of leaf 1. Repeat this system with leaves 4 and 5, 6 and 7, and so on, until all the leaves are arranged in a circle. As you can see in the drawing above, there is no more than a two-number difference between any leaves, which means the pattern shift will be minimal across the entire tabletop and adjacent leaves are more likely to be similar in grain pattern. Compare this with a more traditional system of starting with leaf 1 and just going in a circle with 2, 3, 4, etc.: By the time you get to leaf 16, it ends up right next to leaf 1, so the pattern shift in the grain may be very pronounced.

Taping together the veneers

Start the taping process by taping leaf 1 to leaf 2, making sure leaf 2 is flipped over to create the book-match effect. Tape together these first two leaves with blue tape, making sure to get the sharp points perfectly aligned (this can be a challenge because there isn't much material to tape together at the points). I try to get the tip of the veneer leaves aligned perfectly and then tape them together starting an inch or so back from the points so I can see all the points while assembling the rest of the leaves.

Continue taping leaves together in the predetermined order, making sure always to keep the points

❖ **TIP** ❖ It's important to keep the saw vertical as you cut through the 16 layers of veneer. Take your time as you work down through the stack.

Begin taping together the first two leaves. Take care to keep the tiny points of the leaves aligned precisely, and apply tape in just a few places along the joint for now.

aligned. Often, you'll need to go back a bit and retape a few leaves once you get more of them together because you'll notice the points aren't lined up properly. Just tape across the joints in a few places to start, so if you need to move a leaf, it won't take much effort. Once all the leaves for one half are aligned correctly, add more tape across the joints and a strip down the length of each joint. I still keep the tape about an inch away from the sharp tips of the veneer at this point because you need to see the points for the next step.

Repeat this process for the second half of the tabletop, and you'll end up with two half circles of taped-together veneer. You should notice at this point that

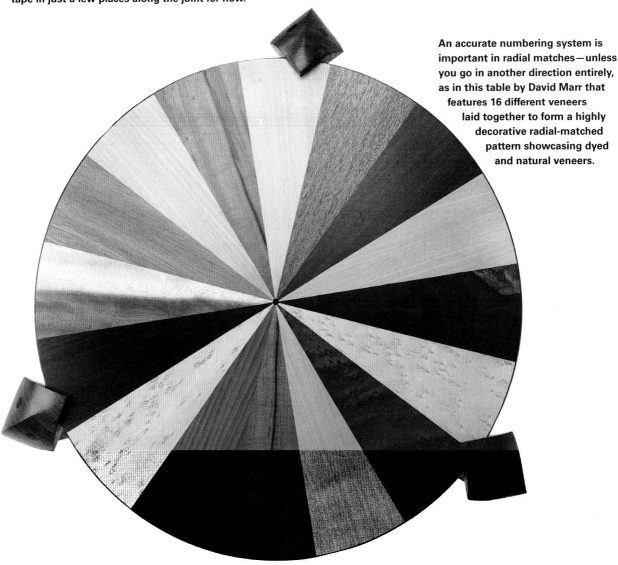

An accurate numbering system is important in radial matches—unless you go in another direction entirely, as in this table by David Marr that features 16 different veneers laid together to form a highly decorative radial-matched pattern showcasing dyed and natural veneers.

2

Add one leaf at a time to the first two, and continue taping them together with a few pieces of blue tape until half of the leaves have been taped together into the first half circle. Repeat this process for the second half circle.

When you place the 16 pieces of veneer in the order described, you'll note that every other leaf is upside down. As long as you placed each leaf in the proper location, it doesn't matter that you can't see the numbers. Just tape them together in the correct order, tape across and along the joints, and you'll be ready for the next step.

if you slide the two halves next to each other, they don't quite meet at the middle—ideally, they will be just a bare ⅛ in. apart at the center (see the photo on p. 102). This is what cutting the parts slightly oversize did for us. We can now tape these two halves together and trim the final joint for a perfect fit while preserving all of the fine points at the center. Imagine if instead of having a gap at the center, the points were touching and the gap was along the outer edge of the joint. That would mean that to get the halves together we'd have to trim off some of the points, and that really ruins the radial-match effect and is extremely noticeable in the final piece. The way we've cut the pieces, there is only a slight bit to trim off the ends of our half circles and that goes essentially unnoticed in the final table. With practice making radial matches, you can bring this amount down to almost nothing.

The easiest way I've found to trim the final joint is to take the two halves and lay them out as though

3

If you've cut your radial-matched pieces of veneer slightly oversize as we discussed, when you place them together, there should be a slight gap at the center where the points should all meet. With a quick trim, they'll all line up nicely. The gap here is exaggerated to make it easier to see clearly; ideally, it would only be 1/8 in. or so.

they were going to be taped together. Instead of taping them together though, flip one half over on top of the other and carefully line up the untrimmed ends of both pieces. Tape them together in a few places along the center joint. Next, use a long straightedge to trim the center joint. You'll want to split the amount you trim off so an equal amount comes off both ends of the joint and essentially nothing comes off the middle where the points are located. Once you've got it trimmed, slide it off the edge of your bench a bit and lightly sand the joint clean and straight with a long sanding block.

Now untape the two halves and flip the top one over so you can line up the final joint. Start at the center and try to get all the tiny points aligned perfectly (now you see why we didn't cover them with tape earlier). Lay a piece of blue tape across the center to hold the halves in place and tape them together along the length of the joint, first taping across the joint, then taping down the full length of the joint. Flip over the entire sheet and double-check that the points are well aligned. If you were careful with your alignment, they should basically be perfect. Apply gum tape along all of the joints on this face (the show face). You'll need to work quickly because there is a lot of tape to apply. Burnish down the tape with a paper towel, and slide the veneer under a piece of MDF for an hour or so. When the tape is dry, flip the veneer over and remove all the blue tape from the glue face. You're now ready to trim the veneer to size and glue it up.

Flip one half on top of the other, and line up the outer straight edges. Tape them together in a few places, and use a straightedge to cut an equal amount from both ends so the points of the veneer pieces meet in the center.

Once the final cut is made, tape the two halves together with blue tape both along and across the center joint to fully tape the glue face of the veneer.

Begin gum-taping along all of the joints. Try not to build up too many layers of gum tape at the center of the tabletop; instead, run several pieces of tape full length across the veneer and then cut all the remaining pieces short so they don't cross the centerline.

Make your substrate slightly oversize (½ in. in diameter), then use it as a template to trim the veneer down to size so it doesn't overhang the substrate in the press. I always make my substrate and veneer oversize so I can trim them to final size after pressing.

Trimming to size

I like to make my substrates a little oversize so I can trim off the edge of the glue-up after the veneer is pressed. Because we're making a 32-in.-round tabletop, I'll make my substrate 32½ in. in diameter. The substrate is easy enough to cut with a router and a long base with a screw for a pivot point at the center of the circle. While you're making the substrate, cut a second circular piece from some ¼-in. MDF to use as a caul in the press. Once you've cut the substrate to size, lay it on top of the veneer and center it over the pattern. Trim off any overhanging veneer with a scalpel or sharp utility blade.

Make a second piece of veneer to use as a backer sheet. The quality of the backer material depends on whether it will be visible or not. If it will be visible, make it from a nice veneer that goes with the design. You might even want to make a four- or eight-piece radial match for the backer just to keep the design continuous. If the backer won't be seen, it can be made from secondary veneer.

> ❖ **TIP** ❖ If you're using a traditional vacuum bag rather than a flip-top press, you'll need a caul for both sides of the part.

Urea formaldehyde glues have a rigid glueline that is ideal for complex patterns in veneer like this radial match. Mix and spread the glue according to the instructions, and allow proper time for curing and final drying after pulling the assembly from the vacuum bag.

Gluing up the veneer

Radial-matched veneer gets glued up the same as any other veneer sheet, typically in a vacuum bag and with a hard-setting glue like Pro-Glue urea formaldehyde. Using a glue with a softer glueline would allow the leaves of veneer to separate over time, ruining all your careful jointing work.

Mix the glue as described earlier (see p. 46), making sure to wear the appropriate safety gear and following the instructions on the container. Roll on an even coat of glue and place your veneer onto it. Flip the panel over and repeat for the second side. Tape

I prefer to do my initial sanding with a hard block and some 150-grit paper. I find this cleans up the veneer surface and levels all of the veneer so that all future sanding has a flat reference surface.

Once you've got the veneer panel pressed, you can add contrasting solid-wood edging around it to make a beautiful tabletop. Here, I'm partway through adding curly maple edging to my walnut radial match; instructions on how to edge this panel are provided in chapter 10.

the veneer in place in a few spots around the perimeter of the circle so it can't move in the press. Cover the assembly with plastic sheet and the MDF cauls, and slip it into the vacuum bag. UF glues need six to eight hours minimum to cure, so I tend to leave mine in the press overnight. When you take the panel out of the press, set it somewhere that allows airflow on both sides of the panel.

Remove the gum tape with a wet paper towel, and allow the panel to dry fully before sanding. Since the grain runs in all directions, the final sanding on radial-matched panels needs to be done with a random-orbit sander. The initial sanding can be done with a long hard block and some 150-grit paper, but don't sand too much or you'll risk going through the veneer. Complete the sanding with your random-orbit sander and 150-, 180-, and 220-grit paper and you're ready for finish.

CHAPTER 7

Marquetry

Marquetry is a form of veneering that incorporates imagery of natural forms and complex scrollwork directly in the veneer work. In years past, it would typically have incorporated wood, metal, tortoiseshell, mother of pearl, ivory, and bone. However, most of today's marquetry is almost exclusively made in wood and metal because several of the other materials are no longer legally available to use (ivory

This blanket chest by the author is decorated in marquetry imagery of gladiola flowers on a tineo veneer background. The white holly of the flowers provides a striking contrast against the darker red background veneer.

and tortoiseshell in particular). There has been a wide variety of styles of marquetry over the years from the more complex scrollwork seen in early 17th- and 18th-century furniture to the more modern and subdued patterns used in most current marquetry. Marquetry imagery can be staggeringly complex or relatively simple (see the Gallery on p. 110); it all depends on the maker's motivation and skill set.

I've been using marquetry as a way to enhance my custom furniture pieces for a number of years and over that time have developed a series of simple steps that make creating marquetry fairly straightforward.

In the text and photos that follow, I'll take you through all the necessary steps from creating the initial drawing to gluing up the cut and sand-shaded marquetry veneer. As with all veneer work, the top face of the veneer is called the show face and the bottom face is called the glue face; we'll be referring to them throughout the instructions.

Creating a Marquetry Image

The first step in creating a marquetry panel is to determine the size of the image. In this case, we are making a small panel of orchid flowers, and the overall image is roughly 12 in. long by 9 in. wide. To create my initial drawings, I typically go to the Internet and search for clear photographs of my chosen subject matter. There are a variety of sites where free images can be downloaded and printed, and with a

Downloading and printing photographs from free image sites on the Internet is a great way to source marquetry material. These printouts can be scaled, rotated, and altered as you see fit to create a unique and original marquetry drawing. Tracing over the pictures you've printed helps get the rough picture down on paper. Feel free to alter the drawing as you go to create the image you have in mind. After you've got the rough drawing done, keep refining it until all the details are correct.

SIMPLE MARQUETRY

In case the Gallery photos on p. 110 lead you to believe that marquetry has to be complex and overpowering, here are a few examples of ways to incorporate rather simple marquetry flowers and leaves into your furniture. These are small enough to be cut with nearly any saw setup, and they don't require much in the way of veneering equipment.

The falling maple leaves on this marquetry cabinet by Brian Condran add a touch of nature to the already elegant design.

I've made a variety of pieces like this end table with dogwood flowers that have some floral marquetry as an added detail to give the design more visual interest.

The marquetry on this desk is meant to be a surprise to the end user, visible only when a drawer is opened. It's a small thing that can bring delight to the owner of the desk for years to come.

home printer or copier you can quickly scale the images to suit your project size. Scale the photographs to fit your project, print copies you can trace over, and then make a rough pencil sketch showing how you plan to lay out each of the details in your picture. This can be very rough, but it gives you a good reference for where to place the flowers, leaves, and branches.

Modern marquetry master Paul Schurch decorated
the surfaces of this dresser in wild white roses on an
imbuya burl background. The chest is further decorated
in Paul's traditional manner with a pietra dure (stone
marquetry or inlay) butterfly, ladybug, and spider.

Silas Kopf has made a name for himself in the world of
marquetry with his whimsical and innovative trompe
l'oeil imagery, like this piece amusingly called "Bricolage"
with imagery of Silas sealing himself inside a box with
bricks and mortar.

John Jeggo of the Staffordshire Marquetry Group
creates some of the most incredible marquetry
pictures I've ever seen. This particular one, called
"Watering Hole," was actually one of the inspirations
for my getting into marquetry in the first place.
The level of detail and realism is simply amazing.

A collaborative piece by Patrick Edwards and Patrice
Lejeune, this "Treasure Box" features amazingly complex marquetry flowers and scrollwork over most of
the exterior surface done in a variety of colors.

Begin tracing the outline of the flowers and leaves you've chosen and try to orient them in ways that look realistic. It's not necessary to trace the photos exactly, and in many cases you can improve the look of the drawing by making slight adjustments as you progress. This stage can take some time, and typically after completing the initial tracing, I'll go back and redraw the entire image several more times, making alterations and improvements along the way.

No matter how complex your marquetry picture will be, the key to successful work is the marquetry drawing itself. Devote as much time as you need to create a fluid and fully detailed drawing of the marquetry picture. Because you'll be cutting precisely what is drawn, it makes sense to put some extra time into creating a complete drawing that fully illustrates whatever image you desire. It's far easier to erase a pencil line and redraw it than it is to recut a line in your veneer packet.

Once you have a final drawing you're happy with, make three copies: one for cutting, one for assembly, and one to use as a shading template later. Take one copy of the drawing and use it to size two pieces of cardstock to the size of the drawing (I use cardstock from a printing-supply house that is about 0.040 in. thick). These pieces will become the top and bottom layers of the marquetry packet. Spray-glue the cutting drawing to one piece of the cardstock.

Use one of your three drawing copies to size two pieces of cardstock for the top and bottom layers of the packet. Then spray-glue the drawing to one piece of the cardstock. This is now the top layer.

Selecting the Veneer

At this point, it's time to select the different veneers that will make up the marquetry image. Assuming you have a piece of veneer for the background already cut to the size of your marquetry image (in this case 12 in. high by 9 in. wide), let's concentrate on the flower and leaf colors. Most of my marquetry flowers are made with holly veneer because it is

The oak leaf and acorn marquetry on these two doors by the author was designed to have leaves in several seasons flowing across the cabinet front. This was done by combining dyed veneer and natural wood veneer to get a full range of seasonal color.

Another example of somewhat minimal marquetry decoration that has high contrast in the coloring, this dogwood flower–decorated side table has white flowers and bright green leaves on a dark walnut burl background.

very white and tends to look quite dramatic against most background veneers once it has been shaded in hot sand (more on that later). Typically, I'll make the centers of flowers from a contrasting color, usually satinwood or another brightly colored material. You can use natural wood veneer for essentially everything except green leaves. There isn't a natural wood veneer that will stay green over time, so I order dyed veneer in several different shades of green to make my marquetry leaves. If you are planning to make colorful flowers, you'll need to order some dyed veneer for them as well because most wood tones will be fairly muted compared with real flower colors.

A selection of veneer for a marquetry image can have many different colors for flowers, leaves, and branches. For the image shown here, we've got two shades of green for leaves, white for flower petals, dyed blue poplar and satinwood for the centers of the flowers, and maple burl for the background.

NATURAL VENEER MARQUETRY

There are a few makers who make marquetry only from natural wood tones and don't use any dyed veneer. Obviously, you'll be limited to more subdued creams, tans, and browns if you opt for this route, but the imagery can be beautiful and still have very nice contrast if you put some extra time into wood selection for each part of the marquetry image.

Brian Condran used just one wood species to create the complex marquetry image of a tree wrapping around this small cabinet. By using both heartwood and sapwood for contrast, Brian was able to display a wide range of colors and tones from just one board.

Peter White used only three colors of natural wood veneer to create this lifelike image called "Stan the Man." Your mind automatically fills in the missing parts of the picture that are only hinted at in the marquetry.

I've found that branches look interesting if they stand out a bit from the background, so I make most of my branches with either straight-grained mahogany or walnut burl veneer, depending on the background veneer color and the look I'm after. For example, walnut burl on a walnut background would be difficult to see, whereas walnut burl on a maple background would look very nice. Select colors that give your branches a natural look; burls work very well at mimicking natural tree growths.

An intricate marquetry frog sitting on a branch adds a beautiful touch to the corner of a cabinet door by Greg Zall. The impeccable grain selection and shading on the branch contribute greatly to the realism of this design.

GRAIN ORIENTATION IN MARQUETRY PICTURES

Grain direction is surprisingly important in marquetry pictures. It can really make or break a picture. The more detailed and lifelike you make the image, the more important it becomes to have the grain of each piece in the picture flowing the proper way. For the picture we are making, grain direction will be most visible on the light green leaves. Typically, you'd want the grain of the green veneer to flow along the length of each leaf. When you tape each piece of green veneer in place, double-check the drawing and make sure you've got the grain flowing the correct way. If you make your leaves out of two pieces of green veneer split down the center, you can orient the grain so it flows away from the centerline of the leaf at an angle that will look even more realistic.

Flower petals are trickier. You could argue that the grain of each petal should flow out from the center of the flower or that it should flow around the flower in a more circular pattern. I usually have the grain flowing out from the center on my flowers, but you can certainly make a judgment call and orient it differently on your picture. You'll be able to tell pretty quickly whether it looks right when you

Make sure the grain in your marquetry parts runs in the most natural direction. This set of leaves and flower petals shows one with a somewhat natural grain direction (bottom row above) and another with the grain running opposite to what would be expected in nature (top row). The grain of the white holly veneer is so light that it is difficult to see; after sand shading, it becomes more visible though, so orienting the parts properly is still important.

assemble the cut image and finally get to see the parts in their proper locations. Sometimes you just need to make a small sample image with a flower or two and a couple of leaves to test out the grain orientation you want to use. It's faster than recutting an entire marquetry picture if you get it wrong. Keep in mind that the grain of holly veneer is fairly light anyway, so it will be harder to see in the final image.

Cutting Methods

There are many different ways to cut marquetry, everything from a handheld fretsaw to old-school French chevalets to powered scrollsaws in a variety of price ranges. Folks in the United Kingdom do quite a bit of marquetry cutting with only a scalpel, and they create some amazing images. I do all my marquetry cutting on a DeWalt® scrollsaw I bought years ago

and an old Excalibur EX30 scrollsaw. They both do a nice job cutting in a nearly vertical path and have a few features that are handy for cutting veneer. Foremost among these is a good speed-control system so you can slow down the cutting speed for precise cuts and speed it up for thicker packets. Easy blade changing for those times when you break blades is a must as well.

The marquetry donkey or chevalet is a time-honored tool for cutting marquetry. Note that using a chevalet requires the packet to be a uniform thickness, unlike a packet made for scrollsawing, which can vary in thickness. The foot clamp on the chevalet depends on the packet being of uniform thickness to hold it properly while you are sawing. You can achieve complete control over the cutting process and create marquetry images of incredible detail and complexity with the chevalet.

Whichever tool you decide to use to cut your marquetry, you'll want to spend some time practicing cutting smooth curved and straight lines before you start on an important marquetry picture. Like most skills, it takes some practice to get the hand-eye coordination necessary to make accurate cuts.

There are a few cutting styles that can be used to make marquetry pictures: packet cutting, bevel cutting, and piece by piece. Because nearly all of my marquetry work is done using the packet-cutting method, that's where the majority of the information here will be focused, but over the years I've found a use for the other methods as well, so a quick introduction to each follows.

Packet cutting

Packet cutting cuts the entire marquetry image at once. Every piece in the image is represented by a piece of veneer in the packet, and all the different pieces are secured to the background with tape. Because you cut the image only once, you are able to remove each individual piece one by one as you cut them out. There also needs to be some extra material around each piece of veneer to allow it to be secured in the packet with tape. However, I find that by carefully placing each piece, I can orient the grain to follow the direction of the individual part

The marquetry donkey or chevalet is the tool originally used in France for cutting marquetry packets. It has grown in popularity over the past 10 years due to the efforts of several individuals, namely Patrick Edwards and Yannick Chastang, who provided this photo of one that he built. It is an ideal tool for cutting marquetry in sawn veneer because the packet is held with a foot clamp while one hand turns the packet and the other drives the sawblade.

A marquetry packet can be quite complex when finished, but the underlying thing to keep in mind when making it is to have a piece of veneer in the packet for every piece in the drawing. Get that right and you'll be fine.

while also minimizing the excess material needed to hold it in place.

Packets for marquetry cutting have lots of small pieces of veneer held in place with bits of blue tape and a cardstock top and bottom layer. The layers of veneer can stack up in busy areas of the marquetry drawing, so the cutting speed will also change as you transition from thick to thin areas of the packet. The marquetry drawing is spray glued to the top layer of cardstock and the entire packet is taped securely closed.

Bevel cutting

Bevel cutting involves cutting only two thicknesses of veneer at a time: the background on the top and the fill piece on the bottom (see the photos on the facing page). Tilting the saw table at an angle allows the bottom piece of cut veneer to slip seamlessly into the hole cut in the top or background veneer. You can flip the layers and cut at the same angle, but you'll need to cut in the opposite direction to get the angle

correct. With bevel cutting, you cut in a single direction around all the pieces, always cutting them one at a time and always cutting in the same direction. As each piece is cut, it gets glued or taped into the corresponding hole in the background veneer and then you proceed on to the next piece. Because you cut only a single piece at a time and then secure it into the background, it's possible to cut very delicate parts with bevel cutting that would be quite difficult if even possible with packet cutting. Since you'll only be cutting two thicknesses of veneer at a time while bevel cutting, there isn't really a packet as there is in the other cutting systems. The two pieces of veneer just get taped together and the drawing is traced on the top piece with carbon copy paper between the drawing and the veneer. You can also sand-shade the individual pieces before gluing them in place for added detail.

Start by tracing the part to be cut onto the top veneer layer with some tracing paper.

Tape the piece of veneer you plan to insert onto the back of the background veneer. It should be located over the traced line from the drawing and the grain direction should flow correctly.

Bevel cutting involves cutting through two pieces of veneer at the same time with the saw table angled so that the bottom piece slips seamlessly into the tapered hole cut in the top piece. For commercial veneer approximately 0.025 in. thick, you'll want to tilt your scrollsaw table to 13°. This will give you a tapered filler piece that should drop perfectly into the hole in the background.

You'll need to drill a small starter hole through both pieces of veneer in order to insert the scrollsaw blade. Try to drill it in a location that will be cut away later so it will disappear.

Pay attention to the direction of cut on the scrollsaw. Turn the part one way and you'll end up with a nice-fitting piece of veneer. Cut from the other direction and your piece will slip right through the hole with a large gap around the edges.

As you add more pieces, you'll find the image starts to develop in detail. Bevel cutting makes it possible to overlap new pieces onto previous pieces to create parts that are thin and delicate.

Bevel-Cutting Angle

Cutting two layers of veneer stacked together at a 13° angle makes parts that nest together perfectly.

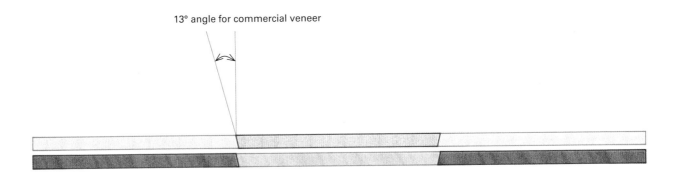

13° angle for commercial veneer

Piece-by-piece cutting

Piece-by-piece cutting is pretty much what it sounds like: You cut each part of the marquetry picture one at a time. It's primarily used when you need to create multiples of an image (up to 10 or more copies). Each detail in the image is cut one at a time from a stack

To create a marquetry picture using the piece-by-piece method, you'll need a separate stack of veneer for each piece you are cutting along with a copy of the drawing of each piece to glue to the packet. This method is ideal for making identical multiples of an image. On this sample, I get five copies of each flower petal each time I cut one, and I've been able to squeeze three different petals into this small packet.

made of multiple layers of the same veneer. Piece-by-piece cutting requires the most skill of all the cutting methods because you essentially cut on one side of the drawing line for the background piece and on the other side of the line for the filler piece. Any mistakes or discrepancies between the two parts can result in either gaps or parts that won't fit together.

With piece-by-piece cutting, the packet consists of a stack of identical veneer pieces typically nailed or taped together with a cardstock top and bottom layer. The cardstock helps minimize tearout on the bottom piece of veneer and gives you something to glue the drawing to on the top of the packet. Because you're cutting only a single component each time, you'll need quite a few packets for a complex design along with several copies of the marquetry drawing that you can cut apart into the individual components.

Building the Packet

Let's get started making our packet for the orchid flower image we'll be cutting. The packet doesn't need to be complex, but it does need to have the veneer accurately placed and secured so the grain runs in the correct direction on each part and so the veneer can't move accidentally while you're cutting.

As we discussed earlier, you'll need two pieces of cardstock cut to the size of your drawing and a copy of the drawing spray-glued onto the top piece of cardstock. Place your background veneer on top of the bottom piece of cardstock, and tape it in place around the perimeter with blue tape. Next, lay the other piece of cardstock with the drawing facing up on top of the background veneer and tape them together along just one edge so you can flip the drawing up to accurately place pieces of veneer onto the background—ideally an edge that is farthest from the busiest portion of the marquetry drawing.

Work in a methodical manner when placing the various veneer pieces onto the background so you don't accidentally forget one. I always work in a specific order: branches first, then leaves, then flowers, and finally any additional detail items like the centers of flowers. This way, I can double-check that I have finished inserting one type of piece completely before moving on to the next. I also mark the drawing as I place each piece, usually with a colored pencil so I know at a glance which pieces remain and which have already been placed.

The easiest way to locate the veneer pieces correctly is to bend the drawing up a bit while looking at both the background and the drawing together. You can see fairly exactly where each piece needs to go and when they are not in quite the right location. It helps to move around to another angle and get a different view of the piece to be placed in reference to the drawing while you're placing it. I tend to look at the veneer along its length and from a side view to make sure each one completely covers the lines on the drawing. Cut your veneer pieces oversize by about an inch all around, which will help ensure that even if you overcut a piece a bit, you'll still have enough veneer to have a piece that fits the background.

As you place each piece of veneer onto the background, tape it on all sides with blue tape to secure it in place, and then mark the drawing with a colored pencil to note which piece has been placed. Continue placing each piece of veneer until you have all the necessary pieces taped in place. You'll probably notice

With the background taped to the bottom piece of cardstock, tape the top cardstock with the drawing onto the background along one edge. This will allow you to lift the drawing up while placing individual pieces of veneer for the parts of your marquetry picture.

Bend the drawing up so you can see both the background and the drawing to accurately locate each piece of veneer. Flipping the drawing up and down a few times makes it easier to locate the edges of each part.

With roughly half the pieces taped to the background veneer, the packet is starting to get quite thick in some areas, while other areas are just the background veneer.

Now that all the pieces are taped in place, double-check your drawing before closing the packet. Make sure each piece in your marquetry picture has been marked by the colored pencil.

Close the packet and tape all around the perimeter with pieces of blue tape. Add extra tape where the marquetry picture goes off the edge of the drawing.

that the packet is quite thick in some areas and thinner in others, and this will affect the cutting speed on the saw. Before you tape the packet closed, go over the entire surface and press the blue tape down firmly to seat all the parts one last time.

Close the packet and tape tightly around the perimeter of the drawing with pieces of blue tape to hold the packet firmly together. Make sure you've got the tape tight, and add extra pieces near any locations where the marquetry picture flows off the edge of the packet. You are now ready to start cutting marquetry.

Cutting the Packet

Before you start cutting the marquetry packet, tape the last copy of your drawing to a bench or tabletop next to your scrollsaw. This is where you'll place the pieces of your marquetry picture as you cut them out. It's also a good idea to have the floor around your saw clean in case you drop a piece and need to find it on the floor. I like to have a large work surface next to my saw so I can throw all the extra parts from cutting into one place. That way, if I need to replace a part or accidentally pulled out the wrong part from the stack, I'll know where all the extra parts are and where to look for the missing piece. It makes searching for the correct part much faster.

I use my DeWalt scrollsaw to cut nearly all my marquetry, typically with a 2/0 blade and the saw set at fairly low speed, around 300 to 400 rpm or so. High blade speed can make it difficult to follow the drawing accurately and makes it more likely that you'll miscut or overcut a line somewhere along the way. If you do overcut, slow the saw down and see if you can salvage the overcut line by making that part a slightly different size/shape. Tighten the tension on the sawblade until it has a high-C ping when you flick it with your finger. It doesn't need to be exact, but slightly tighter is better than slightly looser and slightly slower is better than faster. I also use a momentary power foot pedal on my saw so I can turn the saw off and on with my foot while keeping both hands on the packet. I find that it makes the sawing process much faster not having to reach up and switch the saw on and off repeatedly. Using a momentary power foot switch allows you to simply lift your foot a bit to stop the saw when parts are cut or to check that you are cutting exactly on the lines.

Begin cutting inward from one of the outside pieces, making sure to hold the packet down near the blade to prevent it from slapping around while cutting (the worst injury you'll get if you accidentally touch the blade is a small paper cut). Carefully saw your way around the entire perimeter of this first piece, stop the

CUTTING TRICKS

Cutting smooth, curved flower petals and leaves can take some practice. I find it works best if you cut curved lines without stopping partway through the curve and instead continuously turn the packet as you cut the entire curved line in one shot.

When it comes to sharp corners, cut right up to the point of the corner and stop cutting, but leave the saw running. Then gently rotate the packet around the back of the sawblade while pulling the blade forward slightly with the packet to prevent it from cutting. Once the packet is rotated to the new direction, continue cutting as before.

Long, flowing curved lines are a challenge to cut, but you can make the process easier if you try to cut them in a single movement. Stopping and starting along the line will likely give you sharp points in your curve. Making the curved cut in one move means rotating your body and the packet as you cut. It takes some practice but isn't that difficult to master.

To make a sharp turn, cut right into the corner, then stop cutting but keep the saw running.

Next, gently pull the packet toward you while rotating it around the back of the sawblade. Keeping slight pressure on the back of the blade prevents the saw from cutting while you turn. Make sure to keep the saw running while you do this or the blade will likely break.

Once you've turned the packet to the new direction, continue cutting as before, then remove the stack of parts when you finish the cut.

As you complete cutting around the perimeter of the first part, stop the saw and gently lift the packet while pushing the cut part down with an awl or scalpel.

Sort through your stack of parts, pull out the specific piece you need for the color of the part you cut, and place it on the copy of the drawing.

As you continue to cut parts and place them on the drawing, you'll begin to see your picture slowly develop into the complete image you drew. Having a copy of the drawing on which to place cut parts will make assembly much easier.

Once you finish cutting the final piece, place it on your drawing and you'll get the first look at your marquetry flowers and see how the different colors interact.

saw, and then, using an awl or other sharp-pointed tool, press it out of the packet so you can remove the correct piece of veneer from the stack of parts.

If you are careful while pushing out the parts, they will remain in a clean stack and you should be able to locate the correct part and remove it quite easily. Remember which piece of veneer you are cutting so that you are able to select the correct one from the stack. Place this piece on the copy of your drawing, then proceed to cut the rest of the image.

You'll find as you are cutting that pieces of the background also need to be removed as they are cut away. Take them out of the stack of parts just as you would any other component and place them in the correct location on the drawing.

Assembling Your Marquetry Veneer

Once all the pieces of your marquetry image have been cut and placed on the drawing, begin removing the rest of the background veneer from the packet (see the photos on the facing page). Carefully cut through the tape holding the packet together and

1

When all the pieces of the marquetry picture are cut and organized in their respective locations on the drawing, you're ready to remove the background veneer from the packet. Begin by cutting through all the perimeter tape holding the packet together.

2

Disassemble the remaining packet parts by carefully peeling off the tape and pieces of veneer that you taped onto the background veneer. The background veneer is very delicate at this point, so go easy on it.

3

Cover the entire glue face of the background veneer with blue tape to help hold it together. The tape also works great at temporarily holding all the parts in place as you assemble the marquetry picture.

4

Flip the background show face up, and begin assembling the marquetry picture piece by piece into the background. Start with branches and any outer parts and work toward the center.

5

Continue placing pieces into the background until the entire image is assembled. It can take some time, but the locations will become more obvious as you get more of the image assembled.

then peel back the tape holding all the various veneer pieces to the background. Be careful because the background now has lots of holes in it and is quite delicate.

Once you have the background free of the packet remnants, lay it show face down on your bench. Cover the entire glue face of the background veneer with a layer of blue tape. This creates a nice, sticky surface for you to assemble your marquetry pieces onto and keeps the background veneer from breaking during handling.

Next, flip the background veneer over so you can begin assembling your marquetry image. Pick up the veneer pieces one by one with a pair of tweezers and carefully place them in their respective locations in the background. I find it's usually easiest to start with long branches because they seem to nest nicely into the background and give you a good reference for placing other parts correctly. Continue placing parts into the background, working from the outer edges toward the center until the entire image is assembled. Keep in mind that you'll also want to place the background pieces you cut away.

Don't press the veneer pieces down hard onto the blue tape because you'll need to pick up each piece again for sand shading in the next section and they break easily. If you placed the parts in their proper locations on the drawing as you cut them out, it should be fairly clear where each piece goes (that's the reason for the drawing next to the saw). Take your time and place the obvious pieces first, and then the more difficult ones will become easier to locate.

Sand Shading

To give your marquetry image a more lifelike appearance, each of the pieces needs to be sand-shaded along some of the edges. This creates the look of shadows and greatly enhances the three-dimensional appearance of the picture. There are a few supplies you'll need to gather so you can sand-shade your marquetry parts: an electric hot plate, a small metal pan (something like a 7-in. to 9-in. cake pan works great), terrarium sand, a variety of wood blocks to hold the veneer flat (I use pieces of 1-in.-thick particleboard about 6 in. square), tweezers, and a small bowl of water.

Sand shading involves dipping each piece of veneer into a container of hot sand to lightly scorch the veneer. I use an electric hot plate with an inexpensive metal pan about 2 in. deep filled halfway with terrarium sand from a pet store. This sand is much finer than play sand or beach sand, so the scorching effect ends up subtler. Heat the sand at medium heat and use some scrap veneer to test the heat and how fast

To sand-shade your marquetry veneer, you'll need a hot plate, a shallow metal pan, terrarium sand, tweezers, some small blocks, and a small bowl of water.

the veneer burns. You want it to take about 10 to 15 seconds for the veneer to get the correct amount of burning; faster than that, you'll likely burn your veneer, whereas longer than that, it will seem to take forever to complete the shading.

Now's the time to pull out the third copy of the drawing you saved to use as a shading template. You'll need to frequently refer back to this shading template during the sand-shading process because it shows you which pieces to shade and where to shade them. Make the shading template by coloring in the areas you'd like to see shaded with a colored pencil. It can take some trial and error to get the shading to look right, but this drawing will be useful when you start shading the veneer. Typically, shading would occur where there are natural shadows, such as the inside areas of flowers or underneath an overhanging leaf.

A method that works well for keeping track of parts while shading is to remove an entire small section of veneer pieces to be shaded and lay them on the copy of your drawing that shows the shading locations—something like one complete flower or a bunch of closely placed leaves. Then shade all of those pieces, making sure to keep them in the proper orientation when you put them on the drawing.

Hold the veneer with a pair of tweezers (the sand is very hot) and dip it into the sand about ¼ in. or so.

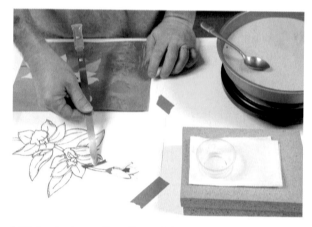

Place your assembled marquetry picture next to the shading drawing. Consider the shading drawing a template for where to sand-shade each piece as you remove it from the background.

I like to shade small sections of the marquetry rather than the entire image at one time. I find this makes it easier to keep track of the locations of the parts in the background. Simply remove a set of parts and place them on the copy of the drawing you'll be using for shading.

❖ TIP ❖ Try to avoid leaving the veneer in the sand long enough to cause it to burn black—a little smoke coming off the veneer is normal, but when it starts to turn black, you've gone too far. Also, don't completely submerge the pieces in the hot sand because that tends to shade the entire piece and the natural veneer color disappears. Just dip the edge you want to shade into the hot sand.

Use tweezers to hold the veneer while you dip it into the hot sand so you don't burn yourself. Dip the veneer in and out of the sand every few seconds to make sure you don't overheat an area.

TEST SHADING

Some veneers like holly and light green dyed veneer sand-shade very quickly and can have nice, subtle shading. Dark green veneer shades slowly and will take longer in the hot pan to achieve the same shaded look. The best method for determining the proper amount of time to shade each veneer is to test a few samples until you get the proper shading effect. Some woods shade quickly and some shade slowly; the only way you'll know which does what is to shade some small samples before you burn your final project pieces.

Getting the correct shaded look from the hot sand requires different burning times for different veneers. The best way to know how long to shade each veneer is to shade some sample pieces. These holly samples show three levels of shading: too much, just right, and not enough.

Shade concave parts by picking up a spoonful of hot sand and slowly dragging the veneer through the pile of sand on the spoon.

Repeatedly insert and remove the veneer every few seconds until the shading is at the level you want—ideally a nice, even dark brown that fades away quickly to the natural veneer color. Some pieces will require shading in multiple areas; simply shade each area one by one until the part is correctly shaded. If

you want to have the shading flow around the edge of a part, carefully rotate the part in the sand as you insert it. The more fluidly you move the part in the sand, the more natural the shading will look.

Parts with concave curves are a challenge to shade in the hot pan, so an alternate method is to pick up some hot sand in a metal spoon and place the curved veneer into the sand piled on the spoon. It may take a few spoonfuls of fresh hot sand to shade these parts as the sand loses heat quickly when out of the pan.

Once the parts from each section are shaded, they need to be rehydrated slightly to compensate for shrinking caused by the heat from the sand. I do this by dipping my fingers into the bowl of water and pressing each piece of veneer one at a time with my wet fingers. You don't need much water, and if you use too much, the veneer will swell beyond the size of the hole it goes into; a drop or two is plenty.

After moistening each piece of veneer, place it back into the background in its proper location. Once all

After shading, the veneer needs a bit of moisture to rehydrate it. Just dip your fingers in the bowl of water and flick off most of the water. Then press your wet fingers onto the veneer piece for a second to moisten it.

After completely shading each section of the drawing and replacing the pieces in the background veneer, cover the wet veneer with a wood block to hold it flat while it dries.

the pieces in a certain area are reinserted, cover the area with a wooden block to hold the veneer flat until it dries (usually an hour or so). Repeat this procedure for all the veneer parts that need shading, and then leave the entire picture to dry for an hour.

Taping and Final Adjustments

At this point, your marquetry image probably looks pretty nice: All the shading is complete and the parts are in roughly their final locations. Now we need to tape the show face and make some final adjustments to the part locations, which we do from the glue face. Start by covering the entire show face of the veneer with a layer of blue tape (see the top left photo on p. 128). Just press the tape down with your hand—don't burnish it down with the brush because you'll be removing the tape later.

Next, flip the panel over and carefully remove the tape from the glue face of the veneer. Go slowly as small pieces tend to stick to the tape while it's being removed. To replace them, just push the tape back down and hold the veneer piece in place with the tweezers while removing the tape.

Once all the tape is removed, use your tweezers or a small chisel to make final adjustments to the locations of the veneer pieces. Some of them have probably moved a bit during taping and need to be rotated or moved slightly. Try to push them outward toward the background veneer edges; that way, any spaces between them are located at the intersection of the marquetry parts rather than between the background and the parts.

Once all the parts are in their final locations and you're happy with how things look, cover the entire glue face of the image with a layer of blue tape. Then flip the veneer over and carefully remove the

1

Your completely shaded marquetry picture is beginning to take shape. Next, we'll make some final adjustments to the pieces and get it looking even better. First, cover the entire show face of the veneer with a layer of blue tape. Don't burnish the tape down because you'll be removing it soon; just press it down firmly by hand.

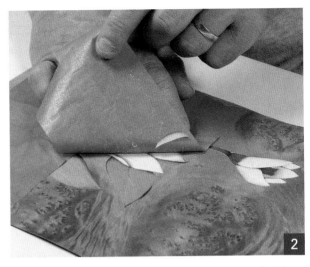

2

Flip the veneer glue face up, and carefully remove the blue tape from the glue face. Go slowly as the tape will try to pull up small pieces as you go. If a piece comes up with the tape, simply press the tape down again and hold the piece in place with the tweezers while you remove the tape.

3

Move the marquetry pieces into their final locations with a pair of tweezers. Try to push them outward toward the background veneer so that any gaps are near the center. Take your time because this is the final chance you'll have to alter the look of your marquetry picture.

4

Once you're done making adjustments, cover the entire glue face with another layer of blue tape. Flip the veneer over, and remove all the blue tape from the show face; go carefully so as not to disturb the parts of the picture. Then tape the entire show face with 2-in.-wide gum tape, working quickly so the veneer doesn't have a chance to distort from the added moisture. Press the tape down firmly with a paper towel.

blue tape from the show face, going slowly to make sure no parts get pulled out of place while you remove the tape.

For this marquetry panel, we're going to gum-tape the show face to ensure that all the small veneer

pieces are held accurately in place while pressing. I'm using 2-in.-wide gum tape for this, but you could just as easily use 1-in. tape if that's what you have on hand. Moisten the tape, and lay it down on the veneer one piece at a time. Press the tape down with a folded paper towel to make sure it's fully seated. You'll want to work quickly because you are applying quite a bit of tape and the veneer could start to buckle if left in the open too long. Once all the gum tape is applied, place the picture under a sheet of MDF and let it dry flat for an hour or two.

When the gum tape is dry, remove the blue tape from the glue face. Be careful not to pull any pieces off the gum tape, but if one comes off, simply place a drop of water on the exposed gum tape and press the veneer back down onto the tape. Cover that area for 30 minutes to let the wet tape dry. Once all the blue tape is removed, you're ready for gluing.

Gather together all the materials you'll need for glue-up before you start mixing glue: breather mesh, roller, tape, backer veneer, substrate, cauls, and plastic sheet.

Gluing Marquetry Panels

I glue all my marquetry veneer work with Pro-Glue urea formaldehyde glue; it dries very hard and does a good job of filling the saw kerfs between the veneer pieces. You can also mix the two colors of the glue to create a new color that more closely matches the background veneer color, which makes it possible to reduce the visibility of seams between the marquetry pieces. Pro-Glue takes roughly 6 to 8 hours to dry and is a dry powder mixed with water. Follow the instructions on the container to mix it properly. You'll also need to cut a piece of backer veneer to glue to the back side of your panel.

You can use clamps to press marquetry panels, but I like to use a vacuum bag. Either method will work as long as the pressure is evenly spread over the panel and the pressure is high enough. In both cases, you'll need cauls on top of the veneer with a layer of plastic between the veneer and the cauls. If using clamps, make the cauls from 3/4-in.-thick MDF; if you're using the vacuum bag, they can be 1/4-in.-thick MDF. Because we're using the vacuum bag for this glue-up, I've made two 1/4-in.-thick MDF cauls just a bit over the size of the marquetry panel—roughly 1/8 in. oversize. Make sure you have all the

The correct amount of UF glue will leave the substrate wet all over, but there won't be enough to form puddles or drips. Add a few pieces of tape around the perimeter of the panel to hold the top and bottom veneer faces in place in the vacuum bag. Cover the veneer with plastic sheet and the cauls, then cover the assembly with the breather mesh and place it in the vacuum bag for 6 to 8 hours so the glue can fully cure.

supplies necessary for gluing your marquetry image assembled and organized before you start mixing glue: both sheets of veneer, 1/4-in. MDF cauls, two pieces of plastic sheet, your substrate, a roller, blue tape, and glue.

My substrate for this panel is a piece of 1/4-in. MDF. Depending on the final application you've got planned for your panel, you could make the substrate out of a variety of materials. All that matters is that you have it sized correctly to match your veneer and, if it's plywood, that you run the grain direction opposite the direction of the marquetry background veneer.

Moisten the gum tape with a damp paper towel until all of the tape is damp and translucent. Don't overwet the tape: Use just enough water to soften the adhesive on the gum tape and make it easy to remove.

When you're ready to glue up the panel, mix about ¼ cup of glue according to the mixing instructions on the glue container. Pour a thin line of glue onto your substrate, and roll it out with an adhesive roller until the surface is uniformly coated with glue. The glue shouldn't be thick enough to puddle but also shouldn't look dry after a minute or two. If it does look dry, roll it out again with a bit more glue. Place your backer veneer onto the glue and press it firmly all over with your hand, then repeat for the marquetry veneer. Add a few pieces of blue tape around the perimeter of the veneer to hold it in place, cover both sides with plastic sheet and the ¼-in. MDF cauls, and place the assembly into the vacuum bag under the breather mesh.

After 6 to 8 hours, the glue will be dry and the panel can be removed from the press. Set it aside and let it continue curing overnight; after that, the gum tape can be removed. Moistening the tape with a damp paper towel will soften the adhesive enough that you should be able to peel off long strips of tape. If the tape tears, the glue has likely bled through the veneer into the tape and you'll need to use a card scraper to remove it. Even if you use a scraper, it's

Once the tape is wet, either peel or scrape it off. I find that using a small putty knife to get between the wet tape and the veneer allows me to peel off long strips of the tape quite easily.

still a good idea to moisten the tape to make removal easier. Peel or scrape off all of the tape, being careful not to damage the veneer, and then set the panel aside for a couple hours to dry before sanding.

Sanding the Panel

Once the panel is dry and all the tape is removed, it's time for sanding. Random-orbit sanders work well

Sanding marquetry panels requires different techniques than sanding straight solid-wood boards. Because the grain in a marquetry picture goes in many directions, most of the sanding should be done using a random-orbit sander. I do my initial cleanup sanding with a sander and 150-grit paper.

After the initial cleanup sanding, a quick flattening with a block wrapped in 180-grit paper helps prevent any dips or waves in the finished surface. Then complete your finish sanding with the random-orbit sander, using 180-, 220-, and 320-grit paper.

on marquetry panels because the grain direction in the veneer goes in multiple directions. I'll typically start with 150-grit on my sander to remove the remaining gum tape residue and bring all the veneer to the same level. After that, a good hand sanding with a hard sponge or cork block and some 180-grit paper will flatten the whole panel before finish sanding with the random-orbit sander. Finish sanding should always be done with the sander starting at 180-grit, then proceeding through 220 and 320; if you hand-sand the final grits, you'll likely see scratch marks going across the grain of some of the marquetry pieces. Once the sanding is complete, your panel is ready for finish.

More Detailed Techniques

For those interested in really pushing their marquetry skills, there are a variety of techniques widely used to create highly detailed marquetry images in the United Kingdom that are rarely used in the United States. This is primarily due to the fact that

Brian Freeman is a British marquetry master who has taken marquetry to a new level with his extremely detailed miniature work. This image, called "Early Morning Milk," is approximately 3 in. in diameter and uses several of the techniques discussed here, including fragmentation and sliverization, to create a stunning level of detail.

This marquetry panel of a Native American by John Jeggo uses a variety of specialized marquetry techniques to create the illusion of lifelike hair and facial details.

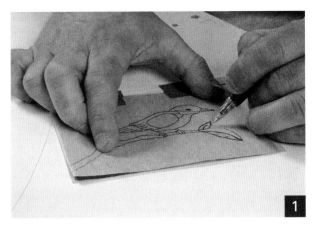

Use a piece of carbon paper and your marquetry drawing to trace the outline of one part onto the background veneer.

Carefully cut along the marked line with a scalpel. Make a few passes so you don't break any of the veneer while cutting and keep the scalpel blade vertical the whole time.

veneer in the U.K. is cut thinner than in the U.S., and therefore it can be cut with a scalpel or utility knife quite easily. But it is possible to cut thicker veneer this way—it just takes a bit more effort to cut. These techniques are somewhat unique, and oddly enough, creating marquetry this way requires fewer tools and less space than the packet method described previously.

Window cutting

The majority of the detailed techniques I'll describe here favor the window method of cutting. This technique entails cutting a hole in the background the exact shape of the piece needed and then sliding a new piece of veneer under the window oriented so the wood grain appearance is ideal. You then cut around the perimeter of the window so the new piece

fits tightly into the hole in the background. This technique requires only a single tool, a sharp scalpel (it does help to have a cutting mat, though, as it keeps your scalpel blades sharp longer).

To use the window method, start with a finished copy of your drawing, your background veneer, and a piece of carbon paper. Place the drawing on top of the background veneer with the carbon paper between them and trace around the specific piece you are planning to cut. Remove the drawing and carbon paper and, using your scalpel held vertically, carefully cut along the line left by the carbon paper. Go slowly and carefully around the piece several times to cut it out completely. This is a skill that takes practice to perfect, and the more you practice, the better you'll

STRAW MARQUETRY

One interesting type of marquetry employs an unexpected material to create shimmering iridescent patterns. Wheat, rye, or oat straw is split open and flattened to create long, flat strips of straw that are dyed a variety of colors or left natural. The straw strips are then glued onto a substrate one by one and cut into patterns of geometric and natural shapes. Straw marquetry takes great skill and is a demanding technique because the straw is quite delicate and the one-piece-at-a-time assembly method is very time-consuming; the end results can be breathtaking, however.

This straw marquetry piece by Arthur Seigneur demonstrates complex geometric patterns that fool the eye and make the shape of this small box difficult to visualize.

Straw marquetry can be used to make a dramatic statement as on these doors by Arthur Seigneur. The sunburst pattern radiating out from the central handles draws your eye in, and the subtle change in color from light to dark as you move from the center outward enhances the effect greatly. Bearing in mind that each piece of straw on these doors had to be cut with a gentle taper and fit one by one to the rest of the pieces gives an idea of the time and patience required for straw marquetry work.

Slide a new piece of veneer behind the hole in the background so you can see what the grain orientation should be for this particular component. Securely tape it to the background veneer from behind. Now carefully cut around the perimeter of the hole in the background with your scalpel to create the new piece that fills the hole.

Press the piece into the hole in the background and push it down until it's flush with the surrounding veneer. Wipe off the excess glue and set it aside to dry.

get at it. There's no avoiding that it takes time to get good at cutting parts by hand with a scalpel. The tradeoff is that you can do this sort of marquetry in your living room while watching TV or at the dining table; you don't need to be in a workshop because there are no power tools and no dust.

Remove the cut piece from the background and slide your selected veneer piece under the background until you can see it in the window you just cut. Orient the grain for the veneer so the grain lines flow in the most pleasing direction, then tape the veneer to the background to keep it from moving.

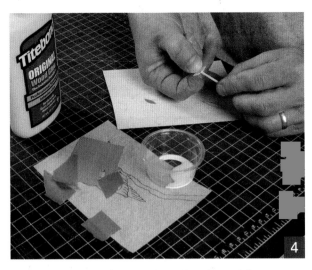

Apply a tiny bit of PVA glue along the edges of the new piece, making sure to get an even bead around the perimeter of the piece.

Carefully cut the new piece along the edge of the window in the background, making sure to keep the scalpel vertical. Take your time while cutting because it should take several passes to cut completely through the veneer. Once you've got the piece cut, insert it into the background from the back and either gum-tape or glue it in place and move on to the next piece. This process requires patience and time, but the end results can be amazing.

Fragmentation

There are a number of other more specialized skills that go along with window cutting that can be used to create marquetry images with even more complexity. The first of these is fragmentation, which involves taking select colors of veneer—brown that would be used for tree branches, for example—and essentially grinding strips of several colors of brown-toned veneer into small fragments of veneer. This can be done by cutting very narrow strips of the selected veneer and then crushing those strips by hand into tiny pieces or by sliding a piece of veneer back and forth across a coarse file.

As an example of fragmentation, let's say you have created a tree that needs a branch in a certain area. You wouldn't want to cut just a brown piece of

A great example of fragmentation used to create realistic trees, leaves, and grass is this impressive picture by Brian Freeman titled "Reflections."

Fragmentation uses bits of colored veneer crumbled or filed into tiny pieces that are then used to fill a hole cut in the background veneer. Depending upon the look you are after, you might mix different colors of veneer to create a variegated effect.

Use the window method to cut a hole in the background veneer where your branch will be located. Cover the back of the hole with blue tape and then fill it with PVA glue.

Pour the fragmented veneer bits into the hole and press them down into the glue. Leave the fragments overflowing for now.

Once you've got enough fragments in place to cover the hole completely, clamp a cork-covered block over the area until the glue dries.

When the glue has dried, sand the fragmented area flush with the surrounding veneer using a hard sanding block and some 150-grit paper. The end result should be a fairly realistic variegated branch. To add more detail, just repeat the process again.

veneer for the branch because that might not look quite right. Instead, use the window method to cut a hole where the branch would go and then apply a piece of blue tape to the back of the hole. Fill the hole with PVA glue and pour in a pile of fragmented brown veneer pieces until the hole is overflowing. Place a piece of plastic sheet over the area and gently clamp a cork-covered block over the hole to compress the veneer pieces into the hole. Let the glue dry completely, then sand the brown veneer flush with the background. You should end up with a much more realistic tree branch than you would have with a single piece of brown veneer.

Peter White used numerous fine slivers of veneer to add detail
and definition to this image of a tawny owl.

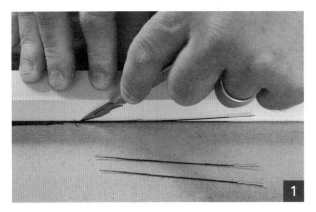

Making slivers of veneer can be done a number of ways. I use a scalpel and straightedge to slice off thin pieces of veneer of the desired color. You could also use a handplane set to a coarse cut to slice thin slivers of veneer.

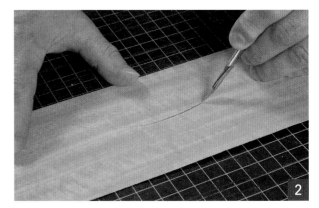

Make a slightly angled cut with the scalpel at the location where you intend to place the sliver, then make another slice in the same location angled in the opposite direction. The resulting cut should be just large enough to insert the sliver of veneer.

Spread a little glue along the edges of the cut, and press the sliver of veneer into the cut in the background veneer. You can use the blunt end of your scalpel to press along the length of the sliver to help force it into the background. Once the glue is dry, sand everything flush with the surrounding veneer.

Sliverization

Another specialized technique that uses good scalpel control is sliverization. In this technique, tiny slivers of veneer are cut from sheets of veneer and glued into knife kerfs cut in the background veneer. Sliverization can be used to great effect to realistically mimic hair, fur, and feathers in marquetry pictures by combining different veneer colors in the slivers (see the photo on p. 137). Essentially, the method is to make a slightly angled scalpel cut in the background veneer followed by another cut along the same line but angled in the opposite direction. The

sliver of contrasting color is then forced into the knife kerf left by these two cuts, thereby creating a thin line of color in an image. Repeated insertions of slivers can create a highly realistic marquetry picture.

Laser Marquetry

One final technique for cutting marquetry that has been growing in popularity with the advent of lower-cost laser cutters is laser-cut marquetry. The process is much the same as hand-cut marquetry and requires all the same preparation as would be done with any other method. The difference comes in that the marquetry drawing must be digitized and translated into vector format in one of several software packages. The vector drawing can then be disassembled into each individual component that makes up the marquetry picture. Each separate component must be isolated and checked for accuracy before cutting. All the components of each color are nested together in a single file that can then be fed to the laser cutter. The cutting process is quite fast once all the prep work is done. Much as the care taken to draw precise lines on a packet-cut picture pays off with easier cutting, care taken in working with the vector lines pays off with parts that nest together

Christy Oates combined a good deal of technical skill in vector graphics with laser cutting to create a unique piece of marquetry art. This project, called "The E-Waste Project," was inspired by the electronic waste at a recycling center. Images of the electronic components were taken and manipulated in a variety of programs to create a radial-matched pattern resembling traditional veneering.

A close-up image of "The E-Waste Project" gives an idea of the precision and repeatability of laser-cut marquetry.

almost seamlessly. There will always be a slight burnt edge to laser-cut marquetry parts, but that can actually be used as a detail in the final marquetry piece.

I've used laser cutting several times in the past when I needed multiple copies of an image cut exactly the same. It is also handy for cutting small and delicate parts because the laser doesn't care about grain direction and applies no force to the veneer while cutting. One thing to note, however, is that laser cutters capable of this level of precision are relatively expensive and the time required to learn the necessary software can be significant. If you're interested in incorporating laser marquetry into a project, I'd suggest finding someone who does laser cutting professionally and working with them to get your project cut. You'll spend much less time and money than if you tried to do it all on your own.

All of the marquetry techniques discussed in this chapter and many more that you can develop on your own can be used to create highly detailed and enjoyable images in marquetry. It just takes time and patience. The more time and patience you are willing to devote to making your marquetry images better, the better they will look. On the next page are a few more examples of highly complex marquetry from the past and present.

This piece by the author features a marquetry panel behind a secret door with a trompe l'oeil image of a castle hallway. There is also a secret door and a drawer hidden in the marquetry imagery.

An example of fine marquetry work from the United Kingdom done by Peter White combines traditional nature-themed marquetry with the realism of trompe l'oeil (fool the eye) imagery of a paint can and brushes. It is appropriately titled "Watching Paint Dry."

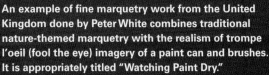

This detail image of an ornate marquetry tabletop by Gregg Novosad takes the creativity possible in marquetry to a new level. It shows that our imagination really is the limiting factor in how complex or visually entertaining our work can become.

A sample marquetry panel from the side of a marquetry commode built by David Roentgen in the 1770s. The commode has numerous marquetry panels depicting musicians in various states; this particular image is of two musicians seated at a table, and the detail level of the marquetry is quite stunning.

CHAPTER 8

Parquetry

Parquetry has been around for hundreds of years and has been used to create complex patterns in veneered projects from furniture to flooring to wall decoration. It was often combined with marquetry in historic furniture to create more visually complex backgrounds for the floral marquetry. Parquetry is similar to marquetry in that it uses small pieces of wood veneer to create decorative designs.

However, parquetry is formed of only geometric shapes to create its own unique and interesting visual patterns.

The most frequently seen form of parquetry is a simple chessboard, its shape defined by a certain number of identical veneer squares arranged in a specific pattern. If you take this idea a step further by changing those squares to

The most common form of parquetry veneering is the chessboard, in this case turned into a freestanding Art Deco chess table by the author in walnut, walnut burl, and holly veneer.

To create a piece of a specific size and shape with parquetry diamonds takes precision layout and cutting. This Art Deco mirror by the author features diamonds in madrone burl and maple highlighted with inlaid mother of pearl circles around the perimeter.

The Tools You Need

When it comes to cutting veneer, there's no substitute for a good veneer saw. I use a French Arno saw that I've resharpened to cut equally well in both directions (you've seen this saw several times throughout the book already). That way, I can use either hand to make a cut and if necessary can reverse the cut at the forward edge to prevent tearing the veneer. The most readily available veneer saw is one made by Two Cherries, although it is designed primarily for right-handed use. If you're a lefty, the Arno saw is your best bet.

You can use a knife or a scalpel to cut parquetry veneer shapes, but I prefer to use a veneer saw because it doesn't tend to follow the grain of the veneer and wander off the cut line as a knife does. If you decide to use a more delicate veneer for your squares, such as burl or heavily figured woods, it may be necessary to cover the face of the veneer with a layer of gum tape to prevent chips and breakage along the cut line. Cut a sample strip or two to check and tape if necessary. Leave the tape to dry before cutting.

> ❖ **TIP** ❖ When cutting with the veneer saw, make sure the blade stays 90° to the cutting board so you will have square edges on the parquetry veneer strips.

diamonds, you create a whole new geometric pattern. Now take those diamonds and rotate some of them in place and you have yet another unique pattern, called Louis Cubes (some of us might have seen Louis Cubes as the backdrop in the video game Q*bert®). You can also use the same cutting techniques to make parallelograms, assembling them in a traditional herringbone pattern to create zigzagging stripes or in a variety of other patterns.

There is an almost endless number of geometric patterns that can be created by simply altering the shape and arrangement of the parquetry veneer pieces. In this chapter, we're going to focus on the three primary ones: squares, diamonds, and parallelograms. Once you've learned how to cut these, you'll be able to take that knowledge and explore new shapes and patterns with a firm grounding in the skills necessary to cut any shape you can design.

We'll be using two kinds of tape to hold the veneer together: regular blue painter's tape from your local home center and gum tape, ideally 2-in.-wide gum tape. Gum tape has a water-activated adhesive on one side and shrinks slightly when it dries to help pull together veneer seams. To use it, have a wet sponge handy and press the tape onto the sponge as you unroll it. You don't want it to be soaking wet, but it needs to be moist to work properly. If you get a bit too much water on the tape, just wipe it off with a paper towel after it's applied to the veneer.

Once we get to cutting parquetry diamonds and more complex shapes, you'll find it handy to have a set of plastic drafting triangles to help you get accurate angles on your pieces. Drafting triangles are surprisingly accurate, so you can use them for detailed work without any worries.

You'll need several rolls of blue tape of different widths along with some 2-in.-wide gum tape to tape up your parquetry patterns. If you can't find 2-in. gum tape, 1 in. will work fine; you'll just need to apply more strips to cover the surface. You'll also need a sharp veneer saw for cutting all the various parquetry shapes. This Arno saw can be used by left- and right-handed workers.

Making a Chessboard

At some point in your woodworking life, you'll probably make a chessboard. This classic parquetry pat-

This detail of an Art Deco chess table by the author features a chessboard made of walnut burl and holly squares framed in ebony, walnut, and holly.

tern can add fun and function to an ordinary table. If you don't often work with veneer, you might be tempted to make your game board from thick squares of solid wood. Don't do it. You'll have to contend with both wood movement and weak end-grain joints. Veneer is much easier to cut accurately and is easy to apply to an MDF or plywood substrate, which won't move at all inside a solid-wood frame. Just be sure to pick a couple of contrasting veneer colors so the different squares will be easily seen.

Standard chessboard squares range from 2 in. to 2½ in. square, but you can make the squares to fit whatever chess pieces you have handy. Let's go with 2-in. squares for this board, which will yield a

A chessboard is really nothing more than a group of identical squares of veneer arranged into a pattern of alternating colors. What you do with it after that is what can make it into something special.

You'll need two pieces of veneer, one of each of two colors, about 10½ in. wide by 18½ in. long. If you don't have pieces that size, you can cut the squares from multiple smaller pieces or tape them together into a larger sheet. You'll also need a piece of backer veneer for the back side of your chessboard to help keep it flat.

JIG FOR ACCURACY

The main jig you'll need is a veneer-cutting board, which is the board you'll use to cut all the parquetry pieces to exact size. Use a piece of ½-in. or ¾-in. plywood about 24 in. long by 12 in. wide. To one long edge of this piece, glue a ¼-in.-thick by 1-in.-wide length of stock to act as a stop to help secure the work and create a straight reference surface. The stop should stand ½ in. to ¾ in. proud of the board's work surface. You'll be pushing the veneer strips up against this stop, so it needs to be securely attached to the cutting board.

You'll also need a straightedge made from a straight square block of hardwood roughly ¾ in. thick by about 24 in. long. Since we're making 2-in. squares for our chessboard, rip it precisely 2 in. wide. This will be the straightedge you use to cut the strips of veneer into equal squares, so make sure it is truly straight and square. You can also substitute a metal straightedge or framing square with a 2-in.-wide leg at least 20 in. long, but only if you are cutting with a knife because there is no side support to keep the veneer saw square to the table with a metal guide. Either way, apply some adhesive-backed 100-grit sandpaper on the bottom of the guide to help hold it in place.

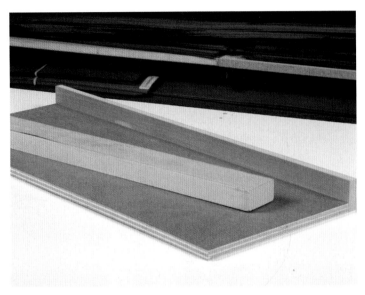

To cut parquetry veneer, you'll need to make a custom cutting board about 12 in. wide by 24 in. long with a hardwood edge stop to hold the veneer securely. The straightedge atop the cutting board is 2 in. wide by about 24 in. long and has sandpaper glued to the bottom face to help hold the veneer while cutting.

chessboard 16 in. square before adding any perimeter inlay and solid-wood framework. You'll need two pieces of veneer, one of each color you've chosen, measuring about 10½ in. wide by 18½ in. long. You can tape together two narrow pieces to get the full 10½-in. width or cut your strips from a narrow stack of matching veneer one strip at a time.

Cutting the veneer strips

Use your straightedge and veneer saw to cut a straight edge on one edge of each piece of veneer. Make these cuts on your regular veneer cutting mat.

Start with a light pass just to create a path for the blade, and then bear down a bit more on the next few strokes until the excess veneer falls away cleanly.

Next, place the freshly cut edge against the stop on the cutting board (see the sidebar above). Place the straightedge on top of the veneer and press both firmly against the stop on the cutting board. Cut the first 2-in. strip of veneer. Repeat this process, using the straightedge on the cutting board as the sizing guide until you have four dark strips and five light strips or five dark and four light (it doesn't really matter which).

Trim one edge of each piece of veneer to get a clean, straight edge to reference the next cut.

is taped. I apply short strips of tape every 2 in. or so, and then when the sheet is completely taped across the grain, I'll run long strips of tape along the joints and burnish all of the tape with a brass brush to help it stick.

The next step is to square off one end of the veneer sheet. This step is critical, so use an accurate square to mark a pencil line where you want to cut the sheet. Use your straightedge and veneer saw to cut a clean, straight edge on the marked line. Now press the just-cut edge against the stop on your cutting board as in the previous strip-cutting step, and use the straight-

Press the edge you just cut against the stop on your cutting board and place the straightedge on top of the veneer, pushing it firmly against the stop. Cut through the veneer to create your first 2-in. strip of veneer. Repeat this process until you've cut all the strips of both colors.

Begin assembling alternating strips by taping across the joint between them every few inches.

Assembling and cutting the sheet

Use regular blue tape to create a sheet composed of alternating color strips, starting and ending with whichever color wood you cut into five strips. You'll want to end up with a sheet composed of five strips of one color and four strips of the other. The face where you did your cutting is the glue face, and the blue tape goes on that face during assembly. Blue tape has some stretch to it, so pull it tight as you apply it to draw the joints together. Start by just taping across two strips at a time, then add alternating strips one at a time until the whole sheet

When the cross-grain taping is done and you have a full sheet of strips, run a piece of tape along the length of all the joints.

Burnish the tape down firmly with a brass brush to help seat the tape on the veneer.

You need to mark a 90° end on the sheet with an accurate square so you can square off one end of the sheet in preparation for slicing into strips. Mark the line with a pencil, and cut exactly on the line using your straightedge and veneer saw.

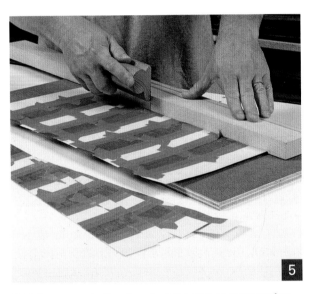

Butt the squared-off end against the stop on your cutting guide and, using the same 2-in.-wide straightedge as before, press the veneer tight against the stop and slice off the first row of squares. Repeat this process until you have eight strips of squares. Keep them in order as they are cut.

edge again to crosscut 2-in. strips from the veneer sheet until you have eight equal strips of alternating squares. Keep the strips in order as they are cut, and be careful as you exit each cut not to tear out the grain. Sometimes I'll run the veneer saw away from me on the first inch or so and then proceed cutting as normal for the rest of the cut.

Creating the chessboard pattern

All of the strips now need to be flipped over so you can see the squares of veneer and align them while taping. Just flip the whole stack of strips end for end so they stay in order and the grain remains aligned. Don't just flip the strips sideways (rather than end for end) or the grain will no longer be consistent. Spread out the strips in the order they were cut so you can begin assembling the chessboard pattern.

Slide every other strip down one square to create the alternating light-dark pattern of the chessboard. Use more blue tape to join the strips one at a time as before, being careful to align the intersections of the squares. Because you flipped the veneer over, the squares are visible and easy to align. Use enough tape to hold the joints together, but don't run tape along the entire joint at this time.

Peel away the overhanging squares that remain outside the playing surface. Now flip the entire veneer sheet over and retape the new joints as before, first with tape pulling across the joints and then with long strips along the joints with a final burnishing using the brass brush.

Flip the cut strips over and lay them out in the order they were cut. Slide every other one up one square. This should give you the beginnings of a chessboard pattern. Tape the alternating squares together in a few spots to hold them in alignment, making sure the corners of the squares are accurately aligned.

Peel away the overhanging squares around the perimeter, then flip the sheet of veneer over and tape across and along all the new joints with blue tape. Make sure to pull the tape tight across the joints so they are held tightly together.

Flip the sheet again and remove all the blue tape from the show face before applying gum tape to the entire surface.

Once the gum tape has dried, flip the sheet again and remove all the blue tape from the glue face of the veneer. You're now ready to glue up your first parquetry veneer work.

After assembling the whole pattern, flip the sheet over once more and remove the small amount of blue tape from the show face so it can be gum-taped. Check that the alignment of all the squares is correct; it's easier to fix a misaligned square now rather than after the gum tape is applied. Apply moist gum tape to the show face one long strip at a time, making sure the strips overlap slightly and cover the entire chessboard. This is a good place to use 2-in.-wide gum tape if you have some handy. When all the wet strips are in place, burnish them down with a paper towel to both dry off any excess water and press the tape down into the veneer better. Place the veneer under a piece of MDF or plywood for a couple hours to let the gum tape dry—otherwise, the gum tape will distort the veneer and pull the squares apart while it dries. Try to move quickly when using the gum tape: As the moisture hits the veneer, it will start to buckle and move, and the faster you get it under a weight, the easier it will be to handle.

After the gum tape has dried, trim off any overhanging gum tape with a razor knife so that it's flush with the veneer edges, and then remove all of the blue tape from the glue face. You're now ready to glue your chessboard veneer to the substrate of your choice, but before we go over glue-up, we'll look at some additional parquetry patterns and how to create them.

There are a number of other ways to use the techniques we've just learned while making a chessboard composed of square parquetry pieces. The two pieces shown left and below have square or rectangular parquetry veneer work at their core. The "White Cabinet" is a compound curved parquetry cabinet by Brian Newell decorated with squares of resawn curly English sycamore veneer.

The unique tabletop design with square and rectangular parquetry shapes in walnut veneer created by Brian Reid shows that parquetry veneer work doesn't necessarily need to have pieces that are all the same size or shape.

Diamond-Cut Veneers

While working on a commission for an entertainment cabinet decorated with hundreds of veneer diamonds, I needed a quick and accurate method to cut all the diamonds the same size and shape. To do that, I came up with the simple techniques I'll describe in detail below. There are many ways to cut shapes like this, so don't feel limited to using just what I'm teaching. If you come up with a faster, more effective method on your own, by all means use it. These techniques require minimal tools and work with virtually any veneer, so you won't need a big investment in equipment to get started.

Once you get comfortable cutting veneer diamonds, you can use them to create a wide variety of interesting patterns using any number of veneer colors. By taking things a bit further, you can also combine your diamonds in new patterns to create Louis Cubes and other interesting designs.

Parquetry diamonds in maple and madrone burl decorate the front and sides of this entertainment cabinet by the author. To create panels of exact sizes requires precision in the layout and cutting of the diamond parquetry.

On my commission project, I alternated two colors of veneer for the diamonds to create a bit more visual interest. On that piece, the veneers were madrone burl and maple. You can add contrast and visual rhythm by combining different colors or changing the grain direction of neighboring diamonds. Using three colors of diamonds lets you create a Louis Cube pattern (see p. 156) that gives the illusion of blocks stacked in three dimensions.

Planning the diamonds

To cut diamonds, you'll need another custom-size straightedge. Set the width of the straightedge according to the size of the diamonds you want to create; this takes some math, so be ready. Diamonds are essentially composed of four right triangles nested

together to form a diamond shape. Sounds confusing, but this actually makes it easier to calculate the height and width of the final diamonds. Let's say you want to make diamonds that are 3 in. high. This one diamond is made up of four right triangles each with a height of 1.5 in. To determine the length of one side (also known as the hypotenuse) of the resulting diamond, you just use the Pythagorean Theorem: hypotenuse (noted as a in the drawing on p. 150) squared equals the height (noted as x) squared plus the base (noted as b) squared, or $a^2 = x^2 + b^2$. Now you just plug the numbers into your handy calculator and it will give you the length of one side of the triangle.

The above information is necessary to calculate the width of your first cutting guide, which is the altitude of the diamond shape. This involves more geometry,

Calculating the Cutting-Guide Width (L) for Diamonds

a = hypotenuse

b = width of base (½ width of diamond)

A = area of diamond

P = height of diamond

x = height of right triangle (½ height of diamond)

L = altitude of diamond

$$a^2 = x^2 + b^2$$
$$A = \arccos(1 - (P^2 / 2a^2))$$
$$L = a(\sin(A))$$

L = 1.50

a

x

30°

b

A

P = 3.00

1.73

and while I lay out the formulas in the drawing above, it might be easier to use an online rhombus calculator to figure out the exact dimensions of your diamond shapes (which are rhombuses). Just do a search for "rhombus calculator," and you'll be able to enter the numbers you have and it will calculate the rest. In these equations, L is the altitude of the diamond (which is the number we're after because it is the width of the first cutting guide). This set of formulas works for any diamond you can come up with, so keep them handy.

You do still need to figure out how many diamonds it takes to get the height and width you need for your panel, but that just involves dividing the width and height of the panel by the width and height of your diamonds. I tend to make quite a few extra diamonds

so I can scrap any that have tearout or flaws in the veneer and so there are extras for the perimeter pieces.

You'll also need the cutting board from the chess-board section and a 30-60-90 plastic drafting triangle. Because the diamond pattern can grow or shrink a bit during cutting and assembly due to accumulated small errors in cutting the many diamonds, it's a good idea to start a project by creating the diamond panels first, whether they are doors, side panels, tops, or other components. Then you can size the furniture to fit those panels. Otherwise, there may be some trial-and-error work in sizing the diamonds to get them to fit a premade panel size exactly.

Paul Schurch used several shapes of parquetry veneer pieces to decorate this small cabinet in satinwood and walnut that is used to store sacred scrolls.

Andrew Varah created innovative and interesting furniture for many years. This small side table features parquetry shapes cut in two colors of shagreen that gradually change in size to create a subtle chessboard effect.

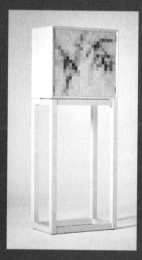

This side table by Brian Reid in bleached white oak and alder called "Cuboid Study" brings parquetry into the third dimension by taking a two-dimensional parquetry veneer pattern and extruding it into columns of varying heights. This was one of a series of tables by Reid exploring the dimensionality of his work.

A great example of using unexpected parquetry shapes to create an interesting design is this cabinet by Silas Kopf that incorporates the "cracked ice" design pattern as its primary form of decoration.

Kevin Stamper created a parquetry image of colored squares from a watercolor sketch of a plum tree he painted. The end result is a light and delicate image mated nicely to a tall cabinet.

Trimming the stacks

Select two colors of veneer with fairly straight grain to use for your initial diamond pattern. The pattern uses quite a bit of veneer, and the wider you make the initial pieces of veneer, the less cutting and taping you'll need to do later. Tape narrow pieces of the same veneer together lengthwise with gum tape to create pieces roughly 10 in. to 12 in. wide by 20 in. long, if you don't have anything wide enough.

Tape together stacks of each veneer color with three or four pieces to a stack, applying tape to all four edges of each stack. Now use your straightedge and a veneer saw to trim a clean, straight edge along one long side of each stack. To make the cut, start with a light pass and then gradually increase pressure on the saw in repeated passes until the cut is complete. Pay close attention to keeping the saw vertical. This edge will serve as a reference for marking the next cut.

Making the angled cuts

The next cut is the first angled one. A plastic 30-60-90 drafting triangle, the larger the better, is ideal for marking it out. Align the triangle along the stack's newly cut straight edge, and mark a 30° line across one end, which will give you diamonds with the grain running straight through the center of the diamond. Place your straightedge on the marked line, and hold it down firmly while slowly cutting through the veneer. Keep the straightedge on the good side of the edge so you are cutting off the waste.

Select two colors of veneer for your diamond parquetry panel (here, walnut and anigre). Each piece should be approximately 10 in. wide by 20 in. long, and you'll need several pieces of each color to make a pattern of any significant size.

Use a 30-60-90 plastic drafting triangle to mark a 30° line on one end of each stack of veneer. Cut the veneer on the marked line, which will be the new reference edge that butts against your cutting guide stop.

Square off one long edge on each stack of veneer with your veneer saw and a straightedge.

❖ **TIP** ❖ By changing the angle of the first angled cut, you can easily change the shape and size of your diamonds. A higher angle makes them shorter and blunter, while a lower angle makes them more pointy and slender.

Press the angled cut firmly against the stop on your cutting board and hold the veneer down and tight against the stop with your straightedge. Cut through the veneer to create the first angled strips. Repeat this process until all the veneer has been cut into strips.

Cutting the strips at this angle ensures that the grain in the final diamonds will run vertically in each diamond.

For the next step, move each stack to the cutting board. Press the stack's 30° edge tight against the stop on the board, with the correctly sized straight-edge firmly on top, and cut through the stack of veneer. Set this pile of strips aside and repeat the process of aligning and cutting until you have four to six stacks of veneer strips cut in each color. Be sure to keep the strips in the order they were cut and right side up.

Assembling the strips

Begin taping together alternating colored veneer strips to create sheets of six to eight strips, again

being careful to keep the strips aligned and oriented in the same direction. Pull the strips together (one by one) and tape across the joints with blue tape. Be sure to pull the tape tight and then run a single strip of blue tape down the length of each joint and burnish all the tape down with a brass brush. Continue taping sets of six to eight strips together until all the strips are used.

Begin taping the strips together, alternating the colors and pulling them tightly together with the tape across each joint. Follow that with a long piece of tape down the length of the joints, and burnish it all down with the brass brush.

Cutting the diamond strips

Now comes the precision part of the process. To make the next cut, we'll use the same 30-60-90 drafting triangle again and align it with one straight edge of the stacked sheets to create a 60° angle from the tip of the stack down across the alternating colored strips. Mark this line and cut through each sheet individually with the straightedge and a veneer saw.

Take the first sheet and press the freshly cut 60° edge tight against the face of the stop on the cutting board. Place your straightedge on top of the veneer, and draw it tight against the stop. Press down firmly on the guide, and cut through the sheet of veneer to create the first strip of complete diamonds. Repeat the process of aligning and cutting strips until all of

Mark a 60° angle on one end of each sheet of strips referenced off the long straight edge. Use the plastic drafting triangle and make sure the angle is correct—otherwise, the points of your diamonds might not line up. Cut this new reference edge on each sheet, keeping them in order as you cut them.

Press the just-cut 60° edge against the stop on the cutting board. Using your straightedge and veneer saw, slice off strips of diamonds, pressing the straightedge tight against the stop. Cut all the sheets until you have a pile of diamond strips ready for assembly.

Flip the strips of diamonds over and begin assembling them into a larger sheet by alternating the colors of the diamonds as you assemble them. Tape across the joints to hold the sheet together.

Once you're done adding diamonds, flip the sheet over and completely tape across all the joints with blue tape.

the sheets have been cut into strips. Be sure to keep them oriented properly throughout the process.

Assembling the pattern

To assemble the diamond strips into a sheet, flip the stack of strips over so the tape side, which is also the glue side, faces down. This allows you to see the points of the diamonds as you tape them together and ensure the alignment is correct. Start with two strips and stagger the diamonds so they alternate

color, making sure the points of the diamonds line up precisely. Tape across the joint of each set of diamonds but don't bother taping down the entire length of the strips at this time. Continue aligning and taping strips together to create sheets of diamonds in the size you need for your panel. As you progress, relocate the outer overhanging diamonds to places inside the sheet where diamonds may be missing.

Once the sheet is completely taped together, flip it over and fully tape all the joints as before both across and along the joints with blue tape. Now flip the

Flip the sheet show face up and remove all the bits of blue tape from the show surface.

Use your straightedge and veneer saw to trim off any overhanging diamond points, checking with an accurate square to make sure your veneer sheet stays square while you're trimming.

Cover the show face completely with 2-in. gum tape. Burnish the tape down with a paper towel and place the sheet under a piece of MDF until the gum tape is dry (in about an hour).

Once the gum tape is dry, remove all the blue tape from the glue face and you are ready to glue up the diamond parquetry sheet.

sheet over once more and remove all the bits of blue tape from the show face. Check the alignment of the diamonds and correct any that need adjusting. To fit your diamond veneer to a panel, you'll need to trim off the excess around the perimeter and make sure the sheet is square. Line up your straightedge with each edge and trim the overhanging diamond pieces so the pattern is complete. Use a square against the first edge you trim to ensure the sheet stays square as you trim the other edges.

Cover the show face of the veneer with gum tape, using 2-in.-wide tape if you have it to save time. Wet the tape with a sponge and lay it on in slightly overlapping strips until the surface is covered. Press the gum tape down with a paper towel and then slide the assembly under a piece of MDF to keep it flat until the tape is dry, usually an hour or so. After the tape is dry, trim any excess flush with the edge of the veneer, then remove the blue tape from the glue face and your diamond panel is ready to glue down.

Parquetry Louis Cubes decorate the top of this circular spinning puzzle mechanism. The geometric diamond shapes make for a mildly challenging puzzle to solve when the pattern is jumbled. The five rings all rotate independently.

Louis Cubes

Louis Cubes are a parquetry pattern made up of diamonds rotated and assembled into a specific pattern that creates the illusion of three-dimensional cubes. This illusion can be enhanced with proper veneer selection; ideally, three different colors of veneer are used. It takes a specific size of diamond to create Louis Cubes. Fortunately, we just cut a bunch of them in the diamond-cutting section of this chapter. You need diamonds with 60° points for Louis Cubes. It doesn't matter what size the diamonds are, as long as they are all the same size. They just need to be

Cut diamonds from three different colors of veneer so you can start assembling the Louis Cube parquetry pattern.

this specific shape to make the pattern work out properly.

To create the Louis Cube pattern, cut diamonds from three different-colored veneers: one light, one medium, and one dark. Follow the instructions for cutting diamonds detailed previously. Once you have a number of each color cut, begin assembling them by taping one light diamond to one medium and one dark diamond. Tape them together so they form a hexagon; this is the first Louis Cube. Continue adding more 3-D cubes to this one until you have a repeating pattern of 3-D cubes across the veneer sheet. You'll need to trim the edges of the sheet square just as we did on the diamond sheet.

Begin assembling the three colors of parquetry diamonds into the final pattern by taping one of each color together to form a hexagon.

Continue making additional matching hexagon shapes and then tape them together to form a larger Louis Cube pattern. The pattern can grow as large as you'd like—or at least until you run out of diamonds.

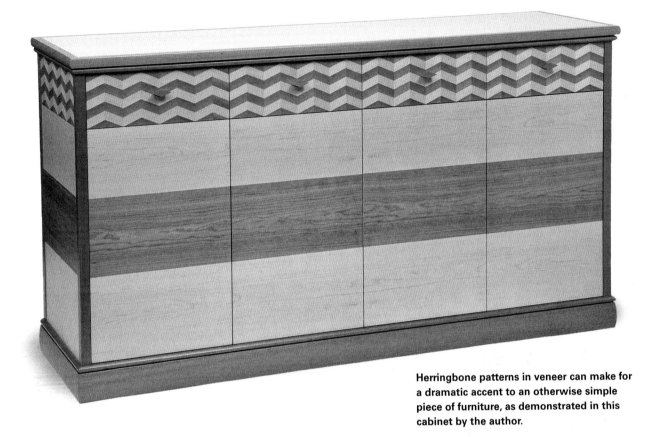

Herringbone patterns in veneer can make for a dramatic accent to an otherwise simple piece of furniture, as demonstrated in this cabinet by the author.

Herringbone Pattern

Another parquetry pattern that can be created with the same tools and methods is the herringbone or zigzag pattern. Herringbones are made in essentially the same manner as diamonds, the primary difference being the need for two different cutting guides because the shape is a parallelogram with one long and one short set of legs. A narrow guide makes the first cuts along the grain of the veneer to create the initial thin strips; a wider guide is used for the angled cuts that create the final pieces.

Start with two stacks of veneer of two different colors. A bit of contrast helps to accent the folding effect, and straight-grained woods work quite well for this pattern. You'll need four to six pieces roughly 4 in. to 6 in. wide and about 20 in. long for each color. Tape them together in two separate stacks with the veneer sheets in sequential order and with one long edge aligned. For the sample sheet shown in this section, we're making herringbone pieces using a 1-in.-wide guide to create the initial strips and a 2-in.-wide guide to cut the 67.5° angled pieces. Make up a set of straightedges with these two widths about 24 in. long and glue sandpaper to the bottom of both straightedges to help them hold the veneer. You'll also need the cutting board we made earlier to help secure the veneer pieces as you cut them.

Cutting the veneer strips

Once again, begin by cutting one straight reference edge on each stack of veneer along the grain of the veneer pieces. Next, press the cut edge of the first

Start with two stacks of taped-together contrasting colors of veneer roughly 6 in. wide by 20 in. long with one edge of each stack cut straight. You'll also need two straightedges, a 1-in.-wide one and a 2-in.-wide one, and the cutting guide we made earlier.

Press the straight reference edge of each stack against the stop on the cutting guide and use the narrow 1-in.-wide straightedge to rip the veneer into even strips.

stack of veneer tight against the stop on the cutting board. Place the 1-in. narrow guide on top of the veneer, and draw it tight against the stop. Cut through the stack of veneer to create the first narrow strips. Repeat the process of aligning and cutting strips until both stacks of veneer have been cut into strips. Be sure to keep them oriented properly because flipping a piece over may ruin the effect when finish is applied. If you have difficulty cutting

through the stack with the guide, you can cut each sheet of veneer individually as long as you make sure to keep them oriented properly the whole time.

Taping the strips

Start assembly by taping alternating colored veneer strips together to create sheets of six strips, again being careful to keep the strips aligned and oriented in the same direction. Pull the strips together (one by one) and tape across the joints with regular blue tape. Be sure to pull the tape tight, and then run a single strip of blue tape down the length of each joint and burnish all the tape down with a brass brush. Continue taping sets of six strips together until all the strips are used. Divide the sheets into two even

Tape together alternating colored strips to create a set of six strips. Tape together as many sheets of six strips as you can with the strips you cut. Then make two equal stacks of these sheets of strips with one reference edge the same on all the sheets.

stacks and keep them separated from here on. Creating taller herringbone panels with more than six lines simply requires increasing the number of taped-together strips.

Cutting the herringbone pieces

Once again, we've arrived at the precision part of the process. The next cuts produce all of the final herringbone pieces, and they need to be precisely marked on all the sheets of strips. The easiest way to mark for these cuts is to use a digital angle gauge. Line up one leg of the angle gauge against the reference edge of the first stack of sheets and mark a

4

Use a digital angle gauge to mark a 67.5° angle across the end of each sheet of one stack of veneer. Cut this line with your veneer saw and straightedge one sheet at a time. Repeat this procedure for the other stack, but flip the angle gauge over and mark the opposite end of the second stack; this gives you the opposite angle on the second stack of veneer.

5

Separate the strips of each stack and keep them separate from here on. Take one sheet and press the 67.5° cut edge against the stop on the cutting guide. Next, use your second straightedge to cut 2-in.-wide strips from the sheet of veneer. Repeat this process until all of the sheets are cut into strips, making sure to keep the two stacks separate.

67.5° angle near the end of each sheet. Place your straightedge on this line and cut through the veneer one sheet at a time. Flip the angle gauge over and mark the same angle on the opposite end of the second stack of sheets. This gives us the opposing herringbone pieces. Cut along the marked line as on the first stack. You now have the two angled pieces needed to create all the final herringbone pieces.

To make the final pieces, cut individual strips of herringbone pieces from each sheet, using the cutting board and your wide straightedge to make all the following cuts. Starting with one sheet, press the 67.5° edge tight against the stop. Place the straightedge on top of the veneer and draw it tight against the stop. Gradually cut through the veneer to create the first strip of herringbone pieces. Repeat the process until all of the sheets from the first stack have been cut into strips; be sure to keep them in order and oriented properly. Set the first stack of strips aside and begin cutting the second stack; note that you are now cutting the opposite angle on the strips. Once cutting is complete, set this stack of strips aside like the first.

Assembling the pattern

Flip the two stacks of strips over so the tape side (also known as the glue side) faces down. This allows us to see the two different pieces that will be used to build the complete herringbone pattern. Take one strip from each stack and line up the pattern so the color flows from one piece to the next; tape across the joints. Continue aligning and taping alternating strips together until you have a full panel of herringbone pieces.

With the first sheet completely taped, flip it over and fully blue-tape all the joints on the glue face, then flip the sheet over once more and remove all the bits of blue tape from the show face. Align a straightedge with the two long edges and trim off the overhanging herringbone pieces so the pattern is complete. Gum-tape the entire show face with 2-in. gum tape as we've done with the other parquetry patterns

Take one strip from each stack and line up the points of the herringbone pieces. Tape the strips together, making sure the alignment of the points is precise. Repeat this process until you have a sheet composed of eight strips.

and set it under a sheet of MDF to dry before removing the blue tape from the glue face. Repeat the process for as many herringbone panels as you need to create for your project.

Gluing Up Parquetry Panels

We've already covered veneer glue-ups in earlier chapters, so this will just be a quick refresher. Prepare your substrate for veneering by cutting it to size, ideally slightly larger than your parquetry veneer. Also cut two cauls from $\frac{1}{4}$-in. MDF about $\frac{1}{8}$ in. larger than the substrate. Prepare a backer veneer for the bottom of the panel the same size as the substrate. It can be decorative or not depending upon whether it will be seen. Make sure you have some

Carefully trim off any overhanging pieces on each of the sheets, then gum-tape the entire show face. Once the gum tape is dry, remove all the blue tape from the glue face and you're ready for glue-up.

> ❖ **TIP** ❖ MDF works well as a substrate for veneering with parquetry because it is smooth, flat, and has no wood movement issues.

plastic sheet cut to size to place between the cauls and the veneer and your glue and roller ready. For veneering jobs like this, I prefer to use a urea formaldehyde glue because of the rigid glueline, but you could also use a good PVA glue like Titebond 1 if you don't have a UF glue handy.

Spread an even layer of glue on the back side of the substrate and put the backer veneer in place. Press all over the veneer to help flatten it, then flip the substrate over and spread glue on the top of the substrate. Carefully place your parquetry veneer (gum tape side up) on the substrate and press it all over to help secure it. Quickly tape it in place with several pieces of blue tape wrapped from the backer veneer over the top of the parquetry veneer. One or two pieces along each edge will be sufficient to hold the veneer in place while pressing. Cover both sides of the assembly with the plastic sheet and then the MDF cauls, making sure the cauls are evenly spaced around the panel edges. Add a sheet of breather mesh over the top caul and slide it into the vacuum bag. Titebond I only needs about one to two hours in the vacuum bag at 70°F to ade-

quately hold the veneer; UF glues will need six to eight hours in the vacuum bag. Either way, when you take the panel out of the press, leave it leaning against a bench overnight so it can dry fully on both sides.

To glue the veneer using clamps, increase the thickness of the cauls to ¾-in. MDF and proceed as we have done in the other sample glue-ups. After the panel has dried fully, remove the gum tape by wetting the tape with a damp sponge; wait a few minutes and then peel the moist tape away. Anything that doesn't peel away can be scraped off with a sharp cabinet scraper.

SANDING PARQUETRY PANELS

Sanding parquetry veneer work is similar to sanding marquetry (see p. 130), though it's a little easier because the veneer is typically going in roughly one direction across the entire panel. I still tend to do the initial cleanup with my random-orbit sander and some 150-grit paper, followed by hand sanding with a cork-covered block and some 180-grit paper to do the flattening of the panel. Finish up with 180- and 220-grit paper on the random-orbit sander and you're done sanding and ready for finish.

CHAPTER 9

Curves and Bent Laminations

When I started out building furniture,

I found any number of articles on how to veneer flat or gently curved panels for doors and tabletops but not much on the tighter curves I saw in my mind's eye. So, I just forged ahead, mixing and matching techniques that I found in various places and making up a variety of my own. In this chapter, I'll show you how I veneer coves and quarter-rounds so you'll be able to skip the trial and error I went through initially. After mastering these shapes, we'll move on to making bent laminations and learn a variety of techniques for creating curved panels.

Veneering Coves and Radii

My system for veneering outside curves or radii works well all the way down to about a $\frac{3}{8}$-in. radius. Because the vacuum bag does most of the work, the clamping sandwich is simpler than the one we'll use for veneering coves. All you need is plastic sheeting, $\frac{1}{8}$-in. gum foam sheet (available from www.mcmaster.com; part No. 9455K92), and breather cloth (which is different from breather mesh but could be substituted with probably the same effect).

This Art Deco chess table by the author incorporates veneered cross-grain coves as part of the overall design. The waterfall Macassar ebony veneer appears to flow off the top of the table and down the sides to the floor; this kind of grain pattern requires extra effort in planning and layout of the veneer.

Layers of veneered quarter-rounds decorate this Italian Art Deco desk. The veneer was softened with an application of gum tape and bent to shape while the gum tape was still slightly moist. The end result: curved veneered surfaces with zero cracks or splits.

David Roentgen's workshops used curved veneering techniques to create a variety of complex pieces of woodwork, including this tea chest from around 1750.

The tools and techniques used to veneer coves and radii are also well within the reach of an ambitious amateur and useful for the professional maker as well. You'll need a vacuum bag, veneer (the thin, commercial kind, not resawn veneer), white Styrofoam® insulation in 1½-in. thickness, plastic sheeting, and ⅛-in. gum foam sheet. I use the white foam as a clamping caul and also to make flexible sanding blocks for smoothing substrates and to sand the final veneered surface. It is surprising how handy it is to have a few sheets in the shop.

Quite frequently, these curved parts become border or trim pieces on larger assemblies. With that in mind, I like to veneer them in long pieces that then get cut into the smaller parts I need for assemblies that will have matched grain and identical shapes. If you're using a chopsaw to cut these parts down to size, I'd recommend making a rough cut first and then taking off just a sliver to leave a truer cut. I sometimes use blue tape on the underside of the cut to prevent blowout. Then I'll hot-glue small blocks to the pieces to create parallel clamping surfaces.

Veneered half-rounds in myrtle burl support the seat on this Art Deco bench, while veneered quarter-round feet and bent-laminated uprights carry the load to the floor. These parts were all made longer than necessary and cut down to size after veneering.

create thicker parts. The layers are glued together using Titebond 1 and clamped overnight to ensure that the glueline is fully dry before shaping the curves. There are many methods to create the curved shapes used for veneering, but I've found that a combination of tablesaw and router table work is ideal.

I use the method described in *Fine Woodworking* issue 168 ("Cutting Coves on the Tablesaw") to lay out and cut all my coves. They usually require some sanding afterward to smooth the tablesaw cut, but if you cut slowly and increase the depth of cut only slightly with each pass, the parts come out very uniform and smooth (see the photo on p. 166).

To create radiused edges, just use the appropriately sized roundover bit on the router table. If your radius is larger than what can be cut with a router bit, start by trimming off the majority of the waste material with angled cuts on the tablesaw. Then use a combination of handplanes and sanding blocks to refine the radii until they are smooth and uniform in size.

Substrates and shaping curves

I like to use MDF as the substrate for veneering curved parts because it's easy to form and presents a uniform smooth surface for gluing veneer. You could also use a variety of solid woods, like soft maple, mahogany, alder, or walnut, as a substrate depending upon your veneer of choice. If I were to use solid wood as my substrate, I would select a wood color that was a close match to my veneer color so potential sand-throughs would be less noticeable. Either way, you'll want your substrate to have some tooth to it, so don't sand it any smoother than about 100-grit sandpaper when you're shaping it. That will make it easier for the glue to grab the substrate.

When using MDF as the substrate, I laminate multiple pieces to

Veneer for curves

The veneer that will be bent over the curved section needs to be gum-taped first to prevent cracking. I like to use 2-in. gum tape on these areas because it covers

---

GLUES FOR CURVED VENEERS

There was a time when I would use Titebond 1 for veneering tight curves, but in the past few years, I've come to appreciate the strength of polyurethane and urea formaldehyde glues on coved veneer work in particular. They both have a rigid glueline when used with accurately mated parts, are highly heat and moisture resistant, and any squeeze-out sands off easily. For these reasons, my go-to glue for veneering these curved parts is now either polyurethane glue or UF glue. For the convex parts like quarter- and half-rounds, I still use Titebond 1 because it is more than strong enough for this type of veneering.

Alternatively, you could use two-part epoxy and get similar results. Epoxy allows quite a bit of open time and creates very rigid gluelines after curing, usually within 24 hours. You'll need to wear a proper respirator, not a dust mask, to protect yourself from the fumes while mixing and sanding epoxy.

Cutting coves on the tablesaw requires two boards clamped to the tablesaw table at the correct angle for the cove to be cut. You usually need to sand the cove afterward to smooth the cut, but if you cut slowly and increase the depth of cut only slightly (¹⁄₁₆ in.) with each pass, the parts come out uniform and smooth.

the area quickly. I use it to assemble joints and to reinforce the veneer on outside curves; it helps keep the veneer flexible and prevents it from cracking while being bent over the substrate. As with any application of veneer gum tape, burnish it down onto the veneer with a paper towel to help seat the tape adhesive.

When it comes to selecting veneer for curved work, there are a few things to keep in mind to make your life easier. First, burl veneer bends easily because of its random grain orientation (if it's been softened first, of course), and it can be used for coves and radii without cracking readily once it's been gum taped. Straight-grained veneer has a tendency to split along the grain when used lengthwise on curved surfaces. Gum tap-ing the veneer can help limit the number of cracks, but if you've selected a brittle veneer like ebony or

rosewood, you should expect some small cracks to appear in your final glue-up. The same applies to straight-grained veneer run across curves, whether coves or radii. If the curve is too sharp, the veneer will crack across its width when you press it into the curved form. This can be alleviated somewhat by gum-taping the veneer first, but brittle veneer will still crack if bent into too tight a radius. I like to make some extra parts that have the same curve as my planned design to use as test pieces.

Veneering a Cove

Veneered coves can be used facing upward, as on my Art Deco chess table, or downward as crown molding. As I mentioned previously, we'll be using clamps and foam cauls to press our veneer onto the coved parts. Once I've cut my cove pieces on the tablesaw, I sand them with 100-grit paper to remove the blade marks.

Once the cove is fully prepared for veneer, I sometimes take the extra step of veneering the flat edges adjoining the cove before veneering the cove itself (which is what I did for the cove piece shown here). This step isn't absolutely necessary, and if you happen to be making coves with waterfall veneer that will wrap over the flat edges, I'd wait to veneer the

> ❖ **TIP** ❖ I've found that a piece of ¾-in. white foam bent by hand into a curved shape makes a great sanding pad that conforms to the curve of the cove with minimal effort. To make it work even better, spray-glue the sandpaper onto the outside surface of the foam before bending it into the cove shape. That will help keep the foam together as you sand, and you won't need to hold the sandpaper in place while you sand.

flats until after the cove is veneered. That way, the grain alignment between them can be fine-tuned on the flats instead of the more complex cove glue-up. Either way works equally well, so it depends on your design and how the cove part will be incorporated into the furniture piece.

Always cut the veneer for the cove parts oversize by ½ in. in each direction, which makes clamping a bit less stressful as the veneer does tend to move when the clamps get tightened. On the piece shown in this section, I'm using straight-grained etimoe veneer running across the width of the cove to create a vertical-grain look in my final part. Because this is composed of a number of short cross-grain pieces, the pieces need to be gum-taped together first, and then the entire face can be gum-taped along its length. We've covered how to cut and tape strips of veneer together already, so there's no need to repeat that information here. Just follow the instructions previously provided and all should go well.

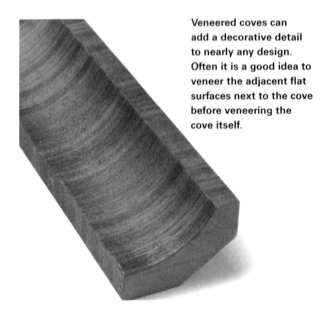

Veneered coves can add a decorative detail to nearly any design. Often it is a good idea to veneer the adjacent flat surfaces next to the cove before veneering the cove itself.

CLAMPING CURVES

There are two ways to clamp curved veneer that I've found work well: in the vacuum bag, or with clamps and foam cauls. I find that the vacuum bag is great for pressing outside curves like half and quarter radii, while clamps with thick foam cauls work well at pressing inside curves like coves. This is partly because of how the vacuum bag works: It is excellent at applying pressure to the outside of an object but has difficulty conforming to shallow areas like cove shapes. The bag simply can't easily stretch enough to fully press an inside curve without a lot of effort from the operator. For this reason, I just use clamps for coves instead, and I've developed a pretty user-friendly way to do this with minimal effort and materials.

Gluing the cove

Start with a dry run by rehearsing the clamping process without glue to make sure the veneer and all the parts of the sandwich are sized right and working correctly. Get all your supplies ready and mix up a small batch of Pro-Glue UF glue to roll onto the cove. Spread it evenly on the substrate using a roller designed for adhesives. Wait a few minutes for some glue to be absorbed and then apply a thin second coat.

MATERIALS FOR CLAMPING COVES

The materials necessary for clamping a cove should be cut and prepped before any glue gets spread. First, you'll need a piece of 1½-in.-thick white foam board cut just a bit longer than your cove part and wide enough that when it's bent into the cove it sticks over the edges ½ in. or so. You'll also need a sheet of ⅛-in.-thick gum foam sheet to even out the pressure between the white foam and the veneer; a piece of plastic sheet to go between the gum foam and the veneer; and a ¾-in.-thick hardwood board sized the full length of your cove and about one-third the width of the cove. The board is used as a clamping pressure spreading device added on top of the white foam. It helps when doing these glue-ups to have the cove part spaced off your bench a couple inches with some spacers, which makes it easier to get the clamps in place.

The basic materials needed to clamp up a cove veneer job are an appropriately sized wood board, insulation foam, thin gum foam sheet, plastic sheet, and clamps. It helps to use a couple of spacers to get the workpiece off the bench, too.

Urea formaldehyde glues have the rigid glueline necessary for holding concave veneer work in place long term. Mix and spread your glue as per the instructions provided with the glue.

Center the veneer over the cove shape and cover it with the plastic sheet, the gum foam sheet, the white foam spacer, and finally the hardwood clamping block. Make sure everything stays centered as you begin applying clamps. Start with a clamp in the center and work out toward the ends. Slowly apply pressure to the hardwood block, clamping it firmly and uniformly along its length a bit at a time until the veneer is pressed fully into the cove. Turn over the glue-up and check the squeeze-out to be sure the veneer is in good contact with the substrate at every point around the perimeter. The white foam will continue to compress, so come back in 10 minutes to retighten the clamps.

Trimming the veneer

Once the glue is dry, remove the gum tape by moistening it with a damp paper towel; the tape will turn translucent and can be peeled or scraped off the veneer. If too much glue has soaked through the veneer, it will soak into the gum tape, and scraping or sanding will be your only option for removing it.

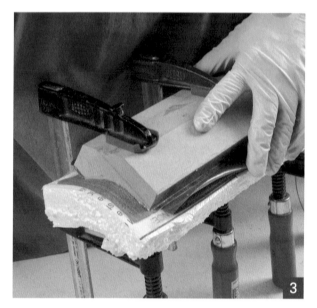

Once the clamps are tight, flip the assembly over and check to see that you've got a little glue squeeze-out all around the perimeter.

Center the veneer over the cove and press it in place with the next layers: plastic sheet, gum foam sheet, white foam, and clamping block. If you can get the foam pressed partway down into the cove by hand, you'll save some time with the clamps.

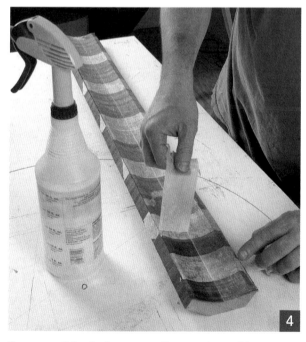

Once everything is dry, remove the gum tape with some water and a putty knife. If the tape has become soaked with glue squeeze-out, you'll need to scrape or sand it off.

You can use a Surform file to break off overhanging veneer and then sand it flush. This is the easiest method if the veneer has become glued to the edges of the part. Or trim it flush with a router table and flush-trimming bit.

There are a few ways to trim the overhanging veneer flush with the edges of the cove (see the bottom right photos on p. 169). If the veneer is sticking straight out and hasn't been broken and glued down by pressure from the foam, a flush-trimming bit works great at trimming it down to the adjoining face. But if the veneer has been flattened down to the edge, use a Surform® or machinist float to file the overhanging veneer down until the excess drops away, and then sand it flush with a hard block and 120-grit paper, going with the grain of the veneer.

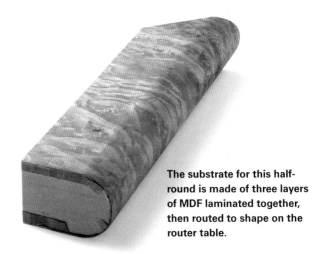

The substrate for this half-round is made of three layers of MDF laminated together, then routed to shape on the router table.

Veneering Outside Radii

All other things being equal, the main difference between veneering coves and veneering outside curves is the method used to clamp the veneer in place. For outside radii, we'll be using the vacuum bag instead of hand clamps; the vacuum system makes it much easier to evenly distribute pressure over the entire veneer surface. Since the bag does most of the work, the sandwich that goes into the bag is simpler. I use breather cloth, available from most composite suppliers, to carry the air from around the workpiece to the hose. There's also a layer of gum foam sheet and a layer of plastic sheet as before. The plastic sheet and gum foam sheet need to be cut to the size of your substrate fairly precisely so you can tape them in place later.

Veneering half-rounds

Prepare your veneer by first measuring the width you'll need with a flexible ruler or a strip of paper. Wrap it over the curve and mark the width directly from your part, and then measure the length of your half-round as well. Take these two measurements to your veneer piece and subtract ½ in. from both when you cut your veneer to size. This will allow the veneer to expand when it hits the glue without

bunching up at the bottom or ends of the substrate. When veneering any of these curved shapes, it's always a good idea to make your substrate several inches longer than necessary so you can trim off the ends later. Any veneer that overhangs tends to get broken up in the vacuum bag, and those breaks can continue farther into the veneer and appear later as cracks in your nice curved veneer work.

Once you've got the veneer sized correctly, begin applying gum tape to the show face of the veneer. Work from the center out and cover all the veneer that will wrap over the curve plus another inch or so in both directions. This will keep the veneer from cracking when you bend it into shape. You can cover the entire face of the veneer with gum tape, but I find it's not necessary to add it on the straight sections (and it just adds more work removing it later). Make sure to burnish the tape down with a brass brush to

> ❖ TIP ❖ When I veneer half-rounds, I'll make my substrate wider than necessary for two reasons: It gives me extra support on the router table when forming the rounded edges, and it leaves room for the vacuum bag to pull the veneer flat past the curved section of the part. After the veneer is applied, you can just trim away the excess substrate on the tablesaw.

I use a strip of paper or a flexible ruler to measure how wide the veneer needs to be to wrap over my part. I leave it a bit short at the bottom to account for the veneer expanding once it gets wet from the glue.

Apply gum tape to the veneer face over the area that will wrap the curve and carry it past the curve an inch or so.

VENEERING WITH WET GUM TAPE

One thing is different about gum taping for curved veneering when compared with all the other gum taping we've done: We don't let the gum tape dry fully before gluing the veneer to the substrate; instead, place the gum-taped veneer under a sheet of MDF to keep it flat, but be ready to pull it out before it's dry. After about 10 minutes, I'll take the veneer out and start gluing it to the substrate. The extra moisture in the veneer from the gum tape adds flexibility and keeps the veneer from cracking while being bent. The timing on this may take some practice because if the tape is too wet, it will come off during handling; too dry, and the veneer may crack. This is also why I veneer only one of these parts at a time.

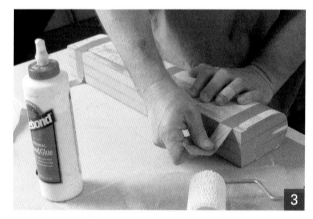

Roll Titebond 1 evenly over the substrate surface, then center your veneer on the substrate and tape it in place with long strips of blue tape.

really seat it on the veneer. Then mark the center of the curve on both ends of the veneer to help center the part on the substrate.

We'll be using Titebond 1 to glue up this veneer; the extra moisture in the glue helps keep the veneer flexible while you work with it. Get all your supplies ready and start rolling a good layer of glue onto your substrate, making sure to get glue on the entire sur-

face. Center the veneer on the apex of the curve, then gradually bend the veneer over the curve on both sides. Tape it in place with a couple of pieces of blue tape to hold it, check that everything is centered, and then add a few more pieces of blue tape wrapped completely over the curve. Pull them tight as you reach the bottom of your part to help pull the veneer over the curve.

Next, completely cover the veneer with the plastic sheet and the gum foam sheet. Tape both in place. Add a layer of breather cloth over the entire surface and slide the assembly into the vacuum bag; continue the breather cloth all the way to the bag inlet. As the air gets evacuated from the bag, pull the bag tight over the curved surface of your part. Try to get the bag to wrap tightly over the bottom corners of the part so it is smooth over the veneered areas. Continue this process until the bag is fully under vacuum. Leave the part in the vacuum bag for three to four hours minimum.

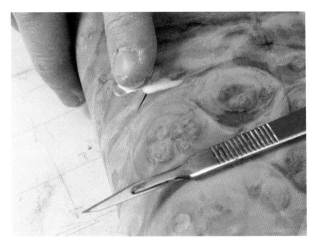

Sometimes, despite your best efforts, you'll find that a small bubble appears in the veneer. Don't despair—bubbles are easy to fix by slicing them open with a scalpel, then smearing glue into the cut. Put the part back in the vacuum bag with the gum foam and plastic to press it flat.

Cover the veneer first with plastic sheet, then a layer of the gum foam sheet, and tape them both in place. Try to pull the sheets tight when you tape them to help hold the veneer down.

Cover the assembly with breather cloth and slide it into the vacuum bag. Make sure to pull the bag tight around the curve while the pressure increases so there aren't any wrinkles in the finished veneer surface.

When you remove your piece from the vacuum bag, take off the breather cloth, gum foam, and plastic sheet, and set the part aside to finish drying at least overnight. Once dry, lightly moisten the gum tape and remove it all, and then check your part for bubbles or cracks. If you find bubbles or small wrinkles, slice them open with a scalpel, work glue into the recess, and reclamp the assembly in the vacuum bag for another few hours.

Veneering quarter-rounds

Veneering quarter-rounds is similar to veneering half-rounds—you'll need all the same materials in the vacuum bag sandwich, and all the same procedures apply. One addition is to add some extra substrate material for the veneer to flatten against past the end of your desired curve. I just screw a scrap board wrapped in packing tape flush to the end of the curve so the veneer flows over the end of my part and doesn't get glued down to the scrap. This piece then gets removed after glue-up and the veneer is trimmed flush. Because I'm putting screw holes into the bottom of the substrate, I make sure to veneer that surface last, after the holes have been filled.

Veneered quarter-rounds are relatively easy to make and can add an interesting design detail to your furniture.

Quarter-rounds need a piece of packing tape–covered scrap added to them to allow space for the veneer to run off the edge of the part. I like to bring the scrap piece flush with the edge of my substrate so the veneer runs straight down both pieces.

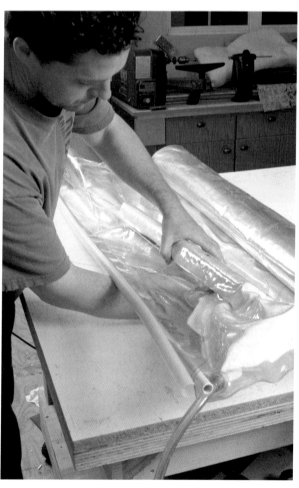

Once again, you'll want to pull the vacuum bag tight around your curved part to prevent any bubbles or wrinkles from appearing in the veneer work.

The process is basically the same as veneering half-rounds. First, apply glue, then tape your veneer in place and cover it with plastic sheet and gum foam, taping those in place as well.

You'll be using the plastic sheet and gum foam sheet in the same way they were used on the half-round. The gum tape also gets applied the same way and is left partly wet during application to allow the veneer to bend instead of break over the curve.

As with half-rounds, use Titebond 1 for quarter-rounds. Tape down the edges of the veneer and then the layers of plastic, gum foam, and breather cloth above it. When you put them in the vacuum bag, you'll want to pull the bag tight over the curved edge and down the face of the scrap board to make sure your veneer presses flat just as before.

Once the glue is dry, unscrew the scrap board and trim the overhanging veneer flush to the bottom of

There are a few ways to trim the overhanging veneer flush; sometimes a sharp veneer saw works best.

your substrate with a veneer saw. The substrate makes a great fence.

Bent Laminations

If you plan on making curved parts for your furniture or boxes, you'll eventually want to learn how to make bent laminations. They help create strong, stable parts that can be used decoratively or structurally, depending on your needs. The core of a bent lamination is multiple thin layers of material glued to each other over their entire face. To the outside of these parts can be added decorative veneer work, marquetry, parquetry, or plain straight-grained veneer.

To create bent-laminated parts, you'll first need to make a form, and you'll find that forms can be used in a variety of ways. Most of my larger forms are used in conjunction with a vacuum bag to bend parts down onto the form shape. You can also make forms that can be clamped together with hand clamps. They just need some additional notches and thickness in certain areas to allow adequate clamping pressure. Other forms that we won't cover here because they aren't regularly used in small shops are larger two-part forms used in hydraulic presses to create larger laminated shapes, like an Eames lounge chair, which has a bent-laminated back created on large forms.

Form design and construction

Designing the form for your bent-laminated part starts with the design of the part itself. If you are planning to make a curved component for a piece of furniture (a curved door, for instance), you'll need a full-size drawing of the curve shown from the top view of the cabinet. This gives you the exact shape and dimensions you'll need in your form. You can create this drawing either by hand with a compass (see the top photo on p. 176) or on the computer if you do your design work in computer-aided design (CAD) software, as I do. Either way, you need to start with a full-size printout of that curved shape. Once you have that, continue the lines of the curve beyond the ends of your drawn lines so your final form will have a curve several inches longer than the final part. This is necessary because the ends of bent-laminated parts need to be trimmed off and aren't usable in the final part.

You'll need a master curve template to make your form pieces. Take your final curve drawing and spray-glue it to a piece of MDF that is several inches taller than your curve (this will give your form some height in the vacuum bag). Make the form part as

Sometimes you get lucky on your furniture design and can use the same form for multiple parts as on this five-legged table made up of five bent-laminated partial curves all made on the same form.

Jefferson Shallenberger used a combination of laminating techniques for his curved desk. The base has resawn solid-wood laminations, whereas the desktop is composed of veneered plywood laminations. Using multiple techniques on the same piece allows the maker to fine-tune the design to suit their vision without technical limitations.

Sometimes you'll need a variety of forms to create a piece of furniture, as on this set of end tables by the author that have a different curve on each side. Four different forms were made up from computer numerical control (CNC)–cut MDF layers to get uniformly smooth curves on each piece.

The author made a matched set of bent laminations for the base of this elliptical dining table. The parts were glued over a large MDF form in the vacuum bag.

This large demilune sideboard required two different forms and three bent laminations to create the two mirror-curved doors on the end and the central curved section. The central section was laminated as a single piece and then cut into individual pieces and fitted to the cabinet. The final parts were then edged and veneered with the gardenia flower marquetry.

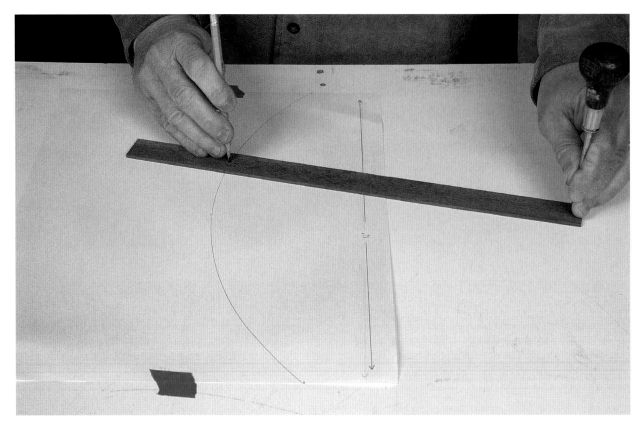

Whether you opt to use CAD or a simple wooden trammel and a pencil, you'll need an accurate full-size drawing of your proposed curve to use as a template for making the bending form.

long as the drawn curve. Cut the template on the bandsaw and smooth the cut surface down to the line with either sanders or compass planes, making sure the curve is square to the face of the MDF template. This is your master curve template used to shape all the form pieces.

You'll also need to know how tall your curved component will be. For the example shown in this section, I'm making a curved door that is 15 in. tall that will be the far-right-hand curved door on the serpentine cabinet in the top photo on the facing page. I want my form to be at least 1 in. taller than my final part to allow for trimming later. Because of this requirement, my form will be roughly 16 in. wide, and, using ¾-in. MDF as the material for my form parts, I'll need 22 pieces of MDF cut to the curved shape, and then glued together to create a single curved surface for laminating that is 16 in. wide.

Creating a highly complex cabinet like this one by Brian Newell requires accurate drawings and precise forms, especially since all of the bent-laminated parts are compound curves.

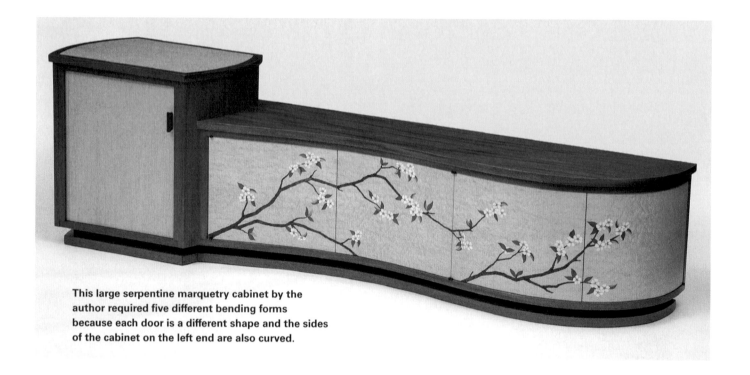

This large serpentine marquetry cabinet by the author required five different bending forms because each door is a different shape and the sides of the cabinet on the left end are also curved.

Use your bandsaw (or a jigsaw) and router table to cut and shape 22 identical curved form parts, and rout them to shape using your master form template as the routing template. This isn't overly complex work because it's just repetitive cutting and routing. Keep the form parts in the same orientation after you cut them so none get flipped around. Begin assembling your form by taking two of the parts and carefully lining up their curved edges. Spread some glue on one face and press the parts together. I'll often shoot a few finish nails through the pieces to hold them together. Repeat this process for all 22 pieces of your form. Make it a point to keep the form flat on the worktable and the ends lined up accurately.

No matter how accurate your routing and assembly process is, there always seems to be a bit of sanding required to smooth the curved face of the form. I do this with a long sanding block and some 120-grit paper. Move the block back and forth across the width of the form and back and forth over the length to create a smooth surface for laminating. It takes a fair

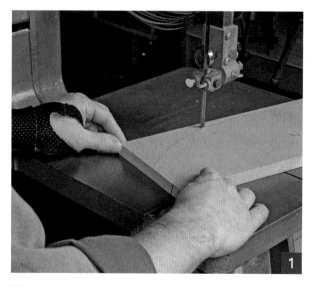

The master template you'll use to make all the form parts is made by spray-gluing a copy of your drawing to a piece of ¾-in. MDF and shaping it to the drawn line. After that, you can trace that curved line on all your form pieces and bandsaw them roughly to shape.

Screw the master template to each form piece and, with a bearing-guided router bit, rout them so they are all identical. To make the curved door we're planning, you'll need a set of 22 matching form pieces.

Glue the form layers together one at a time, making sure to keep them square and straight.

As you press each glued layer into place, shoot a couple of brad nails into each piece to hold it in alignment while you add the next layer.

Even CNC-cut form parts will need some sanding to bring all the MDF layers level and smooth. A long sanding block and some 120-grit paper will make quick work of smoothing the form.

bit of hard labor to do this sanding, and the first time you do it, you'll realize how important accurate form layout and building really are.

Forms for clamping

To build a laminating form to use with clamps limits the size of your form to the size of your clamps. The largest form you can realistically clamp is about twice as wide as your deepest-reaching clamp, because you need to reach the center of the form to clamp it adequately. Given this constraint, I make clamping forms only for parts like stretchers or curved legs that are just a couple of inches wide.

The process is still similar to the one used for vacuum laminating, but for clamping forms I'll make a top form that has a curve closely following the bottom curve minus the thickness of my final part. If you plan your form to have parallel top and bottom faces for clamping, applying the clamps is quite easy. If you make parts that curve too far for flat top and bottom faces, you'll need to plan for some clamping cutouts in both form halves that allow you to clamp across the forms accurately. Without those notches, the clamps would simply slip out of place when you tried to tighten them.

MATERIALS FOR FORMS

MDF and particleboard are the two most common form-building materials. I tend to favor MDF because its smooth surface works well as a base to veneer against, whereas particleboard tends to have numerous holes that need to be filled or covered before veneer can be pressed against it. If you're planning on making bent laminations with thicker resawn veneer, a particleboard form will work fine and be less costly and lighter.

Substrate materials

I use only three materials as substrates when making bent laminations: MDF, Baltic birch plywood, and resawn veneer. All of them are used thin, of course; the MDF and Baltic birch are both ⅛ in. thick and the resawn veneer can vary from ¹⁄₁₆ in. to ⅛ in. thick, depending on how tight the curve I'm making needs to be. The tighter the curve, the thinner the materials required to bend need to be.

The curved doors on this maple-leaf marquetry cabinet by the author are veneered on a substrate of ⅛-in. Baltic birch layers laminated together over a form in the vacuum bag.

Both ⅛-in. MDF and ⅛-in. Baltic birch plywood make ideal materials for laminations. They hold their shape well when glued in multiple layers and take veneer well. You can also use resawn solid wood as your lamination if you need bent-laminated parts that behave like solid wood—legs or stretchers, for example.

Depending on the quality of your resawing setup, you might be able to glue resawn veneers together on your form without sanding or planing them smooth. If the parts aren't smooth off the saw, take the extra step to sand or plane them smooth. You'll get a much better glue bond and the joint between the layers will be less visible.

Glues for bent laminations

There are a few specific things you need from the glue you use for bent laminations: first, a rigid glueline; second, no long-term creep at the glueline; and third, enough open time to spread glue on all the layers of a bent lamination. There are three glues that can provide all of these features: two-part epoxy, urea formaldehyde glue, and polyurethane glue. Any of the three will work very well at creating rigid bent

If you get a smooth cut like the one on the left from your resaw setup, you can easily glue up right off the saw. If, however, your cut looks closer to the one on the right, you'll want to plane or sand your resawn veneer before glue-up.

Before you start spreading glue, make sure you have all the necessary supplies ready and close at hand: glue, plastic sheet, form, substrate, caul, roller, and vacuum bag.

Greg Zall works primarily in resawn veneer to make his delicate marquetry pieces, like this cremation urn decorated with marquetry flowers.

laminations. I use polyurethane glue most often because it doesn't require the safety gear that epoxy and UF glues do and it dries faster, so I can take my bent laminations out of the press in 3 to 4 hours instead of 8 to 10 hours.

> ❖ **TIP** ❖ No matter which glue you decide to use, you need to move quickly to spread glue on all the layers of a decent-size bent lamination before the glue begins to set. Make sure you have everything you need for the process ready and nearby. It helps to recruit a helper, as well, to make spreading the glue go quicker.

Making a basic bent lamination

Let's go through the whole process for making the sample bent-laminated door discussed earlier. You've got your form assembled and sanded smooth, so now you'll want to cover it in a layer of plastic sheet. I like to wrap the sheet over the form and tape it underneath so it can't come off in the vacuum bag. Make sure to stretch the plastic smooth so there aren't any wrinkles that could impact your face veneer. Once the form is assembled, cut the substrate pieces to size (you want them to be the size of the form but no larger in any direction), along with the top layer of plastic sheet and one extra piece of substrate material to use as a caul on top of the lamination. For this lamination, I'll be using ⅛-in. MDF to create my bent lamination. I also make a point to have some longer strips of packing tape adhered to the bottom of the form so I can wrap them over the substrate once it's on the form. It's best to apply these before you start spreading glue.

Lay out your stack of ⅛-in. MDF next to the form and begin spreading poly glue on the first layer. Mist the back side of the next layer with water before you place it on the glued layer and repeat this operation until the final layer is in place. I won't glue the veneer faces to the substrate at this time (see the sidebar on p. 182 for an explanation as to why).

Place the stack of glued substrate layers onto the bending form centered over the form and apply the first two pieces of packing tape across the center of the form. Then bend one side of the lamination down onto the curve of the form and pull it tight with the packing tape at the end of the form. Repeat for the opposite side. The packing tape will hold the parts in place long enough for you to get the assembly into the vacuum bag and under pressure.

Cover the substrate with plastic sheet and the caul and slide it into the vacuum bag. Make sure the caul stays correctly oriented over the substrate while the vacuum presses the part onto the form. Leave the assembly in the vacuum bag for a minimum of 3 to 4 hours, although more time is better. Once you remove the substrate from the bag, set it aside overnight to finish drying, unless you are planning to veneer it first. In that case, go right to applying your veneer faces as soon as you take it out of the bag.

Regardless of what system you decide to use to trim your curved parts to size, the first thing to do is flatten one long edge with either handplanes or a hard sanding block so you can run that edge against your tablesaw fence. From there, you can quickly trim the opposite edge of the lamination, so you'll have two parallel edges that can go against whatever fixture you make to secure the part while making the angled cuts on the ends. To trim my curved part, I use a combination of the rip and miter fences on my tablesaw, but you could do the same work a bit more slowly with a bandsaw and handplanes.

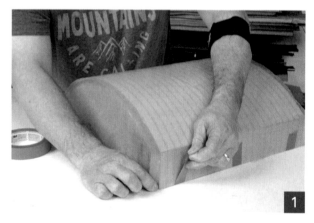

Cover the curved area of your laminating form with a layer of plastic sheet to keep glue from adhering to it in the press. I tape the plastic to the bottom of the form with pieces of blue tape.

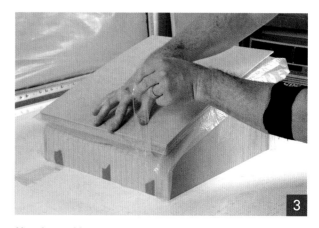

Begin spreading glue on one face of each layer of the substrate. Because we're using polyurethane glue, you'll want to mist the opposite layer before placing it onto the glue.

Use the packing tape you placed earlier to pull the laminations down as far as you can onto the form. This will keep the breather mesh and vacuum bag from getting caught in between the lamination layers.

WHEN TO VENEER

When you apply veneer to your bent laminations depends on two things: what the part will be used for and how fast you can work. I find that trying to get glue on all the layers of the lamination and keep the veneer flat and in place is just too stressful, so I separate the two tasks and do two layups. The first is just the substrate layers, and the second is gluing the veneer faces to the substrate. This can be done as soon as the substrate is dry enough to take off the form, or you can do any fitting and fine-tuning necessary on the substrate before applying the veneer. I do this quite frequently with bent-laminated door panels because they often don't line up perfectly from door to door and need a bit of surface shaping to fit perfectly.

Instead of trying to fix that minor misalignment after the door panels are veneered, I laminate the substrate, edge it, and fit all the laminations to my cabinet openings. Then I can do any sanding or fitting on the door faces before veneering them. It's quite easy to sand a little Baltic birch or MDF off a corner or two but quite a challenge to do that same sanding on a veneered face.

Clean off the glue squeeze-out on one edge before doing anything else so you have one straight reference edge to use for all future cuts.

After cleaning up one edge of your lamination, use the rip fence on your tablesaw to trim the opposite edge straight and parallel to the first edge.

Next, run the first clean, flat edge against the rip fence on your tablesaw to trim the opposite edge smooth and parallel. You'll probably also want to recut the first edge you cleaned up to get a perfectly straight edge.

By using your miter fence and some scrap blocks to support the bent-laminated part, you can use your tablesaw to trim the ends of the curved part to nearly any angle. This is my preferred method for sizing curved parts. I can use an angle gauge to size the scrap support blocks for precise angled cuts on my curved parts as long as I take the time to secure the curved part so it can't move.

We'll discuss techniques for edging this bent lamination in the next chapter. I'll be edging it with solid wood before veneering the faces, and the veneering is done exactly like making the lamination itself. Spread glue on the lamination, press the veneer in place, and repeat for the opposite face of the lamination. Then slide it into the vacuum bag with the ⅛-in. caul, plastic, and breather mesh on top. The only detail to pay attention to is the size of the caul. Because you cut the lamination down in size and added edging, the caul will need to be a dif-

6

Clamp a block to your miter fence to support the bent lamination at the correct angle and then clamp the bent lamination to the fence so you can safely slide it past the tablesaw blade. Using this system and a digital angle gauge, you can make a wide variety of angled cuts on complex curved parts right at the tablesaw.

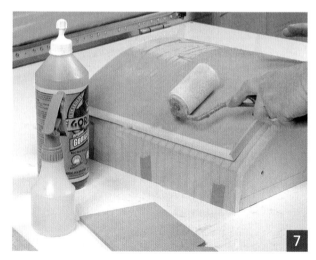

7

Roll an even layer of glue onto the surface of the bent lamination, making sure to cover the surface evenly and get good coverage along the edges.

ferent size so it overhangs the veneer by only ⅛ in. maximum. Once the lamination is made and edged, the veneering becomes pretty easy.

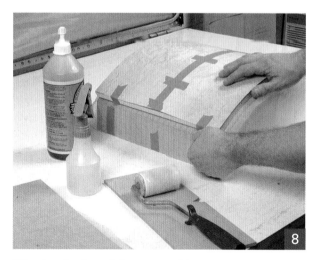

8

Mist the glue face of the veneer with some water, and then lay it onto the glue and tape around the perimeter to hold it in place in the vacuum bag.

SANDING CURVES AND BENT LAMINATIONS

All your sanding on curved pieces should be with the grain of the veneer. Sometimes this makes for lots of short sanding strokes to get parts completely sanded. Sanding larger curved shapes takes a bit more skill and effort than sanding flat ones, because you can't do much of the sanding with power tools—it's nearly all done by hand with shaped sanding blocks. I've found that pieces of ¾-in.-thick white foam make great sanding pads for curved surfaces. I make mine 4 in. wide by about 8 in. long so I can hold them with two hands and the pressure gets spread over a larger surface area. Simply spray-glue sandpaper to one face of the foam and gently bend the foam to the curve you need to sand. Try to sand with the grain all the time because removing cross-grain sanding scratches can take a lot of effort.

No matter what tool you use to sand curved veneer, make sure to sand the entire surface evenly. Don't spend lots of time in one area or you might find a sand-through under your sanding block when you're done. I try to start my sanding routine with 150-grit paper as the coarsest grit and follow that with 180-grit and then 220-grit to get the surface ready for finish.

Sand curved veneer or edging flush to the substrate with a white insulation foam pad bent to fit the curve of your panel and some 120-grit sandpaper. It works great with a bit of spray glue to hold the sandpaper in place; just make sure not to round over the edges of the panel. This system works for roughing up the substrate and flushing the edging to the substrate, as well as for sanding the final veneer surface.

CHAPTER 10

Edging and Crossbanding

Now that we've covered a variety of techniques to create veneered panels, it's time to go over some methods for finishing off the edges of those panels. Edging can be done in a number of ways, and what type you use will be largely determined by the specific project you'll be making. We'll start with something simple like a veneered edge, which is quick to glue up and, if done in the same veneer as the panel, will have nearly invisible grain match with the panel. Edging can also be made of solid wood as you'd typically find on a veneered table or cabinet top.

This small side table by the author has a veneered marquetry top surrounded by solid-wood edging in mahogany that helps protect the delicate veneer while also adding a decorative detail to the overall design. Edging used this way can become part of the design rather than just a way to finish off a veneered panel.

Shown here are some of the many methods of finishing off a veneered panel: from left to right, veneer edging, veneer crossbanding, resawn veneer crossbanding, waterfall veneer edging, and solid-wood edging. On the bottom is a sample of curved solid-wood edging.

This has the benefit of protecting the delicate veneered edge with a solid-wood border and potentially also adding a bit of decorative detail if you choose to use a contrasting wood for the edge material.

In addition to those types of edging, we're going to learn how to apply crossbanding to veneered panels. Crossbanding is composed of either veneer or resawn solid wood, with the grain radiating outward from the central area of the panel. It can be applied during or after veneering depending upon the final design solution needed. Waterfall veneering, which we'll also cover, works in a similar fashion: The veneer on the face of the panel continues down the edges and vertical faces of the assembly to create what looks much like a solid piece of wood with beautifully symmetric grain on all surfaces. With this pattern,

instead of having a single long piece of straight-grained edging going along the edge of a panel, we'll have a long strip composed of short pieces of cross-grain veneer with grain flowing across the length of the edging strip.

We'll also look at methods for edging curved panels with veneer and solid wood. They take the same basic techniques, but solid wood will require more cutting and shaping of the solid-wood edging to get it to follow the shape of the panel.

One big decision to make when it comes to edging is when to apply the edging—before or after veneering the faces. It may not seem obvious, but there are a number of times when you'll want to edge your parts before gluing on the face veneers to hide the edging below the veneer and to make gluing on the edging easier. I'll go over a few of these along the way.

Patrick Edwards used decorative crossbanding in a contrasting wood to accent the perimeter of all the panels on his small Hepplewhite worktable. Used this way, crossbanding becomes another part of a more complex design, adding both detail and interest to the furniture.

Gray Hawk uses some unique veneering in his furniture, including this piece, "Banksia Cabinet," with edging around the doors that utilizes the sapwood of the resawn redgum veneer he used to create truly original frames around his doors.

By combining waterfall edging and straight-grained edging on the same piece, the author was able to create the illusion of solid boards of cherry and maple for the doors of this small side cabinet.

This Art Deco cabinet in palisander and Huon pine by Gray Hawk showcases crossbanding in a variety of ways. Even the glass doors have a pattern of crossbanding that matches the side panels and drawer fronts.

This dining table in walnut veneer has a veneered top and edges. I wouldn't normally veneer the edge of a dining table, but the design for this client necessitated using veneer on all the surfaces.

Basic Veneer Edging

Edging a veneered panel with veneer matched to the face veneer is a great way to create a seamless look on your finished panels. It also offers enough protection to the veneer for edges that aren't going to be exposed to much damage—things like cabinet doors and the like. I wouldn't recommend veneer as edging for something like a dining table unless the design can't be accomplished another way because the sharp edges where the top and side veneer meet can be damaged easily.

Once you've got the faces of your veneered panel glued up and it's fully dry, trim it to final size so it's ready for you to apply edging. Often, I'll trim only the first two edges, top and bottom or left and right, and then edge them so that when I trim the remaining two edges, I end up with perfectly flush cuts on the initial edging pieces. Assuming you cut your panel this way, you won't need to trim the ends of

the first edging you apply because they'll be cut flush with the panel ends when you size the panel down.

I use this technique frequently with solid-wood edging so that I won't need to trim the ends of the edging perfectly flush with the ends of my panels by hand. It can save you lots of fussy fitting of edging, whether the edging ends up being legs for a cabinet or side stretchers. If you can apply the initial edging long and trim it to final size with the panel cuts, you'll make things easier and faster for yourself in the end.

Attaching veneer edging

Edging veneered panels with veneer is really quite simple. Start by cutting a few strips of veneer from the same material as the panel, but make sure they are at least ¼ in. wider than the thickness of your panel. That gives you some leeway when applying the edging in case something shifts while clamping it

Apply an even coat of Titebond 1 to the substrate edge and then press the veneer edging in place, securing it with a few pieces of blue tape along the edge.

all together. A few pieces of blue tape across the edging also help hold it in place until clamped.

I typically use Titebond 1 to attach veneer edging. It's more than strong enough to hold a strip of veneer in place and dries quickly enough to allow

multiple panels to be edged in a single day. Apply an even bead of glue to the first edge and spread it across the edge with either a small acid brush or your finger. Once there is glue on the entire edge, lay the strip of veneer onto the glued edge. Apply a few pieces of blue tape along the length of the edge to hold the veneer in place while you work.

Flip the panel end-for-end and repeat the glue-spreading and veneer-applying operation on the opposite edge. Place a cork-covered caul over each veneer edge and clamp them in place with a clamp every few inches. Double-check that your veneer hasn't moved while you are tightening the clamps. If it has, loosen the clamps and shift the veneer back into place, and then tighten the clamps again. Once the clamps are all tight, set the assembly aside for a few hours to dry.

Clamp the edging in place with cork-covered cauls and clamps spaced every few inches.

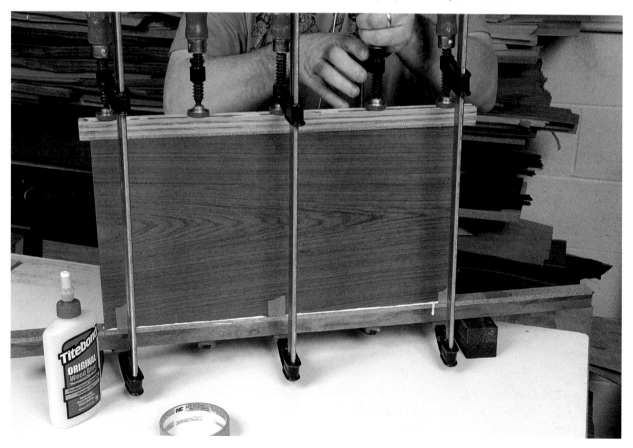

CORK CLAMPING CAULS

My preferred method for applying veneer edging is to use cork-covered clamping cauls slightly wider than my panel edges to press the edging in place. Let's say you pressed a 24-in.-square ¾-in.-thick panel with veneer on both sides. You'll then need cauls that are at least 1 in. wide by 26 in. long, and because we're going to glue edging onto two edges at a time, you'll need two cauls.

Cork-covered cauls help distribute clamping pressure on thin edging and protect the edging from potential damage caused by the clamps. Cork is available in wide sheets from most lumberyards; mine is ¼ in. thick and is sold in 4-ft.-wide rolls. The fastest way to make a bunch of cork-covered cauls is to cut a piece of ¾-in.-thick plywood about 15 in. wide by 4 ft. long. Cut a piece of cork 15 in. wide by 4 ft. long and spray a heavy coat of spray adhesive on one face of the cork (it takes more to glue down cork than it does for paper, so make sure it's a heavy coat). Carefully press one corner of the cork down onto your plywood and slowly press the rest of the

cork down, trying to keep it aligned with the edges of the plywood. You can roll over the cork with a laminate roller to help seat it on the plywood, but I like to just slide the assembly into the vacuum bag for a few minutes. The vacuum pressure makes the cork bond to the plywood nearly permanent.

Next, trim any overhanging cork flush on one edge of the plywood with a utility knife. Set your tablesaw rip fence to about ¼ in. over the thickness of your panel and rip off a few pieces of cork-covered plywood. I like to cut the edging into strips with the cork facing up to keep the blade from trying to pull it off the plywood. You'll want to cover the cork face with clear packing tape to prevent any glue squeeze-out from sticking to the cork. Just run a strip of tape down the length of each caul and press it down over the edges. These cauls will last a long time and the cork recovers well from clamping pressure, so you can use them over and over. I think I've been using some of mine for 10 years or more.

Spray-glue the cork and press it down onto the plywood. I place the assembly in the vacuum bag for a few minutes to help seat the spray adhesive.

Wrap the cork with clear packing tape to keep glue from sticking to your cauls.

Cleaning up veneer edging

There are a variety of ways to trim veneer edging flush with the panel faces, including a router with a flush trim bit, sandpaper on a hard block, or a sharp knife. Through years of trial and error, I've found one method that seems to work on essentially every type of veneer and every panel. I start by gently filing the veneer edging close to flush with the panel with the fine-grit side of a Surform tool. This tool does an interesting job of partly breaking the veneer and partly filing the veneer. Either way, it gets veneer trimmed down with no torn grain in the edging material.

Finish bringing the edge veneer flush to the panel with a hard sanding block and some 120-grit sandpaper. Wrap the front edge of the block with a few layers of blue tape to keep it from gouging your veneer face.

Wrap the front end of a Surform tool or mill file with a few layers of blue tape to keep it from digging in, then file the overhanging veneer almost flush with the panel surface.

There is a specific method to use so that the Surform tool does not damage the face veneer. First, wrap a few layers of blue tape around the front end of the tool to prevent it from digging into the face veneer. This allows you to file the edging down without worrying about potentially damaging the faces. I'll typically stop filing when the edge veneer is almost flush. Trying to file it flush always seems to leave score marks in the face veneer from the sharp teeth of the file. I'll also work inward from both ends of the panel toward the center so that there's no chance of breaking extra veneer off the ends of the panel.

After the edging is filed, switch tools and come in with a long sanding block—ideally something about 2 in. wide by 12 in. to 15 in. long covered with 120-grit sandpaper. Again, wrap several layers of blue tape around the front end of the sanding block and sand the edging flush with the face veneer, stopping when the edging is perfectly flush. In this case, the blue tape prevents 120-grit sandpaper scratches from cutting across the panel face. Whenever I apply edging of any kind, I don't sand the face veneer until after the edging is applied. This helps prevent sand-throughs in the face veneer caused by oversanding. The same goes for sanding inlays: Try to sand only when all the work is done.

Curved-Panel Veneer Edging

The process for applying edging to bent-laminated curved veneered panels is somewhat similar to the

WHEN TO APPLY THE EDGING

There are times when you'll want to edge your panels before applying the face veneers—for example, when you want to add crossbanding to the veneered panel. If you edge after the crossbanding is applied, the edging will be visible on the finished face. Or when you're making curved doors and fit the substrate to the opening before veneering the faces. I'll often do this when applying marquetry or parquetry faces so the alignment of the imagery from door to door is exact; it also prevents the edging from being visible on the edge of the marquetry face.

Edging curved doors with solid wood before veneering also makes gluing on the edging a much simpler operation. Panel edges can be cut at 90° and thicker edging glued on with tape or clamps much more eas-

ily than trying to glue thinner edging onto a curved or angled edge on a curved panel. When I fit curved doors, I'll rough-size the lamination and edge it completely before veneering. Then when I do the final fitting of the door to the carcase, I'll only be cutting into the solid-wood edging.

These marquetry doors were edged in ¹⁄₁₆-in. solid maple on the top and bottom edges and ½-in.-thick maple on both sides. They were then fitted to the opening before being veneered so the marquetry imagery would flow across the doors uninterrupted by the edging.

This marquetry cabinet by the author has a variety of veneered panels that were all edged after veneering with ³⁄₈-in.-thick mahogany edging that was intended to be visible and part of the design of the cabinet.

process used for applying straight edging, at least when it comes to the flat planes of the curved panels. Edging the ends of panels that finish off at odd angles, however, can be challenging. For this reason, I'll often edge these panels before gluing on the face veneers so I can use wider solid-wood edging that is easier to glue in place (see "When to Apply the Edging" above).

Let's assume that you've made a bent-laminated door panel that curves across its face (I'll be using the door panel from the previous chapter as an example). Start by applying the edging to the sides of the panel. The sides are thicker than the top and bottom edging, so we'll apply them first and cover them with the top and bottom edging next to hide the thickness of the edging material.

Curved doors often get thicker side edging to allow for fitting to the cabinet sides and to other doors. The top and bottom edges will overlap the side edging to hide the thickness of the edging.

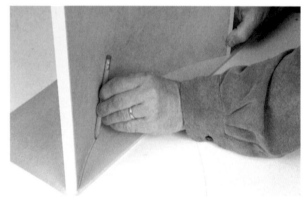

An easy way to size the curved edging required for the top and bottom edges is to simply trace around the panel onto the edging. Then cut out the tracing on the bandsaw or with a scalpel depending on the thickness of your edging.

For a door like this, the top and bottom edging can be any thickness from veneer to ⅛-in. solid wood, but the sides need thicker material to allow for beveling the door to fit the opening—something like ¼ in. to ½ in. thick on these doors. When I edge panels before face veneering, I'll frequently use a material that closely matches the face veneer in tone and color so it blends into the veneer. Titebond 1 makes a good adhesive for solid-wood edging because it dries fast and has a hard glueline.

A fast way to size the edging for the top and bottom edges is to lay out a piece of matching veneer wider and longer than the edge to be veneered. Then place the panel edge on top of the veneer and simply trace around it with a pencil. This gives you the exact shape you need to cover the edge. Leave at least ⅛ in. extra on all sides for alignment. You can use the same system to make matching curved cork clamping cauls or just use larger rectangular ones to do the same job. Gluing and trimming the edging is done the same way as with straight edges.

Once the glue is dry, plane most of the excess material off with a block plane and then sand the edging flush to the panel using a hard block (or a curved block that fits the curve exactly) and some 120-grit paper. Make sure you don't round over the edges when flushing the edging. Then do any final fitting to your cabinet so the panels are ready to be installed after veneering.

You can use wide cork-covered cauls to clamp curved pieces of edging in place or cut curved cauls to match the edging pieces.

A block plane makes quick work of any excess edging overhanging the substrate; just be sure to trim it off at the correct angle so it flows along the curve of the substrate. Finish it off flush with a curved sanding block.

Solid-Wood Edging for Protection and Decoration

There are lots of times when a veneered panel will need more protection than can be found in veneered edging, and these are the times for solid-wood edging to step in. Solid-wood edging can also be used for decorative effect by bringing in contrasting material to frame decoratively veneered panels. Quite often, veneered panels are made from highly figured or burl veneers that aren't available in solid form, and the best option is to create an interesting contrast in the frame material rather than try to get a perfect color match with a rare piece of veneer.

I'll use solid-wood edging for tabletops, cabinet tops, and often for door edging, though I use it in different ways in each application. It's easy to see how a decorative solid-wood frame around a veneered tabletop can add some necessary damage prevention: Solid wood can be easily resanded and refinished several times, whereas veneer has more limited refinishing potential. The same holds true for cabinet tops and doors. For doors, however, I find that I frequently combine veneer edging and solid-wood edging on the same door by using them where their individual strengths lie. Solid wood is great for making integrated door handles and decorative dividers between a set of doors, but veneer works better to blend the hinge and top edges into the veneered panel.

Making solid-wood edging

Solid-wood edging can vary in width from a barely noticeable 1/16 in. for cabinet doors and shelves to several inches for tabletop edges that may get some shaping detail added. I've found that thinner edging can be glued directly to the panel edge (assuming it's been cleanly and squarely cut to size first), but wider edging needs some form of mechanical attachment in addition to glue. Often this can take the form of full-length splines, biscuits, Dominos, or other integrated joints cut into the edging and panel.

When making solid-wood edging, you need to make the edging pieces slightly thicker than the thickness of the panel. How much thicker should vary along with the width of the edging—removing a lot of extra material on 2-in. solid-hardwood edging takes significantly more work than removing the same extra material on 1/16-in.-thick edging.

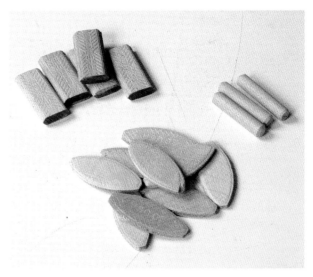

Samples of a few ways to attach wide solid-wood edging mechanically include Dominos, biscuits, and dowels. If you would rather have full-length joints, cut splines to fit a tablesawn groove in both pieces.

If you're ready for a real challenge in your edging, try this piece by David Marr featuring shopmade edging composed of hundreds (or maybe thousands) of alternating pieces of 1/8-in. mahogany and holly rectangles glued edge to edge then glued to the table edges. Quite an exercise in patience!

When matching the face veneer pattern on the edges becomes impossible, it makes sense to use a solid-wood corner edge of similar tone to both protect the fragile face veneer and unify the design, as on this box by Adrian Ferrazzutti.

This small cabinet has veneer edging on the doors on three sides but utilizes solid-wood edging on what would be the handle side to allow for wear and potential damage from handling.

For that reason, I'll typically mill narrower edging about ⅛ in. oversize overall, so there will be around ¹⁄₁₆ in. of excess material top and bottom to remove after glue-up. I like to mill wider edging much closer to the thickness of the panel—more like ¹⁄₃₂ in. over, which leaves ¹⁄₆₄ in. top and bottom to remove later. You'll need to be much more accurate when you line up wide edging with the panel, but that's partly what the mechanical fasteners are there to do. Properly lining up the biscuits, Dominos, etc., will allow you to easily attach your edging in just the right location to save effort later bringing it flush to the panel.

Locating the mechanical fasteners

Milling up solid-wood edging is not something that we need to cover in this book. It requires basic shop skills with a tablesaw, jointer, and planer—all things you should be familiar with if you're making veneered furniture. What we will cover here is how to locate the mechanical fasteners on panels and edging so the correct amount of excess material is exposed after glue-up. I'll be using Festool Dominos as the mechanical fasteners in my edging, but the same method works for biscuits and splines (those would just be cut with a biscuit jointer or tablesaw instead).

This cabinet uses a variety of edging methods in a specific order to achieve a finish design with minimal effort and complexity. Applying the curved lower edging to the side panels first and then cutting the side panels to final width saves time in fitting the parts. After the legs are applied to the side panels, the top edge is trimmed flush. Done this way, none of the edging (be they legs or trim) needs to be precisely located when it's applied.

We'll assume that you've already veneered your panel and have the solid-wood edging cut to size. For the example shown here, I'm using edging that is 2 in. wide, so I'll definitely need some mechanical fasteners to line it up with the panel and secure it long term. Since the edging is so wide, I'm planning to leave it only $\frac{1}{32}$ in. thicker than my panel. When cutting the Dominos, I'll need to place a spacer under the fence only while cutting the slots in the panel; the spacer needs to be $\frac{1}{64}$ in. thick or about three or four pieces of paper or blue tape in thickness. You use the spacer only when cutting into the panel, not the edging.

Lay out your Domino locations by setting the edging against the panel edge and marking straight across the two with a pencil. Set your machine to cut the slot in the center of the edging piece and cut all the slots in the edging. Now place your spacer under the Domino fence and cut all the slots in the panel edge. I like to test-fit my edging with a few extra Dominos that I've sanded lightly so they go in more easily. The edging should end up centered on the panel; if it is, you're ready for glue-up. If it is not centered, you might have used a spacer that was either too thick or too thin or you placed the spacer on the wrong parts—remember, it goes on the panel side only.

Wide solid-wood edging needs to end up just a bit proud of the face veneer. While cutting in the mechanical fasteners used to hold the two parts together, add a thin spacer to the panel face to offset the edging slightly above the face veneer surface.

Remove the spacer when cutting the fasteners into the edging material.

Do any fitting of your edging pieces before cutting the Dominos. On these pieces, I've already cut and fitted the mitered corners. Now mark across both pieces with a pencil every 4 in. to 6 in.

If your spacer was the correct thickness, you should have an edge that requires minimal work to bring it flush with the face veneer.

Curved Edging

If your design has curved edges, they'll likely need applied edging in either solid wood or veneer. Both use similar techniques, but the solid-wood edging takes more time to fit (it's also much more durable). I make curved edging in a specific way that has worked for me for many years. There are many other ways to do it, but this method is fairly foolproof if all the steps are followed.

I'll start by laying out my boards for edging so there are enough to wrap fully around the substrate (in this case, it's the radial-matched walnut tabletop from chapter 6). Mark the inside curve of one board at a time by slipping it under the tabletop surface and tracing around the perimeter of the top panel with a pencil. I'll also mark the outside line of the edging pieces at this time so I can see how the grain will look when they are finished. This is the best time to move the uncut edging pieces around to get better grain orientation, if desired (remember to remark the pieces). On this tabletop, I'll be applying 1½-in.-wide curly maple edging, so I need to trace a line that is at least 1½ in. larger than the tabletop substrate. I use a small wooden spacer 1½ in. wide to locate the pencil the correct distance from the substrate; a pair of dividers would work just as well. I also mark the locations of any extra material I want to leave on the edging strips to aid clamping. On these parts, I leave a flattened-off bump at the end of each edging piece. These protrusions allow me to clamp the edging pieces together with a small bar clamp as I add new pieces so the connecting joints are tight. I'll just bandsaw them off after the edging is completely glued on.

Cut both the inside and outside marked curves on your edging pieces. I'll use a variety of tools to fit the inside curve of the edging pieces to the substrate: A spindle sander works well for fitting concave curves, and a small benchtop belt sander or disk sander does a pretty good job of fitting convex edges. You can also use a compass plane or curved

Trace the perimeter of the tabletop onto each of your edging pieces, making sure to mark which piece goes where if the curve is not uniform.

Use a spacer to trace the outside width of the edging onto each piece. Also, add some marks for the extra material you'll be leaving on the edging to aid clamping later.

sanding blocks to fine-tune your edging pieces to the substrate edges until the fit is perfect. The more time and patience you have during this stage, the better the joint between the edging and veneer will be. I'll often add a decorative inlay to bridge the joint after the edging is applied—not to hide the joint but frequently to add another small design detail to the panel. Once all the edging pieces are fitted to the substrate, fine-tune the joints between the individual edging pieces. The orientation of the joints will depend entirely on the design, but I find that it usually looks best to split the joint evenly between each set of pieces. Because these edging pieces are going around a round tabletop, the joints

3

Once all the edging pieces are cut and fitted to the tabletop, it's time to fit the joints between them. You'll also want to lay out the locations of any mechanical fasteners you'll be using—here, I'm adding Dominos every 6 in. around the perimeter and between each edging joint. This is the time to number and mark the location of each piece with a few pencil marks as they'll need to go back into the proper location for the fasteners to line up. I do this by numbering the edging and tabletop in the same location and then add pencil marks to signify the ends of each piece of edging.

are essentially perpendicular to the curve of the table and are quite easy to fit together using a disk sander.

Glue the edging pieces in place one at a time. (I've found that because of the curved shape of the substrate, it's easier to just glue them on individually.) To add some strength and help with alignment, I added Dominos to connect the edging pieces to the substrate at about 6-in. intervals around the tabletop and at the joints between the edging pieces.

4

Apply an even layer of Titebond 1 to the inside of the edging piece and the Dominos connecting it to the substrate. Then run bar clamps across the tabletop from the edging to the opposite side of the top and tighten them down. Once the first piece is dry, repeat the process for the remaining edging pieces.

Inlaid Edging for Boxes and Cases

Sometimes your cabinet or box design calls for a different look, one not tied to solid edging as we've been discussing. Boxes and mitered cabinets can often benefit from some form of protective edging that can also add a decorative detail to the design. This is when I'll typically inlay a corner bead of solid wood around the perimeter of the veneered panels—something between ⅛ in. and ¼ in. square will usually do nicely. The corner inlay can be a contrasting material for an added detail, or it can be a closely matched wood that essentially disappears into the veneering.

On the small cabinet in walnut and anigre below, I added an inlaid corner bead in wenge to protect the walnut veneer and tie the case to the base materials a bit more. Having the inlay completely wrap the cabinet perimeter completes the look better than just having it at the vertical corners. The veneered panels are mitered together, and the corner bead is added after the case is glued together.

You can notch the corners of small boxes for this type of inlay on the tablesaw, but for a larger cabinet

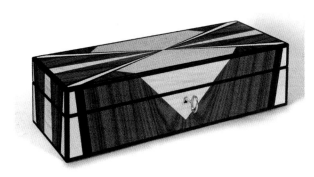

Adrian Ferrazzutti used dark ebony as the edging material on this parquetry veneered box. The ebony serves two purposes: It protects the face veneers and adds a nice framing detail to the overall design.

The mitered veneered sides of this cabinet in walnut and anigre needed some extra protection, so the author added inlays of ¼-in.-square wenge to the corners and tied that to the overall design with matching wenge inlays around the top and base of the cabinet.

These two Macassar ebony veneered boxes by Damion Fauser benefit from an inlaid edge of solid ebony that adds a decorative detail to the boxes and also provides some protection from damage.

like the one shown at left, I used a trim router and rabbeting bit guided by a straight fence screwed to the router. This groove is for ¼-in. edging, so the router bit is set to cut both down ¼ in. and in ¼ in. with the fence. Make some trial cuts in scrap material to dial in the fence and depth settings so both dimensions are the same before cutting into your veneered cabinet.

Mill the solid-wood edging material as you would any other solid-wood parts, but make the final dimensions of the inlay strips just a bit over ¼ in. square. Because the groove is exact, you can use your final groove cuts to fine-tune the size of the

Once the mitered case is assembled, set up a trim router with a rabbeting bit and straight fence to route ¼-in.-square rabbets on all four corners of the case. Be careful when starting and stopping each cut because not much of the router base is supported by the cabinet. It might be worthwhile to make an auxiliary base for your router that is larger and provides more support before doing these cuts.

I use Titebond 1 for all my edging and inlays in solid wood. It gives decent open time and has a rigid glueline. Spread a thin bead of glue into the inlay rabbet, using a small brush or scrap of wood to spread the glue up both walls of the rabbet. Press the inlay strip in place and secure with strips of blue tape pulled across and down, applying a strip every inch or so. Pull it tight across both directions of the joint and leave it in place until the glue is dry.

Corner Inlay

The edging fits into the corner rabbet routed in the assembly. It both protects and decorates the veneer faces depending upon your choice of material.

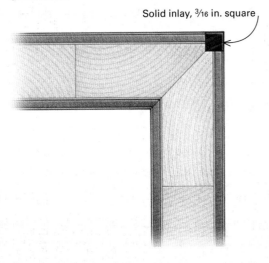

Solid inlay, ³/₁₆ in. square

The entire surface of this table is veneered with a variety of veneering techniques. It needed something around the perimeter of the tabletop to protect the delicate veneer: I used ⅛-in. solid Gabon ebony corner inlays to accent the veneer and add the necessary protection. It helps that there is also an ebony inlay between the different veneers.

inlay to be just a bit proud of the veneer, something like half a ¹/₆₄ is plenty.

Once all the edging is dry, plane or sand it flush to the veneer, being careful not to oversand the veneered panel. The same system works for boxes, cases, and any other location where you need a bit of extra protection. I'll frequently add a corner inlay like this to tabletops when the top and edge are both veneered. Done correctly, it adds a nice design detail that hides its real purpose of protecting the veneer from damage.

Crossbanding

Another way to finish off a veneered panel is to use crossbanding, which is a border of veneer that surrounds a central veneered panel. Typically, the grain direction of the border flows out and away

from the center of the panel, but it can be applied at different angles to achieve different looks. No matter what direction the crossbanding grain runs, the method of application is similar and requires that the substrate be presized to fit whatever opening the finished panel will occupy. Because the crossbanding has a specified width, trimming panels down to size after glue-up can result in borders of uneven widths and mismatched corner joints.

Sizing the substrate

The substrate I'm working with on the following pages has been sized to be a door panel 14 in. wide by 24 in. high, and it has been pre-edged in ¹/₁₆-in. solid mahogany edging so the face veneer will run over the edging and hide it after veneering. Once the substrate is sized and edged, the crossbanding and center veneer can be cut to size. For this door, I want

This cabinet by the author has curved doors with radial-matched satinwood center panels surrounded by cherry veneer crossbanding. It takes proper planning to get a door like this to come out with all the details aligned and even. These doors were edged and fitted to the openings before the face veneer was applied so the face veneer could be accurately measured and cut to size.

1½-in.-wide cross-grain sapele veneer surrounding a central panel of curly maple veneer. Because the crossbanding is 1½ in. wide all around the central panel, I need to cut the central veneer panel down in size to allow for even crossbanding all around. My finished door is 14 in. wide, so I'll subtract 1½ in. twice to get my center veneer width of 11 in. The door is 24 in. high, so again subtract 1½ in. twice from that number to get a final center veneer height of 21 in. Cut your center sheet of curly maple veneer to exactly 11 in. wide by 21 in. high, making sure the corners are clean and the sheet is square. If you need to sand the edges of the veneer to clean them up, do that as well.

Cutting the banding material

Make up a stack of quartersawn sapele veneer from four sheets of veneer about 4 in. to 6 in. wide by about 12 in. long. Tape the stack together at the ends (see the top left photo on p. 204), and trim both sides straight and parallel as we've done before. We don't want the veneer panel to be undersized when we glue it to our presized door panel, so we're going to cut the crossbanding 1⅝ in. wide rather than exactly 1½ in. wide. This will give us a bit of extra veneer overhanging the door panel and allow us to see the corner joints of the crossbanding so they can be accurately aligned with the corners of the door panel during glue-up.

Start by measuring the first strip of crossbanding to be cut, and mark the veneer at exactly 1⅝ in. long. Place your straightedge on this line and slice through the stack of veneer. Repeat the measuring, marking, and cutting until you have four to six stacks of sapele veneer strips. Keep the stacks in the order they were cut and make sure you don't flip any over or the grain might look odd in the final door.

Square both sides and one end of the stack of sapele veneer and tape it together in a few places.

Measure the sapele veneer stack at 1⅝ in. long and crosscut a number of equal stacks of veneer to use for crossbanding. As the strips of crossbanding are cut, keep them in the order they were cut and set them aside.

For slip-matched crossbanding, just slide each piece of veneer down so it sits next to the previous piece. Then tape across each joint, making sure to keep the inside edge straight and even.

Taping the strips together

Because I'm using uniform quartersawn sapele veneer, I'll slip-match the crossbanding rather than book-match it. This means that instead of flipping every other piece end-for-end, I'll just slide them down across the stack one by one to make a strip of uniform-grain crossbanding.

We'll be working on the glue face of the veneer for all the taping operations so the show face can be gum-taped later. Place the curly maple veneer sheet on the workbench and mark the exact center of each edge with a pencil mark. These will be the center points you'll work from while applying the sapele edging. Measure and mark the center of the crossbanding strips as well so they are easy to align with the panel. Then take your first piece of edging and center it on one of the panel edges. Apply a few pieces of blue tape along the length of the joint, pulling the edges tightly together. Repeat this process for the remaining three edges, letting the ends overlap freely.

Trimming the miters

To trim the corner miters, you'll need a straightedge and a scalpel (see the photos on p. 206). Starting with the first corner, lay the straightedge across the two overlapping pieces of veneer and align it with both the inside and outside corners where the pieces cross. Doing this gives you an exactly mitered corner, and it works for miters of different widths and curved work, too. Once the straightedge is perfectly aligned, slowly cut through both pieces of veneer. Cut toward the center from both ends to keep the veneer from splitting while it's being cut. Once you've cut all the way through, remove the excess pieces and press the mitered ends together. You should have a perfectly cut and aligned miter. Tape across the miter to pull the veneer joint together tightly. Then repeat this process for the remaining three joints.

> ❖ **TIP** ❖ Trim the corner miters on your cutting mat to keep the scalpel sharp and work from the glue face of the veneer in case you make a mistake.

With all the miters cut and taped, flip the sheet show face up and begin gum-taping along all the joints between the center panel and the crossbanding. Add a piece of gum tape along each of the miter joints as well. When the gum tape is dry, flip the sheet again and remove all the blue tape from the glue face. Take a look at all the corners to make sure they are straight and precise.

Gluing up the crossbanding

To glue up the crossbanded sheet of veneer, proceed as you would for any other veneer glue-up. Typically, I'll use urea formaldehyde or polyurethane glue for crossbanded veneer work to make use of the rigid glueline they both create. When you are ready to

Mark a centerline on each side of your maple veneer piece. Now line up the crossbanding so it is centered on the maple veneer.

Tape each strip of crossbanding to the panel, making sure to center them. Apply a few pieces of tape along the length of the edging, but leave the last inch or so untaped so it can be trimmed to fit.

glue the veneer to the door panel, make sure to place it facedown so you can see the glue face of the veneer sheet. You can then look at the mitered veneer joint and the corner of the door panel and check that they line up accurately. Adding a few pieces of blue tape around the perimeter of the veneer to hold it in place is worthwhile—it's quite disappointing to take your panel out of the press and find that it's slipped a bit when you weren't watching.

To cut accurate miters on the ends of your crossbanding, leave the ends long and align a straightedge from corner to corner across the banding width. Cut through the crossbanding with a scalpel until both pieces are completely cut through.

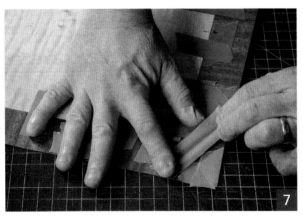

Tape across the miter joint, pulling it tightly together.

Flip the sheet over and double-check that the miters are all clean and accurately cut. Finish by gum-taping the show face of the joints together and remove all the excess blue tape from the glue face when the gum tape is dry.

To ensure that the veneer corners line up with the corners of your substrate, sight down each of the corners and line up the miter with the corner of the substrate. Once all the corners are aligned, tape the veneer face in place with a few pieces of blue tape along each edge.

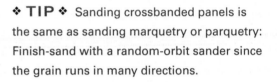

❖ **TIP** ❖ Sanding crossbanded panels is the same as sanding marquetry or parquetry: Finish-sand with a random-orbit sander since the grain runs in many directions.

Solid-Wood Crossbanding

There are times when you'll need to crossband a panel but won't want to do it before the central veneer is glued up. Maybe it's a complex shape with curved edges that would be overly difficult to cut in veneer or it needs to be fitted to the case after glue-up. Or maybe you're making a tabletop and the crossbanding is the edging and needs to be more robust than veneer. In these situations, I add the crossbanding after veneering the panel by using resawn veneer glued into a rabbet cut around the perimeter of my panel. It's relatively easy to do, but a little more time is spent resawing the veneer and fitting the banding to the veneered panel.

Resawing wide veneer sheets is a subject best dealt with in another book, but resawing narrow boards

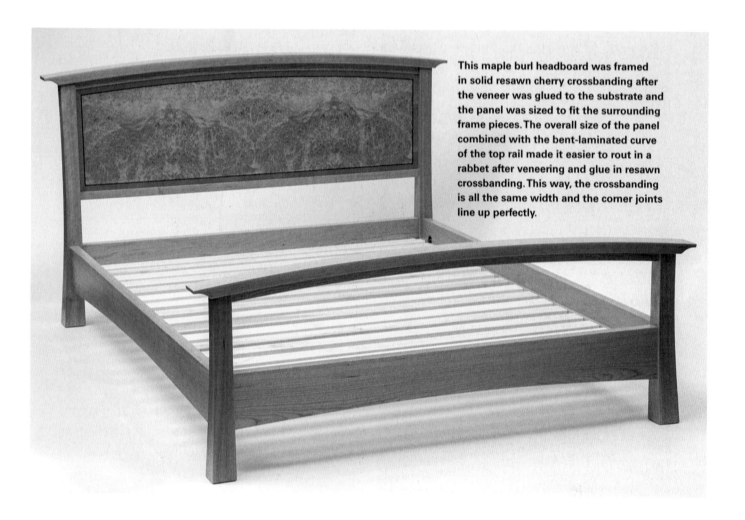

This maple burl headboard was framed in solid resawn cherry crossbanding after the veneer was glued to the substrate and the panel was sized to fit the surrounding frame pieces. The overall size of the panel combined with the bent-laminated curve of the top rail made it easier to rout in a rabbet after veneering and glue in resawn crossbanding. This way, the crossbanding is all the same width and the corner joints line up perfectly.

for crossbanding veneer can easily be done on the tablesaw because the pieces are narrow enough to cut in a single pass. I like to make my crossbanding on the tablesaw because I can cut it to final thickness and not need to plane or sand it smooth after cutting, as I would need to do if I cut it on the bandsaw. Either way, to make resawn banding, you'll need a nice 6/4 or 8/4 quartersawn or rift-sawn board of whatever wood you want to make the banding from, the wider the better. I'll be making one of the side panels for the dresser (shown in the top left photo on p. 83) in maple burl veneer with solid-cherry crossbanding.

Making resawn crossbanding

For this side panel, I'm going to be making my resawn banding from a piece of 6/4 cherry, so first

I'll need to square and surface all four sides of the board so it's ready to be cut down. Next, mark a long diagonal line down one edge of the board so you can keep the cut pieces in order. Once this is done, crosscut one end square to the rest of the board. A miter fence on the tablesaw works fine for these cuts (see the top photo on p. 208). Because my crossbanding groove is 1 in. wide, I'll want to make my banding at least 1⅛ in. wide. Set the rip fence 1⅞ in. away from the blade and clamp a ¾-in. spacer block to the front end of the fence so the pieces don't get trapped between the blade and the fence. Now crosscut the board into 1⅛-in.-long pieces, making sure to clamp the board to the miter fence each time so the board doesn't move (and throw a backer board behind it so you don't get tearout on the back edge).

Square up the block of crossbanding material, then crosscut pieces in order on the tablesaw using the miter fence.

Set the rip fence to just over the depth of your rabbet and rip the blocks into resawn veneer. Keep them in order the entire way through this process. It's not possible to make these cuts with the blade guard in place, so always use a push block to keep your hands away from the blade.

Once all the blocks are cut, lay them out in the order they were cut. Set your rip fence to ⅛ in. and your blade depth to a hair past 1⅛ in., and using push blocks and a featherboard, rip the blocks into as many strips of crossbanding as you can safely cut. Don't try to cut the very last piece because it's unstable. Keeping the parts in the order they are cut, stack them to the side until all the blocks are cut.

Cutting the panel rabbet

There are a number of ways to cut the rabbet in the panel effectively. If you're old school, you can cut it with a handsaw and rabbet planes, or use a dado blade on the tablesaw with the panel flat on the table. While at the tablesaw, you could also stand the panel vertically against a tall fence and cut the rabbet with a regular blade (that's how I'll be doing it and I'll be cutting the rabbet just a little under ⅛ in. deep and 1 in. high).

If your tool of preference is the router, you'll need to make some fences and possibly an oversize base to mount the router because routing off wide swaths of material tends to leave little material for the router base to sit on. You could also go to the router table and rout the material off with the panel flat or vertical depending on your bit choices (flat would be safer and require a smaller bit). As you can see, there are quite a few methods available for cutting the rabbet, but I'll focus instead on cutting the crossbanding and fitting it together, which is fussier and more detail oriented than just cutting a rabbet. (I'm assuming that if you've made it this far into the book, you know how to cut rabbets!) The process for cutting curved rabbets is essentially the same, but you'll likely be using a router and templates to get the cuts exact.

Cutting rabbets for solid-wood crossbanding on the tablesaw is straightforward—as long as you use featherboards and pay close attention to what you're doing. Keep your hands well away from the blade at all times.

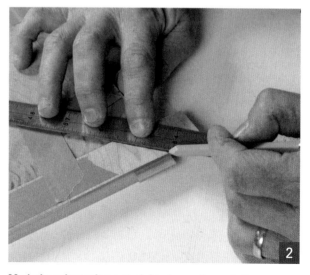

Taping resawn crossbanding strips together is identical to taping veneer crossbanding. The difference comes with mitering the corners: It's not possible to cut through resawn veneer with a scalpel, so the miters need to be cut on the bench and then test-fitted until they are perfect.

Assembling the crossbanding

Take all the strips to the workbench and begin laying them out to form long strips of crossbanding. I'm book-matching these pieces, so every other strip gets flipped end-for-end. Tape across the joints between the strips, making sure to keep the inside edges flush. Once you've made up enough strips to surround your panel, proceed as before, marking the center of each panel side and banding strip and then temporarily taping the banding in place from the center joint outward.

You'll need to cut and fit the mitered corners one by one before gluing the crossbanding in place. I use the same method I use with veneer crossbanding, just marking along the straightedge with a pencil rather than cutting through the material with a scalpel. Mark the top piece of each corner, then remove the crossbanding piece from the panel and cut the miter to the line; you can also sand to the

Mark the miter using a straightedge and pencil, then remove the top piece and cut or sand it to the line.

Tape the cut piece back in place and use it to mark the second miter. Sneak up on the fit of this one so you don't overcut the line.

Resawn crossbanding is easy to glue one single strip at a time. It takes longer to get all the strips in place, but they end up perfectly aligned in the end. Spread an even layer of glue in the rabbet, keeping it a short distance away from the ends.

Tape the strip to the edge of the rabbet, pulling the tape tight to hold the edging against the panel.

Use cork-covered cauls and clamps to hold the banding in place until the glue dries, and then move on to the next strip. Space the panel up from the workbench with some scraps of plywood to make clamping easier.

line on a disk sander quite easily if you make a 45° fence for your sander. Retape the banding in place with the mitered piece on top of the uncut piece and use the mitered end to mark the matching miter cut. Again, remove the banding strip and cut the miter, but this time cut just outside the marked line and test the fit against the first miter. Slowly

fine-tune the fit of the second cut until the miters match perfectly.

Gluing the crossbanding

Remove one complete strip of crossbanding and apply glue to the rabbeted area (using Titebond 1

Darren Fry used techniques of waterfall veneering to create this cabinet in walnut veneer, which has grain flowing down off the top of the cabinet and through all the vertical parts, creating a clean, modern design.

This small side table by the author takes waterfall veneering to the extreme, featuring matched quartersawn pau ferro veneer carried down and across every surface of the table.

again). Spread the glue with a small brush so it's even, but try not to get glue all the way to the end of the strip where it joins the next strip. Place the crossbanding into the glue and tape it firmly to the edge of the rabbet. Place a cork-covered caul over the banding and clamp it firmly down to the panel. Once the first strip is dry, repeat this process for the remaining strips, making sure to glue the corners together as you glue new pieces in place.

Once all the crossbanding is glued and dry, sand or plane it flush with the veneer and trim it flush around the edges of the panel with a flush-trim bit in a handheld router. Then you're ready to sand, using the same method as the one we used to sand veneer crossbanding.

Waterfall Veneer Edging

Waterfall veneer edging gives veneered panels a more uniform solid-wood look as they appear to have wood grain flowing across the face and over the edges of panels. It is achieved in a similar fashion to the veneer crossbanding discussed previously. In this case, however, the edging is cut from an extra-wide piece

Make sure to add enough extra in the length and width of the crossbanding veneer to allow for cutting off the edging strips. Measure for the crossbanding for the top surface of the tabletop and mark each side the same.

of crossbanding before glue-up. When done correctly, waterfall edging takes more effort and precision than plain edging because to create the waterfall effect accurately, the grain of the edge veneer needs to line up precisely with the grain of the face veneer.

The top panel for the side table on p. 211 has a central panel of curly maple veneer surrounded by 1-in.-wide pau ferro veneer crossbanding. The pau ferro is then continued down the edge of the top and all the way to the base of the table, which makes for some rather fussy veneering, but the final look achieved is worth the effort. To make a table like this requires considerable planning in the early stages of veneering because you'll need to make sure your veneer leaves are long enough to span all the vertical and horizontal planes of the piece. This 1¾-in.-thick panel needs edging at least 2 in. wide to allow for alignment during gluing. Because of that, you need to make the veneer for the top crossband 2 in. wider and longer than what is needed for the crossbanding itself. For this piece, that means the pau ferro veneer needs to be at least 3 in. wide. The pau ferro is cut and taped exactly like crossbanding veneer (that's really what it is on the top face of the table). I book-

Mark all four pieces of edging before cutting with a simple number and arrow system so you can keep track of their orientation and location later.

Trim the edging strips off the crossband pieces one at a time, cutting carefully so you don't damage the delicate cross-grain material.

matched the veneer to create a more uniform appearance in the grain.

Along with planning ahead, you'll also want to accurately mark the edging parts to keep track of their orientation and location on the panel. I do this with a simple system of numbers and arrows. Edge 1 gets a 1 on the face near the edge and a 1 on the edge, and the edging gets an arrow pointed upward right next to the 1. This makes it easy to see which edging piece goes where and how it should be oriented.

Attaching the crossbanding portion of the edge material to the face veneer is done exactly the same as previously described in the crossbanding section. Once the face veneer is glued to the substrate, trim it flush around the perimeter and lay out your edging strips according to the number and arrow markings.

The process of gluing up waterfall edging is essentially the same as gluing up straight-grained edging, except that some additional attention needs to be paid to making sure that the grain lines accurately telegraph from the face down the edge. Check the alignment by looking from the face veneer down across the edging; your eyes will pick up any slight misalignment of the grain lines fairly quickly. Simply shift the edging strip until the grain lines up correctly, and then tape it in place securely. I use a few extra strips of blue tape to hold the edging in place when gluing waterfall edging so it can't shift out of alignment while being clamped.

Another example of waterfall veneering is this Art Deco–style chess table by the author that has Macassar ebony veneer running down the coved frame all the way to the floor.

Sanding waterfall edging

Waterfall edging needs to be sanded with the grain of the wood so there aren't any cross-grain sanding lines in the finished piece. This takes time and patience because typically you'll be using a hard block and making lots of short sanding strokes along the edges as you work through the sandpaper grits. Take your time and be careful when using your hard block to keep it flat against the edging face. If you tip the block at the edges, you can easily sand through the thin veneer at the edge and leave the substrate showing. Because the edging isn't very wide, you can't use power-sanding tools to speed up this process.

Check the grain alignment of the edging as you glue it in place by sighting across the face and down the edge. Once it is lined up, tape it securely in place and clamp it until dry.

A Sampler of Veneer Species

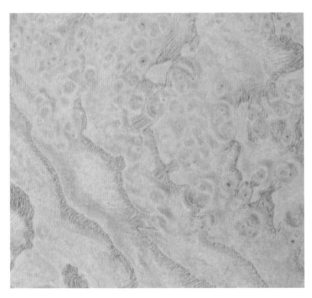

ASH BURL is typically found in eastern North America and is characterized by an even golden coloration throughout the burl. Sheets of ash burl can be quite large—some are nearly 6 ft. across.

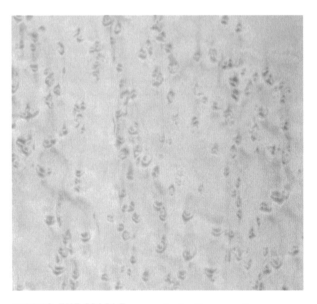

BIRD'S-EYE MAPLE veneer typically comes from sugar maple trees in the northern regions of North America. The bird's eyes are said to be caused by bud growth in the tree that leaves behind numerous tiny knots in the grain of the wood.

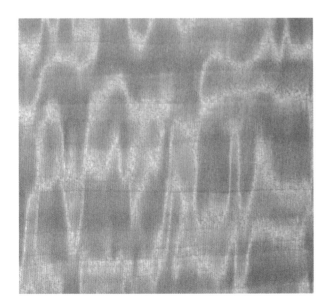

BLOCK MOTTLE FIGURED ANIGRE comes from Africa; the figure is characterized by a somewhat regular pattern of wrinkled blocky shapes visible in the figure of the wood.

Found in South America, BLOODWOOD is well known for its distinctive bright red coloration. Unfortunately, this vibrant red color changes to a darker brownish red over time when the wood is exposed to sunlight.

BUBINGA is an extremely hard, dense wood found in central Africa that can have a variety of highly decorative figure types such as pommele, waterfall, quilted, and mottled. This sample piece has been flat cut to show the cathedral-grain pattern more fully.

CURLY ANIGRE, like all anigre wood, is found in Africa. The curly figure in this riftsawn sample is just one of many figure types that appear in anigre.

CURLY EUROPEAN ASH is found in Europe; there are, however, many other types of ash trees found in a variety of locations around the world, such as Tamo ash in China and Oregon ash in the United States.

CURLY MAPLE is just one of a variety of figure types found in maple trees. This particular one comes from the eastern United States. Curly figure is frequently found in soft maple trees, and the vibrancy of the figure can be increased by quarter- or rift-cutting the wood. More dense curl figure can increase the cost of the wood dramatically.

CURLY SYCAMORE like this sample is actually a type of maple found in Europe and Asia, not to be confused with European plane, which has a grain pattern similar to lacewood.

CURLY WALNUT is most often found in the western and eastern parts of North America. There are many varieties of walnut, from Claro to Bastogne to Black, and each has different color and grain texture. Curly Claro walnut is among the most expensive versions of walnut available.

DOUGLAS FIR is used in the construction and plywood industries. The vertical-grain cut is more decorative and occasionally gets used in furniture making and cabinetry. Douglas fir grows primarily in western North America.

ETIOME is from West and Central Africa and frequently features curly figure. It is most often sliced into veneer and is rarely available in lumber form.

EUCALYPTUS comes primarily from Australia and New Zealand and can have highly figured grain. Oddly enough, the lumber is often also used for railroad ties.

FIDDLEBACK ANIGRE is typically found in West Africa. Anigre is available in several different figure types; fiddleback figure is most prominent when the wood is quarter- or riftsawn.

When a tree is cut through a joint of two branches, the result is crotch figure, as in this HONDURAN MAHOGANY crotch. Frequently found in South America, the genuine version of this mahogany is quite valuable because of its beauty, workability, and rarity. There are several imposter versions of mahogany that don't hold a candle to the genuine version.

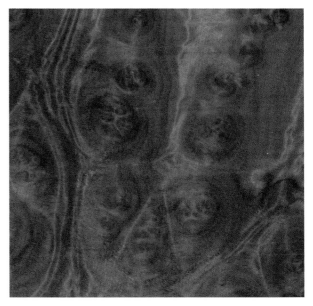

IMBUYA is often called Brazilian walnut, but it is a beautiful wood in its own right as seen in this sample of imbuya burl. Imbuya is most often found in South America.

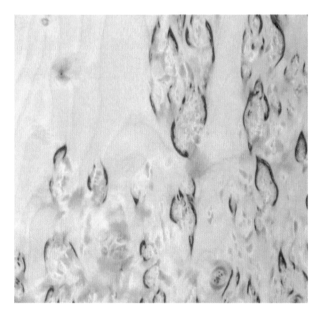

KARELIAN BIRCH is typically found in a region located between Finland and Russia. It has distinctive dark streaks that are caused by an unknown factor in the tree's growth or environment.

KOA is found exclusively on the Hawaiian Islands. It is one of the most exported of the Hawaiian woods and frequently has dramatic figuring.

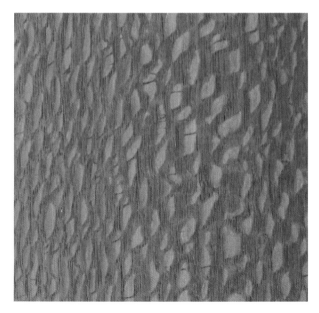

Found most often in South America, LACEWOOD is highly prized for the pronounced ray fleck it has when perfectly quartersawn. The Australian Northern and Southern silky oaks are both often sold as Australian lacewood.

MACASSAR EBONY comes from Southeast Asia and is typically quartersawn. It is becoming difficult to source due to the slow growth rate of the trees and overcutting. It was one of the most prized woods used in Art Deco furniture.

There are many types of MAHOGANY trees. This one from South America is the traditional Honduran mahogany and has better color and workability than its replacements, Philippine and African mahogany.

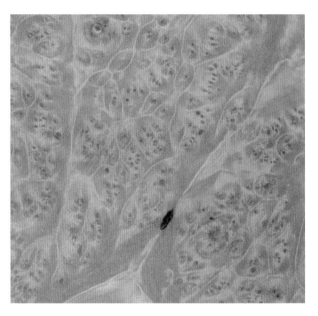

MAPLE BURL comes from the big-leaf maple and is found on the West Coast of the United States. It is typically rotary cut because of the smaller overall size of the burls.

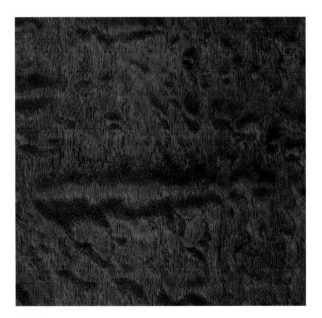

MOABI trees are found in West Africa and can grow to extremely large size. The pommele figure is quite rare and therefore expensive when found.

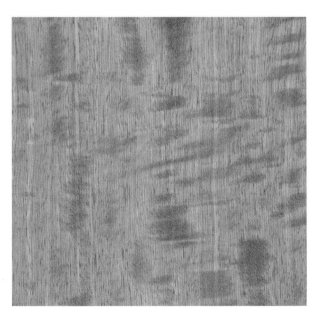

MOVINGUI is found in Africa and is frequently compared with satinwood because of the golden color and interesting figure it shares with satinwood.

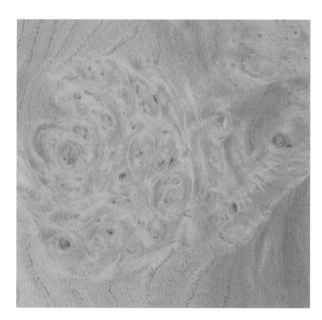

MYRTLE BURL comes from the laurel tree and is commonly sold as laurel burl. Found primarily on the West Coast of the United States, the burl growth in laurel trees is in the roots of the tree. Myrtle burl has a mild texture and is relatively easy to work, taking finish quite well.

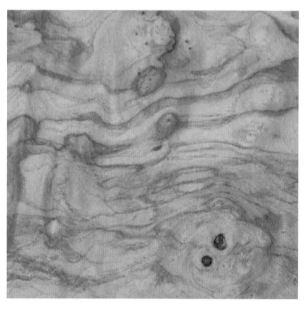

OLIVE ASH BURL comes from ash trees with a distinctive dark heartwood that creates the striking dark/light streaks visible in this sample. Olive ash is found in Europe.

PAU FERRO, also known as Santos rosewood, comes from South America and has been used as a substitute for more expensive rosewoods for many years.

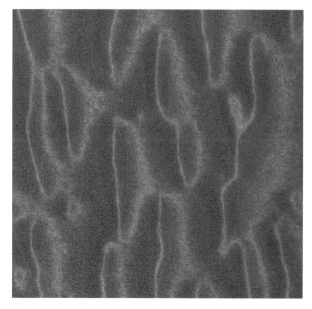

POMMELE SAPELE comes from Africa, and the pommele figure occurs quite often in the sapele tree. It can be strikingly beautiful despite the interlocking grain of the wood.

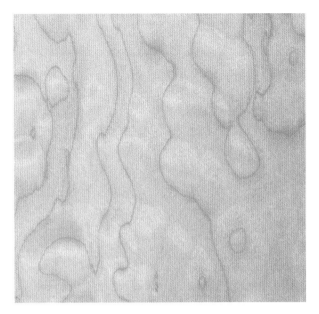

QUILTED MAPLE most often appears in big-leaf maple trees, though it can also be found in both hard and soft maples. The quilted figure becomes strongest when the wood is flatsawn. It is found in eastern North America.

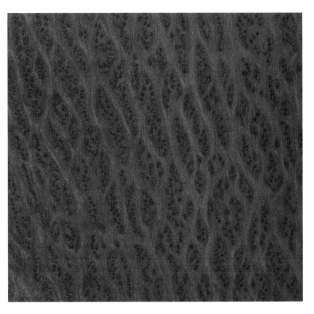

Created by burls formed on redwood trees found on the West Coast of the United States, REDWOOD LACE BURL, or vavona, creates a striking appearance when finished because the burl figure is highly uniform and delicate in appearance.

Another tropical African wood, SAPELE is quite popular because of its uniform grain and availability. It has been used as a substitute for both mahogany and rosewood in the past. It has interlocked grain and is quite hard, but when quartersawn, it can produce a shimmering ribbon figure.

SATINWOOD is found almost exclusively in Sri Lanka and India. The grain is interlocked and the wood is a challenge to dry properly, but it is quite beautiful and highly sought after. The original satinwood is Ceylon satinwood, though West Indian satinwood from the Caribbean is a close substitute.

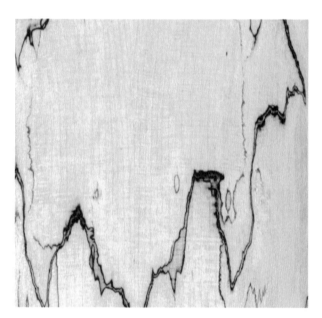

The spalted pattern in SPALTED MAPLE can grow in all types of maple trees if they are left to decay until fungus begins to form. The wood must be sawn and dried before the rot degrades the wood beyond usability, however.

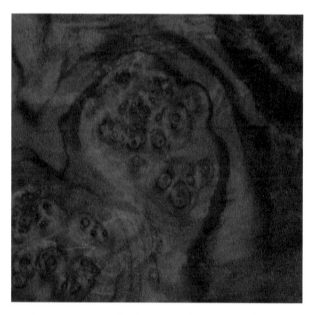

The burl in WALNUT BURL is created by abnormal growth on walnut trees. It is widely used by furniture makers in North America. Walnut trees can be found on the West and East Coasts of the United States, though not many trees will have the growth necessary to produce burl veneer.

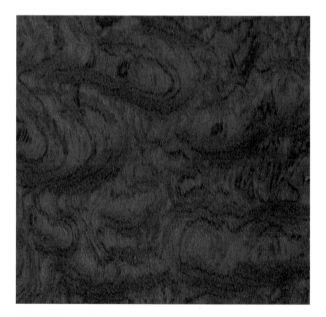

WATERFALL BUBINGA, also known as kevazinga, is rotary-cut bubinga veneer with a wildly swirling grain pattern. A very hard African wood, bubinga is available in a variety of beautiful figure types.

WENGE is another wood from Africa. In this sample, the wood is quartersawn, which produces nearly perfectly straight grain. Wenge is extremely hard and has a splintery texture; care should be taken to remove splinters promptly as they can cause infection.

WHITE OAK is universally recognized as the ideal wood for quarter sawing. Proper sawing can reveal prominent medullary ray flecks and perfectly straight grain. Typically found in eastern North America, it is very popular in furniture and cabinetmaking.

Backer veneer   Lower-grade veneer typically used as a cross-grain layer on two-ply veneer or as the interior veneer on noncosmetic panels to balance the face veneer.

Bird's eye   Small round shapes in the grain of the wood resembling bird's eyes; common in maple veneer.

Block figure   A type of figure with a blotchy appearance that creates roughly square patterns across the wood grain.

Book-match   A set of two consecutively cut leaves of veneer folded open along a seam like the pages of a book to create a mirrored effect in the grain of the wood.

Boulle   A method of cutting marquetry (attributed to the work of André-Charles Boulle) where two contrasting materials are stacked together and the marquetry pattern is then cut through both layers at the same time, resulting in a set of two images made of opposing colors.

Buckled veneer   Veneer, typically burl, that has a wavy pattern of undulating grain due to constantly changing wood grain; usually requires flattening before use.

Bundle   A stack of either 24 or 32 consecutively sliced veneer leaves.

Burl   Swirling grain formed in some trees that creates circular patterns of wild grain, typically caused by abnormal growth in the tree.

Cathedral figure   A type of grain pattern produced in flat and plain slicing that demonstrates a distinctive crown pattern in the grain.

Crotch figure   Figure created by slicing through a joint in a tree where two limbs meet. The figure has a pronounced cathedral pattern.

Curly figure   Uniform straight lines of figure running across the grain of the wood, less numerous than fiddleback figure.

Delamination   A separation of the veneer from the substrate either through a failure in the glue or some other failure method.

Fiddleback figure   Very tight, narrow bands of small, straight curl-type figure that runs across the grain of the wood; often seen in sycamore and makore.

Flake figure   Produced from only certain wood species, notably oak, sycamore, and lacewood, the flake figure is created by cutting across the medullary rays of the wood.

Flat cut   Similar to plain slicing, this method of cutting veneer slices completely across the log to produce veneer with a more traditional solid-wood appearance with noticeable cathedral patterns in the grain.

Flitch   A stack of sequentially sliced bundles of veneer leaves.

Glue face   The face of the veneer that will be glued to the substrate.

Half-round slicing   A method of rotary-slicing veneer from one half of a log that produces wider leaves than would otherwise be possible from small logs.

Leaf   A single piece of veneer.

Marquetry   A method of cutting decorative floral and curved patterns in wood veneer.

Medium-density fiberboard (MDF) A combination of wood dust and a resin binder that is pressed under high pressure and heat to form uniform flat panels frequently used for veneering.

Paperback veneer A type of veneer sheet that is preglued to a paper backer of 10-mil or 20-mil thickness and made in multiple varieties and matches, typically in 4x8 or 4x10 sheets.

Parquetry A technique used to cut geometric patterns in wood veneer, including squares, diamonds, rhombuses, and other shapes.

Pommele figure A type of blistered figure that has the appearance of overlapping bubbles in the veneer; it creates a striking pattern when finished.

Quarter cut Cuts done at nearly right angles to the growth rings of the tree, producing uniform straight grain lines and in some species a characteristic medullary ray flex.

Quilted figure Recognizable by its large, rippling pattern resembling waves in water and the pattern in quilts, quilted figure is found most often in bigleaf maple.

Radial match Multiple leaves of veneer, typically 8, 12, 16, or more, are cut into specific triangular shapes to form a circular pattern resembling slices in a pie. Most often done as a book-matched pattern where every other leaf is book-matched to its neighbor.

Random match A type of veneer match that incorporates random leaves of veneer from a single species to create a more random look in the final panel.

Raw veneer Natural wood veneer sliced directly from the log and kept in the order it was sliced.

Ribbon stripe A version of quartersawing that in some species produces a distinctive reflective stripe pattern in the quartersawn grain.

Rift cut A cut done a number of degrees off a right angle to the growth rings of the tree that produces uniform straight grain without the medullary rays visible in quarter-cut veneer.

Rotary cutting A method of cutting long, seamless sheets of veneer made by rotating a log against a fixed knife; the result is much like unrolling a roll of paper towels. Frequently used to cut burls.

Sequence The order that veneer leaves are cut in and arranged to form uniform grain matches.

Show face The face of the veneer that will show once the veneer is glued to the substrate.

Slip-match Two consecutively cut leaves of veneer slipped beside one another to form a repeating pattern in the grain.

Spalted figure Spalting in wood is caused by fungi that alter the color of the wood. Different types of fungi can produce a variety of colors and distinctive patterns readily visible in lighter woods like maple and birch.

Substrate The material the veneer is glued to; it can be MDF, plywood, solid wood, metal, or any number of other materials.

Veneer Suppliers

Certainly Wood
(small- or large-quantity veneer supplier)
www.certainlywood.com

Cue Veneer
(dyed veneer supplier)
www.cueveneer.com

Herzog Veneers
(bundle and larger veneer supplier)
www.veneeronline.com

Indiana Veneers
(veneer-slicing mill)
www.indianaveneers.com

Interwood Forest Products
(architectural veneer and panel supplier)
www.ifpveneer.com

Reliance Veneer Co.
(UK veneer supplier)
www.relianceveneer.com

Rosebud Veneer
(bundle and panel supplier)
www.rosebudveneer.com

Veneer Tech
(face veneer supplier)
www.veneertech.com

Marquetry Sources

American Marquetry Society
www.americanmarquetrysociety.com

The Marquetry Society (UK)
www.marquetry.org

Peter White Marquetry Instructional Videos
peter@marquetry.org

Vacuum Supplies

JoeWoodworker
(general veneer and vacuum supplies)
www.joewoodworker.com

Vac-U-Clamp
(vacuum press and Pro-Glue supplier)
www.vac-u-clamp.com

Veneer Supplies
(refurbished vacuum pumps)
www.veneersupplies.com

Miscellaneous Woodworking Sources/Suppliers

Australian Wood Review
www.woodreview.com.au

***Fine Woodworking* magazine**
www.finewoodworking.com

***Furniture & Cabinetmaking* magazine**
www.woodworkersinstitute.com/
furniture-cabinetmaking

***Good Woodworking* magazine**
www.getwoodworking.com

Milligan & Higgins
(hot hide glue supplier)
www.milligan1868.com

Old Brown Glue
(liquid hide glue supplier)
www.oldbrownglue.com

***Popular Woodworking* magazine**
www.popularwoodworking.com

Two Cherries USA
(veneer saws)
www.twocherriesusa.com

METRIC EQUIVALENTS

INCHES	CENTIMETERS	MILLIMETERS	INCHES	CENTIMETERS	MILLIMETERS
⅛	0.3	3	13	33.0	330
¼	0.6	6	14	35.6	356
⅜	1.0	10	15	38.1	381
½	1.3	13	16	40.6	406
⅝	1.6	16	17	43.2	432
¾	1.9	19	18	45.7	457
⅞	2.2	22	19	48.3	483
1	2.5	25	20	50.8	508
1¼	3.2	32	21	53.3	533
1½	3.8	38	22	55.9	559
1¾	4.4	44	23	58.4	584
2	5.1	51	24	61	610
2½	6.4	64	25	63.5	635
3	7.6	76	26	66.0	660
3½	8.9	89	27	68.6	686
4	10.2	102	28	71.7	717
4½	11.4	114	29	73.7	737
5	12.7	127	30	76.2	762
6	15.2	152	31	78.7	787
7	17.8	178	32	81.3	813
8	20.3	203	33	83.8	838
9	22.9	229	34	86.4	864
10	25.4	254	35	88.9	889
11	27.9	279	36	91.4	914
12	30.5	305			

All photos by Craig Thibodeau, except as noted below:

Photos by Craig Carlson: p. iii, pp. vi-1, p. 7, p. 9 (top left, top right), p. 10 (right), p. 22 (top left, bottom left), p. 23 (top left), p. 27, p. 33 (top), p. 44, p. 58 (bottom), p. 60 (top), p. 61 (top left, bottom left), p. 65 (bottom right), p. 75 (top left, middle left), p. 83 (top left, top right, bottom), p. 89 (top left), 94 (bottom left), p. 95 (top right, bottom left, bottom right), p. 100 (bottom), p. 107, p. 109 (bottom left, bottom right), p. 111 (bottom), p. 112 (top), p. 140 (top right), p. 141, p. 142, p. 143 (top right), p. 149, p. 156 (top), p. 158, p. 164 (top, bottom left), p. 165, p. 174 (bottom), p. 175 (middle left, middle right, bottom), p. 177 (top), p. 179 (right), p. 185, p. 187 (bottom left), p. 188, p. 192, p. 195 (top, bottom left), p. 196, p. 200 (top right), p. 202, p. 203, p. 207, p. 211 (bottom), p. 213 (top).

Photos by Wayne McCall: p. 83 (middle left), p. 89 (top right), p. 94 (top right), p. 110 (top left), p. 151 (top left)

Photos by Dean Palmer: p. i, p. 9 (bottom left, bottom right), p. 22 (top right), p. 61 (bottom right), p. 65 (bottom left), p. 195 (bottom right), p. 200 (top left)

Photos by Peter White: p. 110 (bottom left), p. 113 (top left), p. 131 (bottom), p. 132 (left), p. 135, p. 137, p. 140 (top left)

Chapter 1

p. 8: Photo courtesy the Library of Congress, Prints & Photographs Division, HAER CAL,54-THRIV.V,2—17

p. 9: (middle right) Photo by Kevin Stamper

p. 10: (left) Photo courtesy Herzog Veneers Inc.

p. 12: Photos courtesy Herzog Veneers Inc.

p. 14: (top) Photo by Nikolai Krawczyk, courtesy Atlantic Veneer Corp. Inc.; (bottom) Photo courtesy Herzog Veneers Inc.

pp. 15-16: Photos by Nikolai Krawczyk, courtesy Atlantic Veneer Corp. Inc.

p. 17: (top left, bottom right) Photos by Nikolai Krawczyk, courtesy Atlantic Veneer Corp. Inc.; (top right) Photo courtesy Interwood Forest Products and Indiana Veneers

p. 18: (top) Photo by Nikolai Krawczyk, courtesy Atlantic Veneer Corp. Inc.; (bottom) Photo courtesy Herzog Veneers Inc.

pp. 19-20: Photos by Nikolai Krawczyk, courtesy Atlantic Veneer Corp. Inc.

p. 21: Photos courtesy Certainly Wood Inc.

p. 22: (bottom right) Photo courtesy The Metropolitan Museum of Art, New York, Rogers Fund, 1933

p. 23: (top right) Photos by Kevin Stamper; (bottom left) Photo courtesy The Metropolitan Museum of Art, New York, Gift of Mr. and Mrs. Charles Wrightsman, 1986; (bottom right) Digital image courtesy of the Getty's Open Content Program.

Chapter 2

p. 25: (bottom) Photo by Nikolai Krawczyk, courtesy Atlantic Veneer Corp. Inc.

p. 26: (top right) Photo by Nikolai Krawczyk, courtesy Atlantic Veneer Corp. Inc.

Chapter 3

p. 55: (bottom) Photo courtesy Vac-U-Clamp

p. 56: (bottom) Photo courtesy Vac-U-Clamp

Chapter 4

p. 65: (top left, top right) Photos by Cherie Cordellos

p. 75: (top right) Photo by Paul Schraub; (middle right) Photo courtesy The Metropolitan Museum of Art, New York, Rogers Fund, 1941; (bottom left) Photo courtesy The Metropolitan Museum of Art, New York, Gift of Mr. and Mrs. Michael Chow,

1984; (bottom right) Photo courtesy The Metropolitan Museum of Art, New York, Purchase, Bequest of Collis P. Huntington, by exchange, 1973

Chapter 5

p. 83: (middle right) Photo by Jefferson Shallenberger

p. 89: (bottom left) Photo by Paul Lapsley; (bottom right) Photo courtesy of Andrew Crawford

Chapter 6

p. 92: Photo by Naman Briner

p. 94: (top left) Photo by Glenn Cormier; (bottom right) Photo by Naman Briner

p. 95: (top left) Photo by Peter Young

p. 96: (top) Photo by Grant Hancock

p. 98: (left) Photo by Frank Pronesti

Chapter 7

p. 109: (top) Photo by Seth Janofsky

p. 110: (top right) Photo by David Ryan; (bottom right) Photo by David Harrison

p. 113: (top right) Photo by Seth Janofsky; (bottom) Photo by Greg Zall

p. 115: Photo by Yannick Chastang

p. 133: (left) Photo by Josh Purnell; (right) Photo by Arthur Seigneur

p. 139: (top, bottom) Photos by Christy Oates

p. 140: (bottom left) Photo by Gregg Novosad/clickdivine.com; (bottom right) Photo courtesy The Metropolitan Museum of Art, New York, The Jack and Belle Linsky Collection, 1982

Chapter 8

p. 148: (top left) Photo by Yoshiaki Kato; (top right) Photo by Chris Pinchbeck

p. 151: (top right) Photo by Paul Lapsley; (bottom left) Photo by Chris Pinchbeck; (bottom center) Photo by David Ryan; (bottom right) Photo by Rowan Morgan/ CR2 Studios

Chapter 9

p. 164: (bottom right) Photo courtesy The Metropolitan Museum of Art, New York, Purchase, Friends of European Sculpture and Decorative Arts Gifts, 1999

p. 175: (top) Photo by Jefferson Shallenberger

p. 176: (bottom) Photo by Yoshiaki Kato

p. 180: (bottom) Photo by Greg Zall

Chapter 10

p. 187: (top left) Photo by Grant Hancock; (top right) Photo by Glenn Cormier; (bottom right) Photo by Grant Hancock

p. 200: (bottom) Photo by Frank Pronesti

p. 211: (top) Photo by Grant Hancock